Hitchcock on Hitchcock

Hitchcock on Hitchcock

Selected Writings and Interviews

Edited by
Sidney Gottlieb

ff

faber and faber

First published in the USA in 1995
By University of California Press

First published in Great Britain in 1995
by Faber and Faber Limited
3 Queen Square London WCIN 3AU

This paperback edition first published in 1997

Printed in England by Clays Ltd, St Ives plc

Photographs courtesy of Jerry Ohlinger's Movie Material Store

Sidney Gottlieb is hereby identified as author of this
work in accordance with Section 77 of the Copyright,
Designs and Patents Act 1988

A CIP record for this book
is available from the British Library

ISBN 0–571–19136–3

4 6 8 10 9 7 5 3

Contents

Film Production

Technique, Style, and Hitchcock at Work

Acknowledgments

What began as a simple attempt to follow up on a few references to writings by Alfred Hitchcock very quickly turned into a much more complicated, time-consuming, but endlessly fascinating project that I could not have completed without a great deal of help. Early support is always particularly important, and I have been extremely fortunate in this regard. Patricia Hitchcock O'Connell was gracious and encouraging from the very beginning and literally made this volume possible by granting her permission to reprint the material herein. And, at the University of California Press, Ed Dimendberg's immediately enthusiastic response to my first query was followed by several years of invaluable critical advice, patience, and continuing enthusiasm.

Much of my research was conducted at the New York Public Library, the Film Study Center of the Museum of Modern Art, the British Film Institute, the Margaret Herrick Library at the Academy of Motion Picture Arts and Sciences, and the Warner Brothers archive at the Library of Performing Arts at the University of Southern California (USC). I am grateful to the librarians and research associates at those institutions for their help, particularly in examining out-of-the-way magazines, newspapers, and clippings files. I am also grateful to Susan and Jonathan Post, who made my various California research trips pleasurable and productive by giving me not only much warm support and encouragement but also a room of my own (with a view and a pool).

Jane Sloan answered many questions and sent me printouts from her exhaustive Hitchcock bibliography before it was published, and this steered me to articles I undoubtedly would have otherwise missed. Sam Gill helped me find my way through the massive Hitchcock Collection at the Herrick Library. Ned Comstock at the Library of Performing Arts at USC uncovered articles by Hitchcock that I had never heard of even as he was bringing me material from the USC collection that is unavailable elsewhere. Charles Silver at the Museum of Modern Art pulled folder after folder of clippings files, which enabled me to find several one-of-a-kind items. Ronald Magliozzi, also at MOMA, did some last-minute checking for me at a moment's notice. Fiona Bolt and Phil Wickham at the British Film Institute answered numerous queries and sent me essential material. Deborah Dutko gave much valuable advice about design and illustrations.

Various people at Sacred Heart University assisted in critical ways. Judith Davis Miller, Kristen Wenzel, and Thomas J. Trebon arranged for much-needed release time and a convenient teaching schedule, which helped make my ideal of balancing research and teaching a reality. Claire Marrone translated an article from the French specifically for this volume. I have received much of my education in film while at Sacred Heart, where Rebecca Abbott, Louise Spence, and Chris Sharrett (no longer my co-worker but always my friend and co-conspirator) have taught a great deal about film history and theory not only to several generations of students but also to at least one very grateful colleague.

I am a scholar by profession but a film lover by inclination, and my later education in film would not have taken hold unless I had been prepared much earlier—by many days and nights working at the Strand Theater with Paul, Ziggy, and Jim and many afternoons at the Whitney Theater with my brother Lou. And now that a VCR has replaced those theaters and the film projector my father gave me, Suzanne Golub helps, more than she knows, in part by reading proofs and watching me watch Hitchcock movies.

S. G.
Somerset and Hamden

Permissions

The Hitchcock Estate has very kindly granted their permission to reprint all the pieces in this volume. Original publication information appears at the bottom of the title page for each article. Additional permissions are as follows:

"Surviving" is reprinted with permission from *Sight and Sound* (Summer 1977). Copyright © 1977.

"Master of Suspense: Being a Self-Analysis," "Core of the Movie— The Chase," "Murder—With English on It" and "Search for the Sun" are Copyright © 1937/50/57 by The New York Times Company. Reprinted by permission.

"Would You Like to Know Your Future?" is reprinted with permission from Guideposts Magazine. Copyright © 1959 by Guideposts Associates, Inc., Carmel, New York 10512.

"A *Redbook* Dialogue: Alfred Hitchcock and Dr. Fredric Wertham" is reprinted by permission from *Redbook*. Copyright © 1963 The Hearst Corporation. All rights reserved.

"Production Methods Compared" is reprinted by permission from the *American Cinematographer.* Copyright © 1949 by the American Society of Cinematographers. All rights reserved.

"Film Production" is reprinted with permission from "Motion Pictures" in *Encyclopaedia Britannica,* 14th edition. Copyright © 1965 by Encyclopaedia Britannica, Inc.

"Direction," originally titled "My Own Methods," is reprinted with permission from *Sight and Sound* (Summer 1937). Copyright © 1937.

"Lecture at Columbia University" is reprinted by permission of The Museum of Modern Art. All rights reserved.

"Hitchcock Talks About Lights, Cameras, Action" is reprinted by permission from the *American Cinematographer.* Copyright © 1967 by the American Society of Cinematographers. All rights reserved.

Introduction

Alfred Hitchcock was an unusually prolific filmmaker and instantly recognizable personality whose popularity and influence show no sign of waning. There is one area of his activity, though, that is neglected, underappreciated, even largely unknown: his writings. Throughout his life Hitchcock was glib, witty, and, if we qualify the term in certain ways, highly literate. He repeatedly emphasized the need for cinema to rely on pictures rather than dialogue, and his most well-known manner of self-representation was via an image, as in his trademark (and nonspeaking) cameo appearances in his films and in the cartoon caricature that aptly identified him. But at other times he was also resolutely verbal and exploited and enjoyed the written and spoken word.

Donald Spoto introduces his controversial biography, *The Dark Side of Genius,* by noting what he takes to be Hitchcock's "deep inarticulateness," confirmed by the fact that he apparently was a "notoriously poor correspondent" and kept no diaries, journals, or notebooks.[1] This premise serves Spoto's purposes, allowing him to read Hitchcock's life in his films and argue confidently that there was indeed much in his life that Hitchcock would want to be inarticulate about: guilt-ridden fantasies, passive-aggressive social habits, forbidden and not always restrained desires, a manipulative if not tyrannical personal as well as directorial style, and so on. Whether or not this is an accurate, fair, and comprehensive picture of Hitchcock is still being debated, but, ironically, Spoto's detailed and formidably documented biography underscores not so much

Hitchcock's "deep inarticulateness" as his constant attempts to show and shape himself—and by no means only in his films.

Hitchcock seemed to live for his work, always deeply involved in one project or another, and in his social life he was shy, even reclusive. But from the beginning of his career to the end he was a remarkably "public" figure, largely through the print media. The writings that came out under Hitchcock's name are surprisingly varied and substantive. I began my work on this material wondering if I would be able to find enough to assemble a small volume of Hitchcock's writings. After much digging and a continuous succession of happy discoveries, I now know that there is more available than could fit in even a very large volume, including, as one might expect, a great deal of studio-generated publicity articles and press releases (which are not without interest, as Robert Kapsis has recently shown)[2] but also personal statements, interviews, stories, humorous sketches, speeches, introductions to books, autobiographical reminiscences, and critical essays. These materials are not completely unknown, although many are hard to find and not many are frequently cited or even listed in Hitchcock bibliographies and are of uneven value, depending on what one is looking for. But even the best critics tend to be dismissive about them, if they are aware of them at all.

Robin Wood, for example, downplays the importance of any material that may distract one from the films themselves. In his ground-breaking criticial study, Wood begins by asking the crucial question, "Why should we take Hitchcock seriously?"[3] He goes on to establish Hitchcock's credentials and status as a serious, major artist in a significant art form, arguing very persuasively that we should indeed take him seriously, but first Wood has to overcome an important "obstacle" placed by Hitchcock himself: the artist's own expressed attitude toward his work. Wood admits, "I used to find maddening Hitchcock's refusal to discuss his work with interviewers on any really serious level" (61). He comes to "admire" this stance, though, not only because it establishes Hitchcock's commendable artistic humility but also because in general one should trust the tale rather than the teller: "What an artist says about his own work need not necessarily carry any more weight than what anyone else says about it." Wood thus complicates my task as the editor of this volume by at least implicitly raising the question, Why should we take Hitchcock's writings seriously?

I do not entirely agree with Wood's assessment of Hitchcock's attitude toward his own writings and comments to interviewers. Wood's characteristic "high seriousness" generates many brilliant critical insights but also occasional blind spots, and even if he is right about Hitchcock's lack of seriousness in his writings and interviews, he may be wrong in concluding that these are therefore any less revealing or important—and that Hitchcock's strong suit in general is his "seriousness."[4] And some of Wood's other objections recede if we envision Hitchcock's comments on his life and art not as *ex cathedra* pronouncements by a teller but rather as parts of the tale, meant, like the films, to be sensitively and thoughtfully experienced, interpreted, interrogated, and appreciated.

Still, though, Wood and others voice important criticisms of and reservations about the value of Hitchcock's writings and public statements that need to be addressed. The most substantive of these are as follows: 1) In what sense are these pieces Hitchcock's own, given the likelihood that many of them were ghost-written or heavily edited? 2) To what extent does the fact that many, if not all, of them may have been intended as part of a public relations or promotional effort undermine their status as useful reflections on Hitchcock's life and art? 3) What do these pieces add to what we already know about Hitchcock, especially through François Truffaut's book-length compilation of interviews, traditionally taken as the one text that is both necessary and sufficient as a summation of Hitchcock's lifelong observations?

Let me take these questions up briefly, not so much to defend as to explore the background of the writings and interviews contained herein and to examine their place in our understanding and appreciation of Hitchcock.

Are these writings Hitchcock's own? Yes and no. Investigating authorship these days involves not only some detective work (Did so-and-so put pen to paper and write such and such?) but also some theoretical work on the concept of authorship. (Was *Vertigo*, for example, authored by Hitchcock or the Hollywood studio system, within which Hitchcock might play a contributing but not determining role?) The romantic emphasis on the individual as the sole agent of creativity has, at least for some critics, given way to an emphasis on art as a mode of social production, involving individual effort and energy in a context of collaboration and editorial intervention. So in determining whether or not these writings are Hitchcock's, we need to be aware of some literal facts and some theoretical complexities.

There is much evidence indicating that Hitchcock's words were often edited and reshaped before they reached print and that he constantly had material written for him that subsequently went out under his name. The early five-part autobiographical series "My Screen Memories," published in *Film Weekly* in May 1936, for example, was, we are told, "written in collaboration with John K. Newnham," and many of his valuable comments elsewhere on films and filmmaking come in interviews or "as told to" articles that we can safely assume were editorially revised. But despite the lack of hard evidence in each case, it is also, I think, safe to assume that Hitchcock in one way or another guided, supervised, reviewed, and/or approved the final copy before it went to press. What may or may not have been his own exact words originally became authorized (by him and then by his readers) as his words.

We get a close view of this authorizing process (distinguished from, although related to, the authoring process) by examining some materials preserved in the Hitchcock Collection, donated to the Academy of Motion Picture Arts and Sciences by Patricia Hitchcock O'Connell. Among a mass of invaluable scrapbooks, notes, typescript documents, and correspondence, there are interoffice memos and other documents about arrangements for particular essays to be ghost-written for Hitchcock. A typescript of "Actors Aren't *Really* Cattle," for example, has the name Lupton A. Wilkinson on each page, but the title reads "by Alfred Hitchcock."[5] Originally titled "Usually I Prefer Props," this piece was intended for publication in *Pageant/Coronet* and contains material on *Spellbound, Lifeboat,* Tallulah Bankhead, and Joan Harrison that was no doubt provided by either Hitchcock or his office. No matter who provided the material, though, the piece was submitted directly "to Mr. Hitchcock for his approval"[6] and ultimately marked with a handwritten note "Okayed by Hitch, June 1/45."[7]

There are other typescripts in these folders of essays written for Hitchcock, including "How and When and Why," with the name Kalma Flake on the first page,[8] and "A Few Secrets About Directing Motion Pictures," with the name Daugherty on it.[9] Perhaps the most interesting of these typescripts is one titled "Mystery Drama," written for a proposed anthology on film called *Their*

Magic Wand, edited by William B. Hawks, younger brother of Howard Hawks. An interoffice memo suggests two possible writers for Hitchcock's contribution to this volume: Cameron Shipp would do it for $500 and Maxine Garrison for $350.[10] There is no indication of who eventually wrote the draft included in the folder, but one of the curious features of this essay is the way it absolutely fails to capture Hitchcock's characteristic tone and style, instantly recognizable in so many of his other essays. To my knowledge, "Mystery Drama" was never published, perhaps because the Hawks anthology evidently got no farther than the planning stages, but perhaps more because Hitchcock or his staff never approved what was to be his chapter, realizing that it was an inept handling of Hitchcock's carefully constructed voice and persona.

For all the evidence of some material being written for Hitchcock, including the well-known important contributions of James Allardice from the mid-1950s onward—he wrote Hitchcock's speeches as well as all of the introductions and epilogues to his television shows, which were a critical part of Hitchcock's public image—we should not underestimate Hitchcock's contributions. He undoubtedly played an important role in choosing topics, anecdotes, and illustrations, and much of the style, wit, and irony is his. That these qualities are indeed his and not just the fabrications of hired hands and publicists is illustrated, if not confirmed, by the published pieces that are fairly direct transcriptions of his production meetings, interviews, and talks. The lecture he gave at Columbia University in 1939, for example, was not—like the speeches he gave regularly later in his life—a finely tuned, highly orchestrated, ghost-written performance but a free-flowing series of comments following his own script. One of the most fascinating bits of material in the Hitchcock Collection is a few pieces of Cunard Line stationery filled with notes and subject headings of this talk, written in Hitchcock's own hand. Hitchcock and his family left England on March 1, 1939 (Spoto, 208), and one can imagine him whiling away at least some of his time on the *Queen Mary* making notes on what he would say about film to Columbia University students at the end of March (and perhaps to Yale University drama students earlier in the month, where he also spoke on melodrama and suspense [Spoto, 213]). Here and in many other places (see, for example, "On Style," "Hitchcock at Work," and his dialogue with Dr. Fredric Wertham) we get a fairly direct view of Hitchcock expressing himself, and there is a striking continuity between these pieces and others in which, some might claim, Hitchcock is being constructed. There is a figure in the carpet of the writings collected in this volume, and my simple point is that we should not minimize the ways in which it is drawn, like his famous cartoon caricature, in Hitchcock's own hand.

But is this figure in the carpet anything more than a publicity image, charming, intriguing, and entertaining, but of no real use in gaining insight into Hitchcock's films or thoughts on film? Hitchcock's lifelong concern for manipulating audiences is well documented, and part of what makes him such a characteristically "modern" filmmaker is his awareness of how this manipulation is accomplished both inside and outside a film, via cinematic structure and style and also carefully calculated publicity, advertising, marketing, and self-promotion. As early as 1930, Spoto notes, Hitchcock "formed a small company, Hitchcock Baker Productions, Limited, which had the sole task of advertising to the press the newsworthiness of Alfred Hitchcock, producer-director" (138). And as Kapsis emphasizes in his invaluable study of "The Making of a Reputation," Hitchcock's frequent interviews and articles, along with the advertising campaigns for his films, were intended to keep his name constantly before the public, above the titles of his films, to focus attention on particular aspects of the films that he wanted to highlight, and to create an image of him as worthy of highbrow critical regard as well as low- and middle-brow mass consumption.[11] Like Picasso (especially as seen by such critics as John Berger) and so many other great twentieth-century figures, Hitchcock must be understood as an artist in and of the marketplace.[12]

At the same time, there is much more to Hitchcock's writings than self-promotion and selling, and we should not overlook the ways in which they are thoughtful meditations on film art in general and attempts to define and refine his own art in particular. His preferred mode of discourse (at least in these circumstances) is the anecdote, and this sometimes creates an image of him as merely chatty, superficial, and anti- or untheoretical. Indeed, he cultivated this image, as in his article "If I Were Head of a Production Company," where he begins, "It's easy and pleasant to theorize, but unsupported theory has explosive properties when exposed to the air, so I propose to confine these remarks strictly to a basis of experience." His writings do not present a fully articulated, abstract, comprehensive theory of film; Hitchcock learned from Eisenstein, but he did not write like him. It is the anecdotal and experiential base, though, that accounts for much of the value of his observations. Like T. S. Eliot's criticism, Hitchcock's comments are typically practical and more often than not revolve around problems in his own films that he had to work through. Articles such as "'Stodgy' British Pictures," "Directors Are Dead," "Director's Problems," and "The Censor Wouldn't Pass It," for example, are unexpectedly polemical and take sides in various debates in film circles, especially of the 1930s, regarding such critical issues as the relationship between the producer and the director, the direction that British filmmakers should take, and the pressures placed on directors by audiences and censors. Others, such as "Direction," "The Film Thriller," "Core of the Movie—The Chase," and "Film Production," take up particular aspects of his own films and filmmaking practices and help him arrive at a statement of what for him is "essential" cinema. At their best, Hitchcock's writings expose a process of Hitchcock forging, more than his public persona, his cinematic method and style by examining his own films repeatedly as well as analyzing such key subjects as the strengths and limitations of German, British, and American modes of film production, the relationship of the artist and the audience, and the ideal components of films that are both "pure" and popular.

He assays these and other topics not only for himself but also for his audience. To Kapsis's insistence that Hitchcock issued such material simultaneously to manipulate his audience and assert some kind of control over a legitimation process by which film critics assigned artistic worth and credibility, I believe we must also add a recognition of Hitchcock's sincere desire to educate his audience. He comments explicitly on this in his essay "Direction," in which he complains about the lack of sophistication and attentiveness in most audiences but also notes that it is the filmmaker's responsibility to cultivate audiences capable of noticing and appreciating subtleties. "In many ways I am freer now to do what I want to do than I was a few years ago," he concludes and envisions a time of "more freedom still—if audiences will give it to me." This was not a vain hope, precisely because he realized the extent to which he might be able to help create the conditions of artistic freedom by explaining his art and instructing his audience.

These purposes harmonize nicely with what we must also recognize as another of Hitchcock's key motives in his writings and public statements: his irrepressible delight in his work. Unlike the classic magician, Hitchcock, the modern magician, always shows his wand. He was endlessly fascinated by the technical aspects of film production, and many of his pieces explain, sometimes in remarkable detail, "how I did it." "My Most Exciting Picture," "On Style," "Hitchcock Talks About Lights, Cameras, Action," and "It's a Bird, It's a Plane, It's . . . *The Birds*," for example, convey his meticulous attention to special effects, camera angles, lighting, and set design and also his underlying assumption that cinematic art is unimaginable without cinematic craft. And one senses that the audience's pleasure is intimately related to that of the filmmaker: Hitchcock is careful to relate not only the details of various technical challenges but the real enjoyment of technical accomplishments as well. His evident pleasure in showing his wand and telling stories in his writings, especially about his life and art, is a crucial and often overlooked aspect of Hitchcock's complicated relationship with his audience and might be used to soften the current critical emphasis on Hitchcock's impulse to torture and manipulate.[13]

Finally, do these writings add substantively to our knowledge of Hitchcock, or do they simply repeat or offer other versions of anecdotes and opinions already familiar from Truffaut and elsewhere? Hitchcock was indeed a master of not only the anecdote but especially the repeated anecdote. Spoto notes that by the end of his life Hitchcock "had perfected a small supply of familiar anecdotes that satisfied the press" (7), and one quickly senses that Hitchcock was well aware that his reputation always preceded him and that he felt a certain pressure to follow dutifully behind, giving his audience what they expected. He sometimes felt imprisoned by his reputation, evident in many well-known statements to the effect that his audience would not let him make anything but thrillers and, as he notes somewhat ruefully at the end of "Why I Am Afraid of the Dark," that if he made a film of Cinderella, everyone would be expecting to find a corpse. But he undoubtedly also felt comfortable within the confines of his reputation, and his writings, interviews, and public statements, especially later in his career, obligingly lean toward the predictable and the expected: he offers endless definitions of the MacGuffin and pure cinema, variations on the "actors are cattle" theme, illustrations of the virtues of suspense rather than surprise, and assertions that, despite the ostensible subjects of his films, he is not a monster but a timid, law-abiding gentleman with a great sense of humor.[14]

Truffaut's book, based on edited transcripts of a weeklong series of interviews with Hitchcock in August 1962, is the great monument to the construction of Hitchcock's persona and reputation and is of inestimable value because it collects and consolidates so much of Hitchcock's many years of commenting on his life and art.[15] Truffaut is sometimes Hitchcock's unwitting straight man, but he also frequently challenges Hitchcock and leads him away from the basically mechanical format of the interviews to comment on some intriguing and unexpected topics. But the result is not, as the blurb on its cover suggests, the "definitive study of Alfred Hitchcock," nor does it provide all the material necessary for a definitive study of Hitchcock—if such is possible. Truffaut envisioned his book as a way of saving Hitchcock from American critics who, unlike French critics associated with *Cahiers du Cinema*, did not appreciate him properly, and he also imagined that he was saving Hitchcock from himself.

It was obvious that Hitchcock, whose genius for publicity was equalled only by that of Salvador Dali, had in the long run been victimized in American intellectual circles because of his facetious response to interviewers and his deliberate practice of deriding their questions. In examining his films, it was obvious that he had given more thought to the potential of his art than any of his colleagues. It occurred to me that if he would, for the first time, agree to respond seriously to a systematic questionnaire, the resulting document might modify the American critics' approach to Hitchcock. That is what this book is all about.[16]

Alongside the barely submerged (and, I should add, characteristically charming and forgivable) egotistical self-aggrandizement of this passage stand a precious truth and a profound mistake. Hitchcock had indeed given more thought to the potential of his art than many of his colleagues, but the proposed interviews would by no means represent "the first time" (or the last time) Hitchcock addressed himself seriously and extensively to the subject of films and filmmaking. There is a Hitchcock before and beyond Truffaut, and we must turn to Hitchcock's writings and other interviews to complete what Truffaut called "the hitchbook" (13).

The pieces I have collected in this volume add to our knowledge of Hitchcock in a variety of ways. Even when they overlap with material also in Truffaut or elsewhere, they allow us to examine Hitchcock's key ideas in the context of their origin and development, rather than in the context of recollection and repetition that Truffaut for the most part provides. The film-by-film organizational structure of Truffaut's book focuses Hitchcock's comments specifically but somewhat narrowly, and though it gives an overview of an entire career, it also tends to substitute chronology for history. Hitchcock's essays, though, return us to the particular events and debates out of which his ideas and techniques emerge (which I will discuss in more specific detail in the introductions to these essays). Not surprisingly, there is a timeliness as well as a freshness and immediacy to, say, Hitchcock's observations on "Films We Could Make," why cinematic "Crime Doesn't Pay," what "Director's Problems" were in the 1930s, and why the chase is "The Core of the Movie" that do not always come through in Truffaut's sometimes grand, sometimes dutiful retrospective. And while Truffaut and other interviewers often record an end product, Hitchcock's essays show his ideas taking shape and even changing: for example, his stress on the importance of one controlling hand in the making of a film ("one-man pictures" he calls them in "Films We Could Make") is modified by the descriptions of creative collaboration in various articles describing production methods; and his understanding of the audiences' relation to cinematic heroes, heroines, and villains gains subtlety and complexity as he returns to these subjects repeatedly in his writings.

Finally, these writings give us access to much that is not available elsewhere, ranging from scattered opinions, autobiographical reminiscences, and backstage stories to fascinating comments on the many challenges of filmmaking. It would be difficult, perhaps impertinent, to summarize all this material adequately. To borrow the words of an old poet, "The beauty lies in the discovery,"[17] and each reader will, I think, find something new and valuable about Hitchcock in these writings. It might be going too far to say that a hitherto "invisible Hitchcock" suddenly emerges from these recovered writings, like the "invisible Orson Welles" that Jonathan

Rosenbaum finds in Welles's often inaccessible and uncompleted projects, a full consideration of which might radically alter our perception of the director's achievement.[18] But we unquestionably gain access to an enhanced and, to use a phrase Hitchcock himself might approve, enlarged Hitchcock.

What follows is a selection from Hitchcock's writings and interviews, arranged in several thematic groupings. A simple chronological arrangement might offer certain advantages, but broad thematic headings help call attention to some of Hitchcock's recurrent focal points and issues; and within each section, I arrange the articles chronologically to make it easier to examine the temporal development of Hitchcock's ideas. Each section begins with a brief introduction, setting out the key concerns of the articles and their relevant contexts. There are also notes on each article, giving original publication information and explanations of any references that might be unclear. At the end of the volume is a full bibliography of all Hitchcock's writings that I have been able to locate. I expect that this list will continue to grow as researchers look through popular magazines and newspapers as well as specialized film publications with an eye toward finding contributions by or about Hitchcock.

In deciding which pieces to include in this volume, I have had to make some hard choices, because there is something of interest in nearly everything. A substantial number of Hitchcock's writings are stories or sketches, usually moody and evocative but sometimes straightforward, almost clinically objective descriptions of crimes, macabre incidents, or unexplained and unexplainable events. We tend to associate these with the later Hitchcock, with the television shows and the mystery magazines and story anthologies that came out under his name (but that he did not write). I include one of these sketches, his first published work, "Gas," to give a good example of this kind of story and also to note that this is a genre he cultivated from the beginning to the end of his career. But although I might have composed an entire section of such pieces, I do not include other examples. Nor do I include any of his various feature articles on food, jaunty comments on current events, out-and-out publicity pieces on his weight and studio activities, fanciful exercises in illustrated storytelling, or brief prefaces to books. I have also opted to include hard-to-find pieces instead of ones that have been reprinted (e.g., in Albert LaValley's *Focus on Hitchcock,* which is out of print but generally accessible in libraries).

My main concern was to gather writings that focus directly on Hitchcock's life, films, and film practice. This led not only to the exclusion of many otherwise intriguing articles but also to an emphasis on his earlier writings. Writings from the 1930s make up a large proportion of this volume: not necessarily because Hitchcock did more writing during this period but more likely because he did more writing on the subjects that I feel are the most significant and interesting. I have tried to include material from every period of Hitchcock's career, but my main goal was to include Hitchcock's most substantive essays, regardless of their date.

I regret having to omit many of the articles, which interested readers will at least be able to pursue on their own, following the citations in the bibliography of Hitchcock's writings at the end of this volume. What remains, though, is substantial. Scholars and critics will find much material here to integrate into new accounts of Hitchcock and his work. Those taking a feminist approach to Hitchcock, for example, while not of course limited to studying a director's comments on actresses and women's roles in films, may nevertheless find particularly interesting Hitchcock's recurrent discussions of his heroines, actresses, wife, and what he imagines to be a primarily female film audience. Critics examining the broad context of the screening and reception of Hitchcock's films may find many of his writings to be a significant part of the complex creation and manipulation of Hitchcock's public persona. And those interested in more closely situating Hitchcock in the context of evolving studio systems (in both England and America), marketing mechanisms, and stylistic models will find that he has much to say about all these subjects.

But this volume is not only, or even primarily, for scholars and critics. Hitchcock was an uncommon director, but he always imagined himself as playing for what he might have called the "common viewer." Casual as well as devoted moviegoers will find that in these writings Hitchcock presents behind-the-scenes views, witty comments, and thoughtful reminiscences and reflections that greatly enhance our understanding and appreciation of film history in general and in particular, his own films, those fifty-three incomparable slices of, as he insisted, not life but cake.

A note on format: The following articles and interviews are transcribed directly from the original texts as they were first published. I include original publication information at the end of each piece, along with brief explanatory notes. Obvious errors are corrected silently, and in a few cases where the original text was unclear or otherwise defective and where other, more legible copies were unavailable, I have given my best guess at the missing letters or words. Spelling is Americanized (e.g., "theatre" is changed to "theater," "colour" to "color"), and I have standardized punctuation, quotation marks, and titles of films (I use the commonly accepted title of a film when there are alternatives, e.g., *Sabotage*, rather than the American release title *A Woman Alone*). I have also standardized details of layout and design, eliminating unnecessary line spaces and indentations, while attempting to preserve significant features of the original versions (e.g., section headings and divisions). Many of the pieces were accompanied and nicely supplemented by illustrations and captions, but although these would be of particular interest to specialists studying the presentation of Hitchcock's image and ideas, it has not been feasible to include them in this volume.

Notes

1. Donald Spoto, *The Dark Side of Genius: The Life of Alfred Hitchcock* (New York: Ballantine Books, 1984), xii. Additional quotations from Spoto are indicated by page numbers only.

2. See Robert E. Kapsis, *Hitchcock: The Making of a Reputation* (Chicago: University of Chicago Press, 1992). Kapsis tends to treat all Hitchcock's writings primarily as publicity material, an approach that I find limiting.

3. Robin Wood, *Hitchcock's Films Revisited* (New York: Columbia University Press, 1989), 55. The original edition of *Hitchcock's Films* came out in 1965. Additional quotations from Wood are indicated by page number only.

4. We have the tortured and torturing Hitchcock in Spoto, the serious Hitchcock in Wood, the feminist Hitchcock in Tania Modleski, *The Women Who Knew Too Much: Hitchcock and Feminist Theory* (New York: Methuen, 1988), and the romantic Hitchcock in Lesley Brill, *The Hitchcock Romance: Love and Irony in Hitchcock's Films* (Princeton: Princeton University Press, 1988). It surprises me that we still have not had a full treatment of the comic Hitchcock, although Hitchcock as trickster and game-player is highlighted in Thomas M. Leitch, *Find the Director and Other Hitchcock Games* (Athens: University of Georgia Press, 1991).

5. Hitchcock Collection, Academy of Motion Picture Arts and Sciences, Margaret Herrick Library, Early Publicity Folder no. 2.

6. Hitchcock Collection, Letter from Loren Wilkinson, June 28, 1946, Publicity Folder no. 2.

7. Hitchcock Collection, carbon copy of "Actors Aren't *Really* Cattle," Early Publicity Folder no. 3.

8. Hitchcock Collection, Early Publicity Folder no. 2.

9. Hitchcock Collection, Early Publicity Folder no. 3.

10. Hitchcock Collection, Early Publicity Folder no. 2.

11. See especially Kapsis, chaps. 2 and 3.

12. John Berger, *The Success and Failure of Picasso* (Baltimore: Penguin, 1965). Andy Warhol is another such figure, and this adds extra interest to Hitchcock's long interview with Warhol in *Interview* 4, no. 8 (Sept. 1974): 5–8.

13. Perhaps Hitchcock's narrative skill and pleasure in telling stories are often downplayed because of his repeated statements that he is more interested in technique than plot and his acknowledgment that the plots for most of his films were not his own. But Hitchcock is an extremely skillful and dedicated storyteller—in "Production Methods Compared," for example, he notes, "I try to make it a rule that nothing should be permitted to interfere with the story. The making of a picture is nothing but the telling of a story"—and narrativity is one of his recurrent themes.

14. At the same time, we should recognize that some of this repetition may also be a function of the modern media environment, generated or accentuated by the common routines and practices of editors, interviewers, and reporters who frequently gravitate toward and then echo the familiar.

15. François Truffaut, with the collaboration of Helen G. Scott, *Hitchcock*, rev. ed. (New York: Simon & Schuster, 1984). The book was originally published in 1967 and included material added since the interviews in 1962 to cover Hitchcock's films up through *Torn Curtain*. The revised edition contains a final chapter covering the period up to Hitchcock's death in 1980. It is worth noting that this book is by no means a direct and complete transcription of the interviews but an edited compression of the very lengthy talks. The original tapes of the interviews as well as some full transcriptions are in the Hitchcock Collection, and it would be well worth examining this material closely to get a firsthand look at exactly how Truffaut shaped his volume.

16. Truffaut, Preface to the Revised Edition, *Hitchcock*, 11–12.

17. George Herbert, second sonnet from Walton's *Lives, The Works of George Herbert*, ed. F. E. Hutchinson (1941; corr. rpt. Oxford: Clarendon Press, 1945), 206, 1. 14.

18. See Jonathan Rosenbaum, "The Invisible Orson Welles: A First Inventory," *Sight & Sound* (Summer 1986): 164–171. Even more than Hitchcock, Welles was also a prolific and very accomplished writer and speech maker. I am currently assembling a collection of Welles's writings on film, theater, and politics.

A Life in Films

Introduction

Hitchcock began to reminisce about his life in films at a fairly young age. "My Screen Memories" and "Life Among the Stars" were published while he was only in his late thirties, but by this time he had already spent more than seventeen years in the rather new industry, which qualified him to speak as one of the veterans. And in any event, at the time of these first reminiscences, Hitchcock was called on not so much as one of the old lions but as one of the bright stars among directors. In the late 1930s, Hitchcock's reputation was at a peak, as was the British film industry in general, and there was a great demand for publicity information, behind-the-scenes tales of film personalities, and firsthand reports of how films were made. Hitchcock was a regular contributor to a variety of periodicals, especially *Film Weekly,* which seemed to take a kind of proprietary interest in him, perhaps because, as the introductory blurb to "My Screen Memories" explains, "his career . . . is, in its way, also the story of British films."

Taken together, "My Screen Memories" and "Life Among the Stars" constitute Hitchcock's most extensive commentary on the first phases of his career, ranging from his first directorial assignment to nearly the end of his "British" period and his move to the United States in 1939. There is some overlapping of material, but various stories become transformed as they are retold, and it is interesting to hear slightly (and sometimes markedly) different versions, for example, of Miles Mander trying to catch a train and, more significantly, how *Blackmail* was shot. Conspicuous by its absence is any detailed treatment of *The Lodger,* which most modern critics feel is his greatest early achievement. But he describes his apprenticeship as, in his own words, a "cub director" by lengthy (and often hilarious) recollections of the making of his first two films, *The Pleasure Garden,* rarely screened these days, and *The Mountain Eagle,* unfortunately perhaps lost forever.

These pieces add considerably to the already substantial storehouse of Hitchcock's droll tales about, as he says, "the queer ways in which filmland sometimes works," and we hear much of such assorted and amusing topics as John Galsworthy's snooty pretentiousness, the essential contributions of a prop man to *Juno and the Paycock* and a slingshot artist to *The Man Who Knew Too Much,* Nita Naldi's nails and underwear, and Hitchcock's own penny-pinching. But alongside such entertaining stories he also gives a great deal of information that fleshes out and sometimes even revises our sense of his development as a filmmaker and his approach to filmmaking. For example, his later "biographical legend" often follows up on his simple assertion in "Life Among the Stars" that he became a director almost by accident: "Quite seriously, I had never thought of being a director," he says, until Michael Balcon urged him on. In "My Screen Memories," though, he notes that when Balcon approached him, "I was already toying with the idea of directing a film myself," and he had in fact directed a film financed by some relatives. His description of the failure of this film introduces a recurrent theme in this memoir: his many insecurities as a beginning director, expressed in melodramatic images of filmmaking as causing "some of the nastiest shocks in my whole life," "terrors" that haunt him constantly.

We may need to revise not only our understanding of Hitchcock's "vocation" as a director but also our sense of his characteristic working method. Some of the descriptions in these essays are not entirely consistent with his later, often-repeated claims that meticulous preplanning was the essence of his art. "Life Among the Stars" begins by contrasting the "disciplined, departmentalized, efficient" production routines of the late 1930s with the much more hectic, exciting, and serendipitous methods of the 1920s, which he recalls nostalgically. And "My Screen Memories" highlights several examples of the kind of improvisation we do not normally associate with Hitchcock: Madeleine Carroll's role in *The 39 Steps* was largely "built up" on the set, for which Hitchcock gives her a great deal of credit, a scene in *Secret Agent* that he praises highly originates not in inventive directing but spontaneous "bandying" by Carroll and Robert Young; and the appearance of the distinguished actor Michel Saint-Denis as the coachmen in *Secret Agent* was not the result of careful planning but sudden inspiration as Hitchcock chatted on the set with Saint-Denis, who was visiting with his friend John Gielgud.

The *Film Weekly* description of Hitchcock's early recollections is not altogether inaccurate: "He tells of small beginnings and great achievements, of colorful people, humor and plenty of thrills." But perhaps Hitchcock's own words are more evocative: his focus is on "the emotional drama that was being enacted on the other side of the camera." His writings, like his films, frequently have bright surfaces but somewhat darker depths, as is especially evident in the next two selections in this section. "The Woman Who Knows Too Much" is at first glance a characteristically rambling, light, anecdotal sketch of his wife, Alma, and their relationship, but even without overscrutinizing it we quickly realize that this relationship is complex, troubled, and troubling. Hitchcock both romanticizes and deromanticizes his attraction to Alma and in a remarkably honest fashion sets their relationship in the context of his deepest worries and fears, some of them obvious and familiar—of policemen and being alone, for example—but others somewhat more subtle and concealed, like his fear of being analyzed and thereby "demolished" by his wife. The silent or silenced woman is a recurrent theme in his films, and this essay is worth reading in the context of, among others, *The Man Who Knew Too Much,* especially the second version, a subtle battle-of-the-sexes film alluded to of course in the title here, and *Psycho,* a not-so-subtle battle-of-the-sexes film in which a silent woman speaks through a man, with pathological consequences. (Alma gets a chance to speak for herself in "My Husband Hates Suspense," *Family Circle* 52, no. 6 [June 1958]: 36–37, 69–70, 72; and Joseph McBride, "Mr. and Mrs. Hitchcock," *Sight & Sound* 45, no. 4 [Autumn 1976]: 224–225.)

The "After-Dinner Speech at the Screen Producers Guild Dinner" was most likely ghost-written for him and used on a variety of occasions. Still, much of the wit and charm are Hitchcock's own, as are the somewhat deeper concerns about the relationship between his self and his image. From the very beginning of his career he not only carefully crafted his public image but also felt and complained about the strain of this self-creation. In this speech, he characteristically projects and pokes fun at his own image, relating a fascinating series of fables of unstable personae, wandering simulations, and masks that will not come off, fables that link Hitchcock's world with that of Pirandello, Ionesco, and Borges. Here as elsewhere, he confirms that he will tease his audience and never give a straightforward answer to "Who is the real Alfred Hitchcock?" But there is also some intimation that he cannot answer that question and that he is worried about the deeper question of whether or not there is a "real" Alfred Hitchcock. Find the director, to use Thomas Leitch's wonderful phrase, is a game played by Hitchcock's audience and by Hitchcock himself.

The end of Hitchcock's life and career has been described in detail by David Freeman, in *The Last Days of Alfred Hitchcock,* and also by Spoto, who paints a particularly grim picture of his final project, *The Short Night,* as the unfilmable culmination of Hitchcock's obsessive fantasies about inescapable entrapment, murder, and sexual violence (574–583). All the more reason, then, to conclude this section with what may be taken as Hitchcock's own valedictory statement. In perhaps the last important interview of his life, aptly titled "Surviving," Hitchcock talks less about his pacemaker or his problems than his patience—"First and foremost, it's a case of the cobbler sticking to his last"—and even his buoyancy as he continues to face up to the challenges of filmmaking. His brief self-analysis is candid and insightful: one could go a long way toward understanding his life and work by following up on his observations that he is characteristically "devious" (by which he means creatively indirect and adaptive rather than manipulative and confrontational) with others and "tough" with himself. And his last words are courageous and prophetic: "I warn you, I mean to go on for ever," he warns us, and indeed, via his perennially engaging films, he continues to haunt us, as a master artist and, in the words of John Russell Taylor, a "champion survivor."

My Screen Memories

I Begin with a Nightmare

Looking back is sometimes amusing—and sometimes humiliating. It is not a thing I care to do as a rule.

I prefer to look forward. I am usually more interested in the immediate future than in the past. But there is, I suppose, a certain advantage in contemplating things that have gone by, for a while, in preference to things to come. It helps one to realize one's mistakes—gives one a sense of proportion.

Having made up my mind to take the plunge, I'll do the job properly by going right back to the very beginning of my association with films.

My first film work was done—after brief experience as a draughtsman in an engineer's office, and as a clerk with an insurance company—when I became a title-writer for the old Famous Players Company at Islington.

I was still at Islington when Michael Balcon, to whom I owe more than I can say, formed the Gainsborough Company and took over the studios. I gained a pretty comprehensive knowledge of filmmaking in all its phases in various jobs there. I was alternately writer, art director, assistant director, production manager, and sometimes all at the same time.

"My Screen Memories," a five-part series "written in collaboration with John K. Newnham," appeared in *Film Weekly* on May 2, 1936, 16–18; May 9, 1936, 7; May 16, 1936, 28–29; May 23, 1936, 28–29; and May 30, 1936, 27.

Birth of an Idea

I was already toying with the idea of directing a film myself. And, in this connection, I'll let you into a secret. I directed one picture, in my early days, of which you have almost certainly never heard. It was not made for any company. Some relatives, carried away by my enthusiasm, put up the money for me to make a film on my own. Out of kindness of heart to the players who appeared in it I won't mention their names. I am afraid the picture never reached the screen.

That was a somewhat chastening experience. But my first real directing effort had much worse terrors in store for me. It gave me some of the nastiest shocks in my whole life. Although it was made over ten years ago, the details of the trials and tribulations I went through are still vivid in my mind. I can smile about them today, but at the time they were ghastly.

The film was *The Pleasure Garden,* and it was made in conjunction with a German company. Michael Balcon, who had conceived the idea of "importing" American stars long before anybody else, had engaged Virginia Valli for the leading role. She was at the height of her career then—glamorous, famous, and very popular. That she was coming to Europe to make a picture at all was something of an event.

But the actual production of the film bristled with difficulties and mishaps from beginning to end, partly because I had to direct it abroad, and in German. Although the company's studios were in Munich most of the scenes were shot around Lake Como.

Trouble with the Customs

I set off from Munich to Genoa while Alma Reville—now my wife; at that time my assistant director—went over to Cherbourg to meet Virginia Valli on the liner. She was to bring her on to Lake Como, where I would meet them. Things went wrong even before my journey had started. We went to Munich station by taxi. I was accompanied by Miles Mander, the leading man, and a couple of cameramen.

We got to the station with five minutes to spare before the train was due out; and just as we were boarding it Miles realized that he had left his makeup box in the taxi. We hurriedly made plans for him to go and get it while the rest of us went on. He would have to catch the next train and meet us at Genoa. Then we had a bit of luck. The train was half an hour late in going out and Miles recovered the makeup box in time to catch it after all.

The next spot of trouble came when we reached the Brenner Pass and had to get through the Customs into Italy. We airily said: "Nothing to declare," without realizing that we had. A keen-eyed official came across the film negative and confiscated the lot. It represented the whole of our stock. Without it we were as helpless as a cinema without a screen.

Stolen Money

We had to negotiate for the return of the stock—on the payment of a suitable fine—and went on to Genoa, praying that it would be returned all right. But time went by and still it was not delivered. Eventually, we had to send into Milan for a fresh, and expensive, supply. Our man got back with it just as the confiscated stock turned up.

The next day we went down to the harbor to shoot scenes. It was while I was down there that I received the worst blow to date. I discovered that the whole of the money to cover our expenses on location, 10,000 lire, had been stolen. Apart from the little I had of my own I was penniless. I frantically borrowed money all around, but it was just sufficient to meet current expenses and to take us, after a delay, to Alassio.

Here I had to film crowd scenes with the local people. There were 5,000 of them, and every one of them treated it as a huge joke. They were supposed to be watching Miles Mander dragging a dead body from the sea, but, from the way they carried on one would have imagined they were watching a pierrot show. The best "take" of all was utterly ruined at the critical moment by an Italian woman walking right in front of the camera. I would have liked to tell her what I thought of her—but I couldn't speak Italian. We got those scenes finished at last.

I wired to London for £50 of my own money. Then we went back to the most luxurious and expensive hotel on Lake Como with hardly enough in our pockets to buy a drink.

Meanwhile, Miss Reville was meeting Virginia Valli on the ship at Cherbourg. Tom Mix had paid a visit to Europe just previously and there had been an enormous turn-out to greet him. Virginia Valli, not unnaturally, expected a similar welcome. Instead, there was only my wife. And I might mention that she is only 4 feet 11 inches in height, and slim with it.

Unpleasant Surprise

If Virginia Valli was surprised, so was Miss Reville. She had expected Miss Valli alone; but she had with her Carmelita Geraghty, one of Hollywood's current "baby" stars. The two were traveling together and intended to stick together.

By the time my wife had bought all the necessary film frocks for Miss Valli and had paid expenses for the two actresses she had spent all her money. When they arrived at Lake Como she had no more than I had.

It rained the first day. Then, when we started shooting Virginia Valli's scenes, I was in a cold sweat. I wanted to disguise the fact that this was my first directorial effort. I dreaded to think what she, an established Hollywood star, would say if she discovered that she had been brought all the way over to Europe to be directed by a beginner.

I was terrified at giving her instructions. I've no idea how many times I asked my future wife if I was doing the right thing. She, sweet soul, gave me courage by swearing I was doing marvelously. And Virginia Valli played her scenes sublimely unconscious of the emotional drama that was being enacted on the other side of the camera.

My £50 arrived from London all right, but it was only a drop in the ocean compared with the amount I needed. I wired to Munich for some more—but the only money they would send was sufficient merely to help me along with our current expenses.

The time drew near for the hotel bill to be paid, and most of my money had gone on production. The film went smoothly enough and we got everything we wanted "in the can." But, overshadowing it all, in my mind, was the thought of that impending hotel bill.

"Confidence Trick"

The critical day arrived. In desperation I hit upon the idea of using Carmelita Geraghty as a means to extort some money from Virginia Valli. The ethics of a director playing such a trick on a star didn't trouble me. But, like a man, I left Miss Reville to do all the dirty work. She went to Valli and explained that, owing to the unexpected presence of her friend, we had insufficient expenses money to meet our obligations. Could she possibly advance us some cash? I was not present at the interview. Women can do these things more discreetly than men. At any rate, Miss Reville came back to me in triumph bearing a couple of hundred dollars of Virginia Valli's money.

By the time I had paid the bill I had got the equivalent of ten English pounds left. I reckoned it all out carefully. There was just enough to pay for Valli to have a cabin on the train back to Munich—the rest of us would have to sleep in the ordinary carriages.

My luck was still out. The next blow came when I found that Virginia Valli's luggage consisted of a large number of very big trunks which cost me an extra £6 baggage fare. I still had enough to pay for food for the stars; the rest of us would have to live on a few sandwiches. This time, however, fortune smiled on us. When I sent along a message to Valli's compartment to ask what she wanted to eat, I received the reply: "Miss Valli doesn't like food on foreign trains. She has brought sandwiches from the hotel with her."

Assets Fifty Shillings

Then the good luck disappeared. The train was late. It got into Zurich station half an hour after the Munich connection had left. There was no other train until the morning. It meant stopping at a hotel for the night. We unloaded the various trunks and equipment. I gave a helping hand. It was an expensive one. I succeeded in catching one of the windows of the train with the corner of a trunk. The plate glass smashed into several hundred pieces. That little accident cost me thirty shillings.

I had about £2. 10s. left. I knew very well that it wasn't anything like enough to pay for a hotel of the type a film star would expect to stop at. Once again I had to use bluff. I asserted that it was necessary to stop at a hotel right next to the station. Thus a humble little commercial hotel in Zurich had the unexpected and unsuspected honor of putting up a famous Hollywood film star for one night.

Ordeal Over

Luckily for me Virginia Valli had nothing but rolls and coffee for breakfast next morning. I paid the bill and looked at the change. There was just enough to buy Valli and her companion a meal on the train.

We boarded the train for Munich. When I sent along a message about a meal I received a similar reply to the one I had had on the previous day: Miss Valli still didn't like the idea of eating on a foreign train. So the rest of us ate! I arrived in Munich with exactly one pfennig left—the smallest German coin minted, worth considerably less than a farthing.

Thus ended my first directing venture—and adventure. It sounds now more like a far-fetched film scenario, but I can assure you that every incident actually happened. As far as I am aware, Virginia Valli doesn't know to this day of the comedy-drama that was played behind the production of *Pleasure Garden*.

Fortunately, the picture turned out quite well. My directing career, though it began in such stormy waters, sailed into smoother seas on the success of that launching.

In the years that followed I was associated with a number of interesting films, and with many famous and once-famous stars. I have been credited with "discovering" several well-known people for films.

I have certainly been fairly lucky in my choice of newcomers, but I have never gone out talent-hunting with the idea of finding new film faces. All I have done has been to search for suitable players for my own pictures.

For instance, I had a scene in *Easy Virtue* in which I wanted a young man to propose to a girl (Isabel Jeans) and be told her answer over the telephone. My idea was to let the telephone operator play the entire scene with her face, so that the audience could tell from watching her that she was overhearing the young man pleading; the girl rejecting him; the young man pleading again; and the girl finally accepting him.

It wasn't an easy scene. I tried one girl and she was no good. So I thought of Benita Hume, whom I had noticed in a Seymour Hicks play on the stage, and asked her to take a test for the part. She played the scene perfectly. Although she was on the screen for only a minute or two she won a round of applause at the trade show, and she received a good many Press comments. I haven't directed her since, and often wonder if she remembers that picture.

Finding Gordon Harker

Most of my other "discoveries" resulted in much the same way, from my seeing the players on the stage and realizing how suitable they would be for my current picture. When I was making *Downhill* I started Ian Hunter on his film career simply because I saw him in a Basil Dean play at the St. Martin's theater when I was casting this film, and he happened to suit one of the roles.

I found Gordon Harker on the stage, too. I was looking for a Cockney "second" for Carl Brisson in *The Ring,* and I happened one night to drop into Wyndham's Theater to see Edgar Wallace's *The Ringer.* Harker was playing a Cockney part, and I saw in him the very man I needed.

Incidentally, it has always seemed to me to be rather a waste of Harker's talents that he should almost invariably be cast as a Cockney. He is a brilliant character actor, and perhaps you'll remember that I gave him the role of a Devon farmhand in *The Farmer's Wife.* He made a very good job of it. This was in certain respects a tragic film, for tragedy came to two of the leading players in it.

The star of the picture was Jameson Thomas. He had, of course, been in numerous films before this, and he was undoubtedly one of England's most popular players. He is in Hollywood today, playing supporting roles. He left England to take his wife to California. She was very ill. The Californian sunshine seemed to offer the only hopes of a cure. So Jimmy Thomas packed up everything in this country and moved to Hollywood—in vain. His wife died in spite of the sacrifice.

Temperament

Thomas's leading lady in *The Farmer's Wife* was Lillian Hall-Davis. She was an amazing girl. On the set she suffered from acute self-consciousness. She had an acute inferiority complex in regard to her ability to play certain parts, and I remember that she turned down an extremely good role because she wasn't sure she could do it well enough. Actually, she could have played it with ease.

Yet, in private life she was an altogether different person. She possessed a terrific personality, and amazing vivacity. It was with the deepest regret that, two or three years ago, I read of her death in tragic circumstances.

The Story Behind *Blackmail*

Few people know that *Blackmail,* the first all-talking feature film to be made in this country, was originally produced as a silent picture.

Cinemas that were not equipped for talkies booked the silent version, which is still being shown on 16mm films for amateurs.

The picture went into production at that critical time when no one knew quite what was happening. Studios and cinemas alike were chary of risking fortunes on the installation of equipment for something which might be nothing more than a ten days' wonder.

In the end it was decided that *Blackmail* should be made as a silent picture. This may seem strange to you in view of the fact that when the film was released as a talkie it was described as being a long way in advance, technically, of any other talking picture.

It was a lucky film for me. It established my reputation as a talkie-maker right at the beginning of the new era. And the explanation of its technical construction is really quite simple.

I was bitterly disappointed when I was told it was to be a silent picture. I was convinced that talkies were no mere flash in the pan, and that the day of silent films had passed. I felt certain in my own mind that, when the picture was finished, I should be asked to add dialogue to it, or to remake it entirely as a full-length talkie.

"Talkie" without Sound

Therefore, when producing the film in silent form, I was imagining all the time that it was a talkie. I was using talkie technique, but without sound.

As I had anticipated, when the film was finished it was decided to add dialogue to it. Originally the idea was to "dub" only a few reels.

I fought against the part-talkie idea. In the end I had my own way. I was allowed to remake practically the whole of the picture in talkie form. There were certain difficulties. I had the same cast, except for Phyllis Konstam, who had gone off to fulfill a stage engagement. Phyllis Monkman replaced her.

But Anny Ondra, who was still the feminine star, presented a pretty problem. She could scarcely speak English. I got over the difficulty by calling in Joan Barry to speak the lines for her. Joan stood at the side of the set and read the dialogue while Miss Ondra mouthed the words.

Making a talkie of a film I had only just completed as a "silent" with talkie technique gave me a tremendous advantage over most other directors. For one thing, I was able to improve on my original ideas; and for another, I was not handicapped by having a stagy subject to handle.

Apart from the technical aspect of the picture I found it particularly interesting to make because of the players in it. It introduced two or three new people.

Donald Calthrop, for instance, had his first big part, after appearing in several small roles.

He was superb on the set. He has more to give as a motion picture actor than most people I have ever handled. He has such a wide range of expression—he could be compared with a Wurlitzer organ, which can give you everything from tremendous volume to the softest notes.

Faux Pas

Blackmail also marked Sara Allgood's talkie début, and I remember a terrible moment in connection with her.

As it was her first film we got to discussing the technique of the screen, and I was pointing out how stage actors rarely used their expressions and only their voices—they never had to project their expressions. Filmmaking was exactly the opposite; everything depended on pantomime.

"How does one acquire the technique of pantomime?" Sara asked me.

I told her that it was mainly instinct, though there were artificial ways of teaching it. In the early days of films they would make a star look agonized by telling her bad news or releasing some rats at her feet.

"How would you look, for example," I asked, "if I suddenly told you your mother was dead?"

To my surprise, Sara's face suddenly went into tragic contortions, and she turned her head away. Then she explained. I had hit upon the unhappiest example I could possibly have chosen. Her mother had only just died.

After *Blackmail* came another picture that turned out well for me—*Murder!* This was Herbert Marshall's first talkie, and the part he played was ideal for him. He immediately proved himself a natural talkie actor. Most people remember the picture by one particular scene—the one in which Marshall spoke his own thoughts without opening his mouth (the same idea was used more extensively some time later in *Strange Interlude*).

It was considered a somewhat startling talkie innovation. Actually, the idea was one of the oldest in the acting world, adapted to the talkie medium.

When an actor wanted to express certain thoughts he used to speak them himself. The soliloquy was one of the prominent methods of stage technique handed down from Shakespeare. Then it went out of fashion. Nowadays, a second character is brought on so that the actor can speak the lines to him.

I have always hated the idea of bringing in an unnecessary person, and this was why I set out to find some way of avoiding it when I had to direct that scene in *Murder!* I merely went back to the oldest form of all and introduced the soliloquy, brought up to date by making it unnecessary for Marshall to open his mouth.

My Strangest Year

Following *Murder!*, I brought the Irish players to the screen in *Juno and the Paycock*.

In don't think many people realized how daring were two of the casting selections. Among a whole company of genuine Irish people I had a Scotsman and an Englishman appearing in Irish roles—and they got away with it.

The Scotsman was John Laurie—whose performance as the crofter in *The 39 Steps* will probably be quite fresh in your mind (incidentally, his grandfather was a crofter).

The Englishman in *Juno and the Paycock* was Edward Chapman, who had been brought along to me and suggested for the part by John Longden. I was unable to get Arthur Sinclair, the original Irish star of the play, for the picture, as he was on tour. The film turned out to be a triumph for Chapman.

I remained with British International on contract for some time after this. *The Skin Game* was one of the most successful of the pictures I made during this time. It gave both Edmund Gwenn and Phyllis Konstam very good parts. I can remember very distinctly Miss Konstam's woebegone expression when I told her that we should have to have a tenth "take" on a scene in which she had to be rescued from a lily pond.

Over to Korda

From B.I.P. I went over to Alexander Korda on contract, and thus began the strangest year in my filmmaking career. I was with Korda for twelve months, and during that time I didn't make a single picture. It was not my fault; nor could Korda exactly be blamed. It was just one of those things.

There were plenty of plans, but somehow they simply didn't materialize.

You may recollect that it was announced that I was going to make a picture called *Wings Over the Jungle*. Numerous people have asked me what became of it, without realizing that it actually reached the screen in an entirely different form, though I had nothing to do with it.

What happened was that Korda had a German film of which he intended to make an English version. The story as it stood was not going to be used; only the general idea.

I spent quite a time hunting for a new story, and eventually got to work on the rough script of one I came across.

Changed Plans

That was as far as I went. The story I was adapting was dropped and some more stories were purchased. By this time my contract had expired.

When the film was finally made it was *Sanders of the River.* I want to make it clear, however, that I was not associated in any way with the actual picture, but only some of the preparatory work that led to the making of it.

That gives you a pretty good idea of the queer ways in which filmland sometimes works.

Talking of preparing stories, this seems to be an opportune time for me to reply to a question that is often put to me: "Why," people want to know, "do you take books and then rewrite them almost completely—as you did with *The 39 Steps*, for example?"

"Ruthless" Methods

Here we come to a subject about which I feel very deeply. I believe that I owe much of the success I have been lucky enough to achieve to my "ruthlessness" in adapting stories for the screen.

A book may have the germ of a screen idea in it. This germ may be in the plot; it may be in the characters; it may be in the background; or it may be in certain of the situations. But that does not mean that the book itself would make a good film.

I have always maintained that it is supreme foolishness to take any book and film the whole of it just because one angle of it is really worth screening.

There can be no doubt that *The 39 Steps* is a rattling good book, but I couldn't see it as good film material.

I found that by taking certain of the characters, part of the plot, and the excellent locales, I had the background for a very good screen story. Therefore I ignored the book as it stood, and developed the story with the screen in mind.

This I always do, and always have done. I never soak myself in a book before starting to adapt it. In fact, before now, I have written a scenario without even completely reading the original book, knowing only the bare plot, the characters, and rough outline. It has been interesting to discover afterwards just where the author and I have hit upon the same developments.

A good original screen plot is very, very hard to find. But if you can see an idea in a published book, why shouldn't it be developed? It is far fairer to acknowledge the source and pay the original author for his idea than to develop a new story from his plot without giving him any credit (though I have known this to happen in filmland).

Anyway, after my unproductive year with Alexander Korda, I signed a contract with Gaumont-British, thus renewing my association with Michael Balcon.

Before I actually took up this contract in earnest I made a pic-

ture which was produced for G.-B. release, and with G.-B. collaboration, by Tom Arnold. This was a talkie version of the popular
stage musical *Waltzes from Vienna,* and I made no attempt to get
away from the successful stage play as it stood. After all, a musical
is not like an ordinary film story.

Back to Form

Then I managed to get back into my stride again with a story after
my own heart, and with a free hand. The picture was *The Man
Who Knew Too Much.* I had been wanting to make this for some
time—ever since I was with B.I.P., in fact. Charles Bennett, Edwin
Greenwood, and I had worked up the story together, but for a
couple of years nothing had been done about it. Michael Balcon
saw the possibilities in it and decided to let me make it.

The personalities in this picture were intensely interesting. The
cast, as you know, consisted of Leslie Banks, Peter Lorre, Edna
Best, and Nova Pilbeam, to mention those most prominent.

What can I say of Leslie Banks? Here you have a very great personality; a very accomplished actor. Quiet, cultured, and charming,
he plays his scenes with ease and without worry to the director.

Nova Pilbeam impressed me for different reasons. Her first film,
Little Friend, had made her something of a sensation; but this
hadn't gone to her head. Her part in *The Man Who Knew Too Much*
was comparatively small, but she didn't mind.

What struck me most about her was her common sense. There
was no question of directing a child. Even at that time she had the
intelligence of a fully grown woman. She had plenty of confidence
and ideas of her own.

Making *The 39 Steps*

Peter Lorre's first English film was *The Man Who Knew Too Much,*
and I have recently had the pleasure of directing him again in *Secret Agent.* He is a remarkable personality.

The Peter Lorre of the screen and the Peter Lorre of private
life are two entirely different people. In real life he is a genial little
man with a great sense of humor and enjoyment of fun; fond of

leg-pulling; and conspicuous in his long overcoat which reaches his feet and has won for him the nickname of "The Walking Overcoat."

His "gag" of sending a crate of canaries along to my flat remains one of the classic leg-pulls of Britain's filmland.

On the screen, of course, he has been viewed so far as a menacing villain with drooping eyelids. But the character he plays in *Secret Agent,* though purely fictional in its unpleasant aspects, has in it something of Lorre's humorous personality as his friends know it.

You see him in this picture as a little flashing-eyed Mexican type, still a ruthless killer, but for most of the time more or less a clown.

Peter is a great individualist. There is no question that he represents the successful actor purely on account of his utter devotion to whatever he is doing for the screen. He lives for his work, and this has put him where he is.

He could hardly speak English when he was making *The Man Who Knew Too Much.* He was taking lessons all the time, and he was coached regularly every night in order that he could speak his lines clearly the next day.

He had a pretty villainous makeup in that picture, as you may remember. He had a terrible scar right across his temple, put there by the makeup department—a process by which fish skin is put over the real skin, which is then drawn up round the edges of the fish skin by means of collodion.

Married in Makeup

Peter got married, during the production, to Cecelie Lvovsky. It's always a dangerous thing to try to fix up a wedding while a picture is still being made, as he learned to his cost.

The wedding was timed for noon one Friday morning at the Caxton Hall Registrar's Office.

Without being deliberately perverse, I found I had to keep him at work nearly all that day. We hurried through some scenes in the morning—and he had to dash off in full-make to his wedding. I believe the scar actually remained on his forehead throughout the ceremony. He was back again on the set within an hour of becoming a husband.

Ambition Achieved

Having completed *The Man Who Knew Too Much,* I started to prepare *The 39 Steps.*

I have already told you how I wanted to make *The Man Who Knew Too Much* more than two years before it actually went into production.

The making of *The 39 Steps* was an even more long-delayed ambition come true. I had been wanting to turn John Buchan's novel into a film for over fifteen years.

I first read the book round about 1919 or 1920, a long time before I started my directing career.

I said that if I ever became a director I would make a picture of it. It was, therefore, on my suggestion that Gaumont-British decided to make the film so many years later.

I hadn't read the book again in the meantime. When I did so, with an eye to turning it into a film, I received a shock. I had learned a lot about filmmaking in the fifteen odd years that had elapsed. Though I could still see the reason for my first enthusiasm—the book was full of action—I found that the story as it stood was not in the least suitable for screening.

So many of the scenes, which were convincing enough in print, would have looked unbelievable on the screen—as, for instance, when Hannay saw a motor car approaching; realized that he would be captured if it reached him and he were spotted; saw some stone-breakers, and in a minute or two had disguised himself as one of these workmen.

Dressed up in Buchan's powerful art of description you could believe that in the book; but you wouldn't if you saw it in a picture.

The novel had Hannay running away from spies. For screen purposes I deemed it better to have him escaping from the police and searching for the spies so that he could clear his own name.

I could not have wished for a better Hannay than Robert Donat. One of the chief reasons for his success—in addition, of course, to his natural looks, charm, and personality—is the good theatrical training he has behind him.

He is blazingly ambitious, but difficult to satisfy. He is a queer combination of determination and uncertainty. He is determined to do only pictures that satisfy him. He will be enthusiastic about an idea, then suddenly discard it completely.

These are qualities of temperament that only a great actor like Donat can enjoy.

At Short Notice

There has been a good deal of controversy over my handling of his leading lady in *The 39 Steps*, Madeleine Carroll. As a matter of fact, Miss Carroll was not cast for this picture until production had actually started. Jane Baxter was originally to have played the part. But Jane had given a verbal promise to appear in *Drake*. Production dates clashed, and she kept her promise.

Madeleine Carroll was therefore asked to come into *The 39 Steps* at short notice—and in a part that was by no means the starring role—particularly at the beginning of the production. It was, however, "built up" on the set, and it turned out to be considerably more important at the end than we had originally intended. For this, much of the credit must go to Madeleine Carroll herself for the way in which she played up to the part.

"Let's Be Natural"

She had the good sense to realize that it doesn't take a long role to make a successful screen appearance. The average actor or actress is inclined to value the quality of a part by its length. This is quite wrong.

Madeleine Carroll's previous films had shown her in cold, unfeeling, humorless roles. So I said to her: "Why not put *yourself* on the screen and cash in on your own personality? It's a bright and likeable one. At the moment you're suffering, like a lot of English actresses, from self-consciousness in front of the camera. Let's get rid of it and be natural."

On the set she entered into the spirit of the whole thing with terrific zest. I was determined not to "let up" at all. Dignity or self-consciousness is impossible when you're being dragged along the ground, which I made Donat do to her.

It was a challenge. She had to answer it. It completely killed any self-consciousness. Madeleine, with her natural sense of humor, appreciated the position. I remember, though, that she had a friend watching on the set one day, who came up to me and reproached me for my rough handling of her!

My Spies

It was purely a coincidence that three of my films in succession—
The Man Who Knew Too Much, The 39 Steps, and *Secret Agent*—
should all have a background of spying, though not such a coincidence that they should all be "comedy-thrillers."

When making a picture, my ambition is to present a story that
never stands still.

Therefore, I always look for a subject that has plenty of action. I
introduce the comedy myself.

You will find very little humor in the original stories of *The 39
Steps* and *Secret Agent* (which is based on Somerset Maugham's
"Ashenden" tales).

I am not setting out to be an expert on screen spies. Those
three stories all contained the elements of good motion picture action. My next picture, which I am making with Sylvia Sidney (at
present called *Sabotage,* though this title is to be changed), is a
straightforward criminal thriller, without a spy in it, in spite of the
coincidence that it is adapted from Conrad's novel, *The Secret
Agent.*

Three Stories in One

But to return to the film *Secret Agent.* This consisted of two of the
Ashenden stories by Maugham—"The Traitor" and "The Hairless
Mexican"—and also a play about Ashenden which was written by
Campbell Dixon.

The story of "The Traitor" told how Ashenden caused the rene-
gade Englishman Caypor to return to England and thus be arrested as a spy.

"The Hairless Mexican" told how Ashenden was sent out with
the Hairless Mexican to get a Greek spy and kill him—and they ultimately got the wrong man.

We switched the two stories round completely; made Caypor
the innocent victim; turned the Greek into an American; introduced a train smash for dramatic purposes; and obtained the love
interest from the play.

My main difficulty all the time was this fact, that I was handling
two separate stories at the same time and weaving them into one.

Introducing the American at the beginning presented something of a problem, and a hint at the eternal triangle was the solution.

Good for Gielgud!

John Gielgud's performance in the picture is remarkable, especially when you consider that, throughout the whole production, he was rushing away every evening to play in *Romeo and Juliet*—and declaiming Shakespeare on the stage is in direct contrast to playing such a matter-of-fact, natural part as that of Ashenden in *Secret Agent*. Gielgud switched from the one to the other with complete conviction.

Comparatively strange to the screen, he was rather on the nervous side at first, but he gained confidence every day.

I found a great deal of interest, too, in directing Robert Young. He is typical of the polished Hollywood actor. He is easy to handle because of his long training in films. He is completely at ease on the set, and he always knows his lines to the dot. His is a faultless technique.

But he is adaptable as well. There is a little scene in which he and Madeleine Carroll are sitting in an open carriage bandying words with a coachman. The whole of that scene was made up on the studio floor—and Robert Young proved himself ready with his wit and ability to handle a situation on the spur of the moment.

It was rather a dramatic moment when he met Percy Marmont for the first time. Here were two leading representatives of the old Hollywood school and the new. Bob Young, as a schoolboy, had been a Percy Marmont "fan."

Percy Marmont

Marmont, of course, plays the relatively small part of Caypor in *Secret Agent*. I can't understand why the studios don't use him more, although I am aware that he has every right, if he wishes, to rest on his laurels.

Cinematically, he has most players skinned. His personality still stands out the moment he steps into a scene. He has that difficult-to-achieve possession—a real screen presence.

Several people have commented on the appearance of Florence Kahn as Marmont's wife in the film. This is the first screen effort of a very talented actress. Miss Kahn is the wife of Max Beerbohm, and I selected her for this part when I saw her playing in *Peer Gynt* at the Old Vic.

Not only was this her first picture, but it was her first visit to a studio—and she had never before seen a film in her life! It was all very much of a novelty to her. She put herself entirely in my hands. I sighed a little when I compared her willingness with the stubbornness of some players.

I mentioned just now that scene with Robert Young, Madeleine Carroll, and a coachman.

Distinguished Actor

The coachman was that very distinguished French actor, Michel Saint-Denis. Important though I like even my small-part players to be, I should never have dreamt of engaging him for such a brief part.

What happened was that he was on the set one day, visiting John Gielgud. When I was chatting to him I suddenly had the idea that he could make that coachman scene very amusing. I asked him if he would care to try it, and the idea appealed to him. His handling of the part was quite spontaneous and delightfully done.

I think I can claim, therefore, that in nearly all my pictures there has been as much interest for the discerning filmgoer in the small-part playing as in the star roles.

I should like to mention Peggy Ashcroft's appearance as the crofter's wife in *The 39 Steps*. It was brief but significant, especially when you consider that this was only her second film role. I am convinced that this delightful Juliet of John Gielgud's stage *Romeo and Juliet* has a brilliant career in front of her. The greatest thing about her is her extreme simplicity.

To conclude this series of reminiscences, let me bring them right up to date and say a few words about the film I am just starting to direct.

I must confess that at the time of writing I have not had very much opportunity of speaking to my star, Sylvia Sidney. I had a short conversation with her before she arrived. I telephoned her while she was in mid-Atlantic, and she was so overcome with surprise that she could hardly talk.

A Great "Team"

Meeting her, I found her to be exactly as I had expected and as I had hoped, when I asked for her to be in the picture . . . a quiet, extremely natural young person. I think we are going to get on well together. And I believe that Miss Sidney and Robert Donat—whom I am delighted to be directing for the second time—are going to make a "team" as interesting as any of the Hollywood-made star combinations.

To me, as I have said before, my most interesting picture is always my next one. I have enjoyed delving into the past in these reminiscences. But the future is much more fascinating.

Life Among the Stars

Have you ever been on location with a film outfit? Or watched one at work? If not, let me tell you just how many people are transported.

There is, of course, the director. There is the production manager, who looks after the finance and organization, to leave the director's mind free for the actual acting problems. There is the first assistant director and the second assistant director.

There is the cameraman—who nowadays never touches the camera except to peep through the lens to see how the scene will photograph. There is the camera operator—for we don't crank today, we turn by electricity. So there's an electrician as well.

There is a focusing boy. There is a number boy—who holds out a slate with the number of the scene and the number of the "take" chalked on it. A "take," by the way, is the individual shooting of a scene. One scene may be "taken" a dozen times.

There are two stagehands and one painter. There are two property men. There is a wardrobe mistress. There is an accountant. There is a location man, whose job it is to fix up accommodation and arrange for facilities for the company—permits to put up cameras, permits to photograph the local hunt, the local pub, the local whatever it may be.

There is a sound man, who supervises the talkie apparatus. He

"Life Among the Stars," a five-part series, appeared in the *News Chronicle,* March 1–5, 1937. (Page numbers were not visible on the BFI xerox and microfiche copies I examined.)

has a first and a second assistant. There is a clapper-boy, who signals with his clapper when a scene begins and ends.

There is a continuity girl, who notes down exactly what each character in the play is wearing at each moment; exactly what "props" are on each set, and in what position. There is a makeup man. A star will have a personal sewing maid. The leading man would have a dresser.

If there are any "tracking shots"—when the camera moves to and from the scene—there are a couple of "dolly" men—the trolley is called a "dolly." If two cameras went on location, there would be two entire camera crews.

They would be given first-class transportation, first-class hotel accommodation. They would be in constant touch with head office, who would smooth out any little difficulty that might arise.

It's like an army today: disciplined, departmentalized, efficient.

It was not always so.

The first picture I was ever given to direct—it is only 13 or 14 years ago—will serve as a model.

I was then engaged at the old Famous Players Studio at Islington. I wrote titles. I wrote scripts. I was art director—that means I designed the sets. I was production manager, which means I controlled the costs and times of the pictures. I was assistant director.

I was all these not turn and turn about, but all at once.

Micky Balcon sent for me one day and told me I was to be a director. Quite seriously, I had never thought of being a director. I was too darned busy on the job. The trouble with half the modern directors is that they don't know how their departments work.

However, Micky called me in and told me I was to direct a script called *The Pleasure Garden*. He was importing an American star—Virginia Valli—he was the pioneer of importing stars.

I was told that the picture is being half financed from London and half by a German company. I was told that not only was this to be my first picture but I was to direct it in German. That's all right, I thought: I know German.

But I was also told that I was to shoot some of it in Como. That was not so good. I don't speak Italian. But Micky said I didn't need to because the cameraman was Baron Ventimiglia, and he is Italian.

So I went to Munich and took over the unit. The unit consisted of:

Hitchcock—director.
Miles Mander—leading man.
Ventimiglia—cameraman.
"Tops"—a Topical News photographer, to do one scene.
A German girl—who is to walk into the sea to be "drowned" by
    Miles Mander.
10,000 feet of film.

We got into a taxi and headed for the station at Munich. We were off on location to Genoa, for some ship scenes; to Alassio, for some beach scenes, where Mander was to do his drowning; and to Como. Apart from personal money, which we hadn't a lot of, I had £100 to handle the whole issue.

We had our tickets; second class. We had instructions to pay duty on nothing, but try to smuggle everything through. We had the company's blessing—and we were away.

We got into a taxi and went to the station. When we got to the train Mander discovered he had left his makeup box in the taxi. We made frantic plans to meet at some point on the way and sent him back to get it.

It wasn't Hitler Germany and the trains didn't run to time. Mander got to the hotel, found his taxi by sheer blind luck, snatched up his makeup box, belted back to the station—to see the train just moving out—20 minutes behind schedule.

Mander got to the barrier. A guard stopped him. German spattered all over the place. Leaning out of the window, I just caught the word "*Verboten*." I heard a couple of English words—no matter what. And Miles socked the guard on the jaw, dashed down the platform, and got into the train.

We in the German train reached the Italian frontier. We prayed for the film in the luggage van. We took apart the cameras—Ventimiglia's and "Tops'"—and put the pieces among our luggage, in the racks, under the seat. I sat on a crank.

We got the cameras through—but the film got pinched. Worse, it was confiscated. We agreed to pay the fine. We agreed to pay the duty. But they would not release it: they said they'd send it on when the formalities were completed.

We rushed about. We telephoned. We telegraphed. The film was "on the way." It was "lost." It "hadn't been dispatched yet." I sent into Milan to buy £20 worth of film. "Tops" and Ventimiglia appeared with it just in time to start shooting. Simultaneously, the confiscated stock was returned—£20 and the expense of fetching the new stuff gone out of my £100.

The next day we started shooting. We fixed "Tops" in one place. We got Ventimiglia in another. We were doing fine. But while I was on the quay in the crowd I got jostled and bumped around. And when I put my hand into my pocket to pay for something, I found my wallet with my £80 had been stolen.

I rushed round to the police. I had to take Ventimiglia to tell them. I rushed back and got him back to his post. I borrowed a few lire from Mander. I borrowed another few from Ventimiglia. We shot the scenes.

When Mander got off the liner he had to drop into the tug we'd chartered. The tug began to seep away from the ship's side. Mander was left dangling at the end of a rope ladder with a camera in one hand and his life—or at least his comfort—in the other.

We maneuvered the tug nearer. Mander, hanging on for dear life, swore he'd drop the so-and-so camera if we couldn't get the so-and-so boat nearer and why he ever signed on with such a so-and-so outfit he so-and-so well didn't know.

We got near. We got Mander. We got back to the shore. And we'd got our shots.

I mopped my brow and got back to the hotel. I sent off to Munich. They refused to send any more money. I cabled London, asking for a personal advance on my own salary to carry the picture through. I borrowed from Mander and Ventimiglia. We pooled our resources. We'd just enough to get to Alassio. I told London to wire the advance there. And we went away.

When we arrived we looked out a nice deserted stretch of beach. We saw there wasn't a soul in sight from morning till night. We thought: "Fine." We went on location the next day.

But my little German girl told me she'd got so bad a chill she couldn't go into the water. We couldn't wait for her to get well again: the hotel bill was running up. Mander's salary, my salary, Ventimiglia's salary were all running up.

So I got the waitress at the hotel. I convinced her she would like to be in the pictures. I told her all she had to do was wade out to sea and let Mander "drown" her. When I say I told her, of course I mean Ventimiglia told her for me.

I meant to learn the language while I was in Italy. What a chance I had!

The waitress was tickled to death. We went on location bright and early. We carried our own equipment. "Tops" had gone back home. Ventimiglia carried the camera. I carried the tripod. Mander carried his makeup box.

We set up the camera. We went through the scene a couple of times. We were all ready to start when our nice deserted beach was suddenly magically full of people. Where they came from, how they knew what was going on, who they were, what they wanted, I didn't know. I don't know now.

We started on the scene. We got a fine take. We were doing fine. I thought maybe my first picture would not be such a flop. I thought maybe I was not such a bad director after all. I began to pat myself on the back: the worst was over. I had 50 quid waiting for me at the hotel. Alma would meet me at Como and she would have a bit more money. I'd had all the bad luck I was going to have. That's what I thought. . . .

I looked at Mander, dripping, shivering from rehearsal after rehearsal, carrying the "dead" body of his victim out of the sea. The girl looked grand. I thought the scene was a wow when an Italian woman walked straight across the camera-line. I shouted. She took no notice. I waved my arms. She didn't see me. I rushed up to her, just bursting. I opened my mouth. . . .

And I'd nothing to say. I realized whatever I said she wouldn't understand. I shut my mouth. I felt the biggest fool ever.

Sadly, we retook the scene.

Did I say I had a bad time? Pity poor Alma! She went to Cherbourg to pick up Valli. Valli had heard how the Mayor of Southampton welcomed Tom Mix. Valli was big stuff, and knew it. Valli expected the Mayor of Cherbourg. She expected the brass band. She expected the red carpet. But she didn't get them.

Instead, she got one woman assistant director standing four-foot-eleven in stockings and a trifle more in high heels. And nothing else. Valli was peeved. She got less than she expected.

When we went on location I was sweating with terror. What if this high-hat star should rumble I was directing my first picture? She'd throw a temperament for certain—if she didn't walk out.

Alma told me I was the snake's hips and the cat's pajamas on the set, but maybe she was prejudiced. Valli seemed to be sweet enough, so maybe, I thought, I was getting by.

But Munich answered my frantic wire for cash with just enough

to carry on with production. I was short. I skimped on the picture.
I skimped on drinks. I reckoned I could just get through.

Then Mander came along. He said he had lent me 15 quid in
Genoa. He said he must have it back. He said he must send some
money to his tailor. He got his 15.

We finished the work on location. We were leaving the following day. And that night the bill came up to my room. I reckoned
up every penny I had. I was £30 down the drain. And still I had to
keep up my dignity, the dignity of the company, the dignity of the
country.

There's only one way to keep up your dignity when you've no
money: get someone else to sacrifice theirs. Get someone else to do
the dirty work. I did. I got Alma. It's the assistant director's job to
cover the director! I know. I've been it.

I sent Alma to see Valli. I primed her to put over the story
(which was partly true) that Carmelita's arrival had upset the accounts and that if Valli would lend her £40 until we hit Munich
she would be very grateful. Valli fell for it. Alma came back to me
with a broad grin and $200 in American money.

I paid the bill. I put the odd tenner in my pocket. I booked
first-class seats for Valli and Geraghty. Alma, Ventimiglia, Mander,
and I went second. I thought the £10 would get us through.

But Virginia Valli was a star. And stars travel with clothes. Valli
had three or four Innovation trunks. So had Geraghty. Excess baggage cost me £6.

With £4 I reckoned we could just about feed the stars in the
restaurant car. The others—well, I could tighten my belt, and maybe
sandwiches were cheap. Maybe they were sustaining, too.

But fortune turned. Valli and Geraghty "couldn't eat the food
on trains." They had sandwiches from the hotel. So we ate.

We steamed into Zurich, where we were to change trains. We
steamed in—and the Munich train steamed out. Italian trains were
even later than German ones. There wasn't another till morning.

We unloaded the equipment. We unloaded the trunks. We unloaded the bags. To save a tip—pence were beginning to count
with me—I lent a hand. Then I wished I hadn't. I put a studded
suitcase into a window. The window didn't like it. It broke. "Broke"
is right again.

Up came the Swiss station master. I could talk to him in German or French. I said—in both—how sorry I was. He smiled. It

was O.K. by him. I breathed again. "Quite O.K.," said he—"*when it's paid for.*"

I began to sink at the stomach. I began to sweat. The perspiration on my forehead was cold. The perspiration round my neck was hot. I asked in as firm and light a voice as I could—Valli was on the platform—"How much?" "Thirty-five francs."

I began to breathe again. The franc was worth about $2\frac{1}{2}d$. I handed out the amount. Then he told me, not 35 French francs or Belgian francs. Swiss francs. They were worth $1s. 2d$.

I paid out. I asked him—quietly—the cheapest hotel in Zurich. He directed me to a little dive near the station. We went. I told Valli that "we must be near the station." She quite agreed.

Valli didn't like a big breakfast. That was lucky—for both of us. I paid the hotel. I had fifteen bob left—enough to pay for Valli's meal on the way to Munich.

But Valli still didn't like eating train food. We did. So we ate.

We arrived in Munich—you always lose on the exchange when you change currencies on the train—with exactly one pfennig: the hundredth part of a mark, worth between a quarter and half a farthing.

But the luck had turned. The company sent a car to meet us.

And they liked the picture.

Nita Naldi, Vamp

When I was a cub director there was only one theory of making a successful European picture. Get an American star. Those were the days when stars were stars.

Not that they made the money they do today. The star I had for the second film I directed was a very considerable star in her day. Her name was Nita Naldi: you probably remember her with Valentino in *Blood and Sand*. But she came across the Atlantic to make one picture in Germany for £1,500.

Compare that—say, rather contrast that—with the £84,000 which Marlene Dietrich took from one of her recent films. Compare that with the salary paid to a character actor today: £75 a day. Two years ago he was glad to work for £30 a week on the stage or £60 a week on the screen.

But though the modern stars make more money, the old stars sold their pictures just as well.

I was still in Munich, working for a joint control: half an English company, half a German one. I was given a script. I was told to go on location and get some pretty shots. I was told my star would be coming out for the studio stuff later.

When I read the script I found it was set in the Kentucky hills. My heroine was a pleasant, simple, homely schoolmarm. My star was glamorous, dark, Latin, Junoesque, statuesque, slinky, with slanting eyes, four-inch heels, nails like a mandarin's, and a black dog to match her black, swathed dress.

But the worry was for later. First of all I had to get my mountain scenes. I had no time to go looking for them. I had to ask. I asked everybody in sight: "Where can I get a nice thatched village with snowy mountains in the background and nice tree stuff in the foreground, and no modern stuff that would be out of the picture?"

I was recommended to this place, to that place, to the other place. But this place's only claim to fame was a new glazed-tile town hall; and that place had been recommended because it had just had lamp posts installed; and the other place because the beer was good.

But as I walked along I glanced into a picture shop. I saw a postcard of the perfect location. I went in and asked where it was. "Obergurgel," said they. Yes. You do remember it. It's where Professor Piccard came down from the first stratosphere flight.

I took the German assistant director I had just been given and went out to see the place. To get there we took a train to Innsbruck. We then drove for 7½ hours in an open victoria. We then walked for 2½ hours on our feet—no transport could reach it.

With every step we swore conditions would be so primitive, the place so out of the way, that to film anything there would be out of the question. But it had cast a spell upon me, that postcard. That was the ideal place to shoot the Kentucky hills (in German). Snow on the high ground, woods on the village level, thatch, a forgotten, almost a vanished, civilization. Grand.

I reached the place. For once it was up to the pictures of it. It was perfect. I went back to Munich as happy as a sandboy. But on the way I wanted to speak English. I was tired to death of German gutturals. I was sick of flogging my brain to think in another language. I was as mad to hear the sound of an English voice, as mad to speak and be understood in my own tongue as a claustrophobe

is anxious to get into the open air. I know that feeling too: I had it
in an Italian seaplane.

However I got back to Munich. There I picked up my company: Malcolm Keen was one of them. He was the most important
to me: he brought out my engagement ring. Nita had not yet arrived, so we went out to do the out-of-doors shots.

We got to Obergurgel. We settled in a cottage. We went out in
the evening and plotted out the work for the next day. A few long
shots of the snow and the close-ups and medium shots amid the
woods. Content as a dog promised a nice bone we went to bed.

When we woke up next day the village was a foot under snow.

That washed us out. The snow meant that we should have to
wait six months at least to make the picture at Obergurgel. We took
our snow scenes and made our way down the valley, hoping just to
beat the falls as they, too, made their way steadily to the lower
ground.

We got to a place called Umhaus. It seemed only a fraction less
perfect than Obergurgel. We made all our arrangements. We went
to bed.

And the next morning the village was under snow.

What made it even better was that we were snowed up. It was
still snowing. We couldn't shoot a foot of film. We couldn't stick
our noses outside the door.

We spent four days sitting round a German stove. I had bought
a few delicacies to take: 100 lemons, for I love lemonade and all
soft drinks; a bottle of Cointreau; a couple of bottles of whiskey,
and some biscuits. One of the actors was head-over-heels in love
with a girl in England. He wrote to her every day. That was grand
for the rest of us. It was grand for him. It wasn't so good for the
girl: the post only went once a week!

When the snow stopped snowing we seemed sunker than ever.
It had traveled farther and farther down the valley. The long shots
we had taken committed us to this valley and the whole place was
under feet of snow.

There was only one thing to do: produce a thaw.

I got hold of four men who formed the local fire brigade. I
convinced them that they must get out the fire engine and wash
the snow away. They argued, finally they agreed. They pulled out
the great manual pump with its leaky hose and they turned it on the
village.

We washed the snow from the houses, from the roofs, from the trees, from the ground. But one of the houses had a leaky roof, and the old peasant woman who lived there complained she was being really washed away.

I saw the Mayor. I told him my troubles. He said that a rich film company could probably get what it wanted—at a price. I asked him how much I should give her. He said "A schilling"—the Austrian coin then worth 7*d*. I gave her two. If I had given her ten I think I could have flooded the whole countryside, she was so pleased.

And on that small area of land, washed clean of snow with a fire engine, our exteriors were made.

I went back to Munich to meet my star. As she stepped off the train Munich quite audibly gasped. They had never seen anything like her before. She traveled with her father, who looked like Earl Haig. Her Louis XIV heels clicked down the platform. The dog on its leash was long and gleaming with brushing. Her maid followed her. It was like the royalty Germany hadn't seen for five years.

But I was thinking of a simple Kentucky Miss in a gingham gown and a cotton apron. I had to produce a strong woman of the midwestern mountains who handled a gun instead of a lipstick.

First we quarreled about her nails. They came down from half an inch beyond the finger to a quarter. We had another discussion. They came down to an eighth. Another discussion and they were all right.

The heels came down layer by layer. The makeup was altered shade by shade. The hair was changed curl by curl.

Nita put up a magnificent fight for the appearance that had made her, but it was nothing to the fight that she put up for the clothes she wanted to wear. Fortunately, I was not concerned with that: it was Alma's job.

But Alma, who took her round and made her buy cotton aprons instead of silk and compelled her to choose cloth instead of satin frocks, nearly fainted when she saw her lingerie.

Munich is a cold city, and it was winter. But Nita under her frock wore just one garment: such scanties as even today would be considered—well, scanty.

However, Nita turned out to be a grand person. For all her entourage, there was nothing high-hat about her. She talked to everybody in her heavy New York drawl. The Germans, accustomed to the starchiness of the Hohenzollerns, fell hard for this American royalty, with her father and her dog, and her maid, who was more democratic than the stagehands.

I shall never forget one afternoon. We had been working hard all the day, and Nita was nearly all in. She had to play one more scene, where she was cleaning Malcolm Keen's rifle when a face appeared at the window and she pointed the gun at him.

The scene was going well when, just as she turned the gun to the window, I saw it waver. It veered from side to side. It moved up and down. It went round in circles.

Then, without a word, Nita tilted to one side and fell headlong.

The floor was very hard. The set was built on a foundation of stones set in cement. Before the camera had even stopped turning, she had recovered. And all she said was: "Why don't they build these lousy sets right over here. This floor's too gol-darned *hard* for comfort!"

She got to her feet and wanted to go on playing, but we called it a day.

Owing to that delay, and the delay caused by the snow, we got a little late with the production. Nita had one bit scene still to play. It was half-past four in the afternoon and her train—for Paris—left at half-past six.

Nita was playing a scene where she had been run out of town (unjustly of course) by the Kentucky farmers. She had to turn on them and tell them just what she thought of them.

In silent days, we never wrote dialogue, except for close-ups where anyone could lip-read. In a big emotional scene, we let people say just whatever came into their heads. It helped them to get over the atmosphere.

When Nita finally turned on these "farmers," I called, "Give them all you've got."

She did. She gave them, in English, Italian, American, Bowery, Park Avenue, and, maybe, double Dutch. She called them anything and everything she could lay her tongue to. She told them where they got off, where they came from, where they were going to. She used words we had never before heard.

When, shuddering and shaking with emotion, she stopped and I called out "Cut" the whole studio—none of whom understood a word she had said—burst into spontaneous applause.

She caught up her dress, her dog, her maid, her father. She piled into a taxi. She rushed to the station. She caught her train still in her gingham gown, with the makeup still on her face.

She went to Paris. A few weeks later, when Alma and I were married, we went to Paris for our honeymoon and spent the first day of it with Nita. But that is another story—and one I'm *not* going to tell.

One Scene that Made a Girl a Star

Film directors spend their lives manufacturing farce and tragedy. Often and often the manufacture of these commodities creates farce more farcical and tragedy more tragic than anything we put on the screen.

When I was making *The Lodger,* for instance, the thing I wanted above all else was to do a night scene in London, preferably on the Embankment. I wanted to silhouette the mass of Charing Cross Bridge against the sky. I wanted to get away from the (at that time) inevitable shot of Piccadilly Circus with hand-painted lights.

The story demanded the dragging of a body out of the river. Here, I thought, was my chance. But Scotland Yard said "No."

We wrote, we called, we implored, we besought. Scotland Yard said "No." We pulled strings. We used influence. We went from step to step until we were within shouting distance of the Home Secretary. Scotland Yard says "No." But we were told that, if we did shoot the scene, we should not be stopped.

That's how we always used to get our permission: told, usually in a hint, that the authorities would turn a blind eye on us.

So we went down to the Embankment. We took two sets of light-vans—that does not mean vans for light work. It means vans to carry lights. We had "sun arcs"—huge, powerful lights to give a real background. Otherwise, the brilliantly lit close-up shots would seem to have been photographed against black velvet.

We parked the vans in the middle of the roadway on Westminster Bridge. We massed the arcs on the parapet of the bridge. We went on to the Embankment and started shooting.

We took our short shots. They were fine. But I was concentrating on the long shot. Every time a tram passed we had to disconnect the cables that lay across the lines. Work below had to be held up until the lights came on again.

But finally, we shot the big scene. The sun arcs turned night to day. The artists did their stuff. The bridge stood out clear and sharp. The camera turned.

The number of this scene was 45. It should have been 13. For when we went to the projection room, to see the "rushes"—the first prints of the day's takings—there was no scene 45.

We looked through all the reels. We looked through all the prints. We looked through positive and negative. There was no scene 45.

The cameraman had forgotten to put his lens in the camera.

That has happened more than once: call it tragedy or farce. Tom Mix once had to jump from a second-story window on to the back of his horse. It was to be one of his biggest stunts. But though he jumped and the camera turned, the scene was never filmed.

That cameraman had stuffed his handkerchief into the mask to prevent dust getting into his beloved camera.

The film has been left out of the reel over and over again. It is a fact that these accidents always happen not in the studio, where everything can be put right with a retake, but when a couple of thousand people have been specially engaged, when we are shooting something we can never shoot again, when the mistake costs thousands.

When that happens in America there is a legend that the cameraman is automatically doomed to death. There is no other possible punishment! But he never waits for sentence to be delivered. He just vanishes there and then.

Then there was *Easy Virtue*. That picture first put Benita Hume on the map.

There was a telephone scene in the picture: the hero was asking the heroine to marry him. She accepted.

I wanted to do it a new way: to show neither the man nor the woman. I wanted to put the whole conversation over by means of dumb show produced through a third person: in this case the telephone operator who was listening in.

It wasn't easy. She had to reproduce the effect on herself of the man's anxiety, embarrassment, eloquence, fears. She had to convey the girl's excitement, doubt, wonder, decision.

And she had to register her own interest in the affair, her own apprehension that the girl was on the point of refusing, her own overwhelming relief when at last she said "Yes."

I tried girl after girl. Finally, I tried Benita. Her scene drew from a hard-boiled trade-show audience a spontaneous round of applause. The next picture she made she played the leading lady.

Blackmail was exciting. The last sequence only was to be shot with sound.

I had an idea to turn the whole picture into sound. I did it by shooting a lot of scenes where sound could be tacked on afterwards and making a lot of other scenes, not in the script, with sound. When they were all assembled the whole picture was a talkie.

But I shall never forget the first time I heard the first "rush" of the first day under the new conditions. We all went to Tussaud's at midnight. We had directors there—financial as well as moving picture—and director's wives.

The lights went out. The picture came on the screen—it was an interrogation at Scotland Yard. There was the close-up of the woman being questioned. Her lips moved. We held our breaths. Her lips moved again. We held our thumbs. A third time her lips moved. And a sound came from the screen.

"Ennnnng."

Nothing more. Just a nasal grunt. The sort of noise you might hear in a nightmare. The sort of noise that could be produced only by a talkie that didn't talk.

That was, perhaps, my greatest disappointment. But my greatest talkie thrill as well as my greatest disappointment came in *Blackmail*. This wasn't as you might think the perfect sound reproduction of a great speech. It was when we were shooting a scene where Donald Calthrop had to eat some bacon-and-eggs.

And when we saw the rush, we heard the scrape of his knife on the plate.

Early talkie days were amazing. We had only one stage equipped for sound.

In *Juno and the Paycock* we wanted to get over a medley of noises: the machine guns that were firing down the street; the tinny note of a cheap gramophone playing in the room; the chatter of other people in the room; the tread-tread tramp-tramp of a funeral procession going by.

The funeral was that of a man whose death John Laurie had encompassed, and the scene was a close-up of him by the fire, and the effect these various blending noises had on him.

So we filled the studio with the noises. In one corner was a crowd of people talking in low voices; in another, half a dozen people marking time; in a third, a stagehand was beating a sofa with two canes to make the machine-gun fire.

But we couldn't get a record of the tune we needed. So the fourth corner was filled by the property man singing the tune through a megaphone. But that just sounded like a man singing, not like a cheap gramophone. So we clipped a clothes-peg on his nose.

And the scene reproduced perfectly.

June and the Paycock was a bad picture for my property man. There was one scene when a tin bath had to fall at the psychological moment from a wall. "Props" was to hold the nail from which it hung and release it at a given cue.

That was all right, but the set was what we call a "combination"—that is, it backed on to another set with only a few inches between them. Into this Props made his way and stood on a stepladder clutching the nail.

All would have been well, but the scene called for the cooking of some sausages. We'd rehearsed it, and the sound of the sizzling came through well. When we were shooting, we built a fire of paraffin rags. The sausages were really cooking.

But the fumes from the fire and from the burning sausages had to escape up the gap between the scenes. And the property man was being smoked out.

We heard muffled groans: "Ca't ho'd od buch logger . . . be quick . . . hurry ub." And the bath fell long before we were ready for it!

The drama behind the scenes is, as I said before, verging from comedy to farce. When I produced *The Ring,* with Carl Brisson and Ian Hunter, the high-spot of the picture was the last round of a boxing match. Brisson had to win.

Brisson was a trained boxer. He was, actually, a boxer before he was an actor. Hunter was only an amateur. It was, incidentally, his first—and very successful—film.

On the day we were shooting this last round—the previous rounds had been photographed before with trick photography to speed up the effect by "undercranking" (turning the camera more slowly)—I ranged four cameras round the set and told them to go all out.

Ian went off to the local tavern with Gordon Harker. He lunched off bread and cheese and beer. How he must have regretted it!

I exploited Brisson's knowledge of boxing. I told him to box as he would if it were a genuine match. So Brisson, with the eye of a practiced athlete, attacked Ian's body.

Every time he connected, Ian remembered the beer. It was a raging hot day. He was sweating like a bull. They fought on and on, Hunter swinging at Brisson's handsome elusive face; Brisson plugging blow after blow to the mark; Hunter puffing and blowing and grunting with every smack he took.

Finally, I gave the signal for the last of it. Brisson was to knock out his opponent. He launched a blow at Hunter's body.

Hunter caught his breath with a gulp, that sort of gulp you give when a football catches you amidships. He swayed, tottered, sat down.

He was congratulated on a brilliant piece of acting. I got some kudos for a good piece of direction.

Actually, neither of us deserved any credit. I was not directing. Hunter was not acting.

He really was "out."

Handcuffed, Key Lost!

When you have seen pitched battles on the screen, did you have any idea how they were made? Come behind the scenes with me, and I'll tell you.

There was one free fight in *The Man Who Knew Too Much*. People flung chairs at one another; people seized chairs and beat their opponents over the head. The chairs broke but, obviously, the heads did not—though they seemed to.

We did it by using balsa wood—a rare timber from the steamy South American jungle. It is so soft you can bite chunks out of it. You can hit someone with balsa—and it will hurt less than a rolled newspaper. But you can turn it on a lathe as if it were mahogany.

But balsa wood is tricky stuff to use on a set. Anyone who is standing about waiting may think: "Ah! there's an empty chair. I'll sit down." They sink into the chair and they do sit down—on the floor. The chair just crumples up under them.

Quite a few members of the staff were offered a chair by "polite" colleagues during that fight sequence. Off the screen as on it, someone sitting unexpectedly on the floor is a surefire laugh.

There was another fight in *The Man Who Knew Too Much*. That was a virtual reproduction of the Sidney Street siege of 1911. We used real bullets in that scene, but the men who held the guns were trained marksmen.

But there was a lot of faking for all that. When we wanted to show a wall actually being pitted by a fusillade, we carefully drilled the wall first and filled the holes with plugs of plaster. The plugs were all fitted with a piece of cotton. When we showed a close-up of the wall, cut into a shot of men firing, we just pulled the cotton and the plugs came out, leaving a properly bullet-pitted wall.

It's a strange thing but none of the artists engaged worried a bit about the bullets. What they did worry about was—a catapult! A member of the floor staff was, at 40, as expert a catapultist as he had been 30 years before.

When we wanted something hit where it would have been really dangerous to use bullets—nearer, for example, than eight inches, which was the mark hit nearest to S. J. Warmington's head—we used our catapult expert.

This fully grown man of early middle-age took the forked stick from his trousers' pocket, tugged back the elastic, and let fly with a steel ball half an inch in diameter. He hit the mark—but the "shot" ricocheted, and that couldn't be gauged.

Quite a lot of people were "caught bending" by him!

It was in that picture, too, that Peter Lorre got married. He was leaving for America immediately after we had finished shooting and for one reason or another we were a little behind schedule.

Peter had to get married before he left because he was taking the future Mrs. Lorre with him, and the regulations on Ellis Island are so strict that two engaged people cannot travel together to America on the same boat without risk of unjustified scandal and delays with the immigration authorities and, occasionally, charges of "moral turpitude."

So I gave Peter two hours off in the middle of a scene. He was getting married at Caxton Hall. He jumped into a car just as he was—makeup on, and a frightful scar painted on his forehead with collodion, an astringent that puckered the skin.

He had no time to take it off. If he had taken it off he would have had no time to put it on again! So you might have seen the scar bobbing on and off his brow during the picture, for we do not make a picture as you see it: the scenes are shot in any order that is most convenient or most economical.

Picture Peter, rushing from the studio to Caxton Hall and worried to death he might be held outside for coming in from a "brawl" where he had got scarred! He had to brush his hair forward to conceal it, go through the ceremony, and rush back and go on working.

John Galsworthy's *The Skin Game* was responsible for the most cultured dinner party I ever attended and for one of the best malapropisms I have ever heard.

The dinner party was at Mr. Galsworthy's house. When we sat down, Galsworthy himself "set" the subject for discussion. "Let us discuss," he said, "words. Words in relation to their meaning and in relation to their sound."

One guest suggested the word "fragile" as descriptive. Another advanced the opinion that the French "*fragile*" was even more delicate in its sound.

A third stressed the claims of "crepuscular" as being "filled with the nuance of the twilight."

I sat amazed at the feeling the guests had for the sound-sense of words.

A course or so later Mr. Galsworthy gave out another topic. "Let us discuss," he said, "the various states of consciousness." Then he amplified the topic in answer to my question. "The states of consciousness are like stratified layers of earth. The crust is complete consciousness and the core is the subconscious. Between lie an infinite series of gradations of consciousness."

That was my first contact with *The Skin Game*. Now for the contrast. Edmund Gwenn had to wear a toupee—a sort of hair wig—in the production. We got it from Clarkson's. It cost three guineas.

One day someone from the accounts, keeping an eagle eye on the pence, came rushing down. "Why go to Clarkson's for a three guinea toupee?" he asked angrily. "Do you think the firm is made of money? You can get one at Austin Reed's for a guinea."

"Really?" I asked. "Have Austin Reed started a makeup department?"

"Makeup?" said he. "Makeup? I thought you were buying a tropical helmet!"

Once—it was when I was making *Secret Agent*—I had to go to

Greece to get some local color. I wanted to photograph a Greek station and some Greek engines and rolling stock to be a guide for the real production at home.

I went out to Salonica and tried to get permission to take my pictures. I couldn't get it. I pulled strings—but they broke. I threw my weight about—but 19 stone was not enough. So I had to take my pictures without permission.

I got up to a little wayside station—it was to act as model for a real frontier station—and began to take my snaps. I snapped a train. I snapped the platform. I snapped the rolling stock and the engine.

But an army officer was having tea on the platform, and he saw me. He asked me if I had permission, and, if so, from where. I said "Salonica"—and hoped for the best.

But he didn't believe me. He said he didn't believe I was a film man at all. He didn't believe I was an Englishman. I was, so he thought a spy, and a Bulgarian spy at that. They have not yet forgotten the Balkan War of 1912 in Greece!

I didn't care so much what he thought. But he went away to telephone and verify my "credentials"—which I didn't have. So I got in our car and scooted. I got back to Salonica as fast as I could.

I got down to the train early—only to find there were soldiers on guard with fixed bayonets. I hung about the station wondering what on earth—or off it—to do. I had visions of myself flung into prison as a spy. I thought of a firing squad and explanations afterwards.

Finally, I got into the train just five minutes before it left. I stayed in my sleeping car. I wouldn't move out. Whenever I looked out of the corridor window I saw a soldier with a rifle and bayonet on guard. I saw more soldiers moving about whenever we stopped. I heard them tramping up and down the train.

I didn't feel happy until we crossed the frontier.

Then—and only then—did I learn that there had been a revolution in Greece!

We had a lot of fun making *The 39 Steps*. One of the sequences required Robert Donat and Madeleine Carroll to be handcuffed together. One day I lost the key! There they were, inextricably bound—and they couldn't get away from one another until, providentially, I found it again.

It was in that picture, too, that I pulled a gag on Donat. He complained that the waterfall scene had ruined his clothes. The ruining of actors' clothes and the demand that the company should replace them is a long-standing bone which actors and directors pick amiably enough during a production.

When Robert demanded a new suit, I gave him one out of my own pocket. I sent round for a 14*s.* child's suit from a neighborhood cheap store. . . .

Yes. We have lots of fun, but there's a lot of work in making a picture. In the old days we always took artists on location. We rarely do that today. The scenes where Madeleine and Robert were going through the Highlands were all made with "doubles."

"No," you will say. "I saw them talking in close-ups during the Highland sequences."

But there's an answer to that: a pair of scissors. You take the first shot of the moorland with the two figures running across it—these are the doubles. Then you cut to a close-up which you have taken in the studio.

How I Make My Films

All the stories I've told so far have been stories about the actual production of pictures. That's about a quarter of the work of making them.

Today I want to tell you about what goes on when there are no artists waiting to make love or kill each other on the screen.

We want to find a story. We meet and talk. We read the reviews— we have no time to read the whole books. We pore over notices of plays. We discuss every possible type of story—and that brings me to the first prime requisite for a film story.

It must blend two things which seem almost mutually exclusive: it must hang on one single central idea which must never get out of the mind of the audience for one single solitary minute, either consciously or subconsciously; and it must offer scope for the introduction of a number of elements, which you have read about every single picture that has ever been produced: glamour, suspense, romance, charm, drama, emotion, and so forth.

The formula for making a picture is to find a single problem which is sufficiently enthralling to hold the attention of the people who are watching the play unfold, and yet not sufficiently difficult to demand uncomfortable concentration.

The reason murder mysteries are not often great successes on the screen is because they demand too much acute concentration: the audience is keyed up to watching for clues, listening for clues, trying to glean from every line of dialogue some light into the mystery.

The true motion picture formula is to state in the first reel your single central theme which must be a problem. It may be of the simplest: "Boy meets girl. Boy falls for girl. Boy quarrels with girl. Boy and girl come together again."

There the problem is: Will they be reconciled? And the corollaries are: How long before they are reconciled? How will they be reconciled?

Take all the recent pictures I have made: *The 39 Steps*—Problem: Will the man get out of the mess? And how will he do it, if he does? *The Man Who Knew Too Much*—Problem: What will the man, whose daughter has been kidnapped because he knows of a murder plot, *do*?

Will he speak and sacrifice his daughter? Or will he keep his mouth shut and save his daughter at the cost of the threatened man's life?

Now, to give you an example of the difficulties a film company has to contend with, I'll tell you the story of the picture on which I am working at the moment.

Last September, I began looking round for a story. I always swear I'll never work on a story again. I'll buy one ready-made. But it never comes off like that. It hasn't this time.

I got into touch with various authors. I began to scan various books. I never read a book through if I am considering making a picture of it, by the way.

If I do read a book through, I get so saturated with the novel that I cannot discard easily what often must be discarded to make a real film and not a mere photographic reproduction of a book.

Anyway, I got into touch with various authors. One came over from the Continent. Another was a Londoner. A third was from the provinces. None of them could give me exactly what I wanted.

Then it was all fixed for me to go to Canada and get into touch with Lord Tweedsmuir—John Buchan—to get a sequel to *The 39 Steps*. I was looking forward to that. Not only did I look forward to seeing Lord Tweedsmuir again, but I've never been to America or Canada.

But the Governor-General of Canada refused to do any work

while he was still Governor-General. He was too busy. So that was knocked on the head.

We rooted about among more manuscripts. We covered more books, more reviews. We talked endlessly about ideas.

For it is ideas that we want in films far more than stories. Give us the idea and we can turn you out a story any time.

We read the "Book of the Month" selections. We discarded some of them as too highbrow; others as too slight; others as too tragic. For we are controlled by popular appeal. It is no use for a director to make a success artistically if the company loses money on the picture.

Finally I read a review of a book called *A Shilling for Candles,* by Josephine Tey. It was a first novel. It was a murder mystery with all the recognized false clues, suspects, complications that such a book always possesses.

But you won't see that when it appears on the screen.

We have used three chapters of the book as a basis for our star material. These deal with the central theme of the picture—not of the book. There is a young man, a nice young man, who escapes from the police who hold him on a charge of which he is innocent.

He is helped by a 17-year-old girl who is the daughter of the Chief Constable. In the book the girl drifts out of the story. In the film the girl—who is Nova Pilbeam—*is* the story.

We began working out our own version of the tale. I am not going to tell you those, for you will, I hope, see them on the screen much more vividly than I could relate them in print.

We engaged a writer to produce the dialogue. We went into a huddle and slowly from discussions, arguments, random suggestions, casual, desultory talk, and furious intellectual quarrels as to what such and such a character in such and such a situation would or would not do, the scenario began to take shape.

The difficulty of writing a motion picture story is to make things not only logical but visual. You have got to be able to see why someone does this, see why someone goes there.

It is no use telling people; they have got to SEE. We are making pictures, moving pictures, and though sound helps and is the most valuable advance the films have ever made they still remain primarily a visual art.

There are very few—astonishingly few—people who can write a

screen story. There are no chapter headings, no intervals between the acts. The fading in and fading out are so quick that they do not give the audience time to discuss and work out and think over what they have seen and why they have seen it.

Incidentally, have you seen Frank Capra's picture, *Theodora Goes Wild*? You will remember, if you have, that it deals with a village girl who has written a best-seller which is "scandalous" to the set in which she moves. It is terribly hush-hush. She refuses to appear as the author of the book.

Josephine Tey is another Theodora, though her book is not scandalous. But she is a mystery woman. I have not seen her, although I have asked her to collaborate with me on the script. Her publishers have not seen her.

But she produced the central idea on which I hope to make my best picture—as yet.

We're still working on *A Shilling for Candles* although we haven't turned a foot of film. Although we are basing our scenario, as I said, on three chapters of the novel, it is only the theme that is contained in them. We are using a lot of atmosphere and a certain amount of incident that appear elsewhere.

The treatment of a film built on a novel can be seen clearly in *The 39 Steps*. That was originally a story with no woman in it; it was set in London during the June of 1914—immediately before the War. When it reached the screen—with the author's complete approval—it was a modern film, with a leading lady, and a sequence in a London music hall and a character—"Mr. Memory"—that the author had never created.

The new picture is concerned with the "Gentlemen of the Road"—the tramps who wander, unconsidered, derelict, comic or tragic by turns, along the highways and byways of Britain.

Much of the material is already in the book—a very fine and careful piece of work by a very talented author. But that is not enough for the films. I must know enough about tramps to avoid making a single mistake. I must learn their idiom. I must get their clothes right. I must get their gestures, their appearance, their whole atmosphere.

In the early days, a picture would often tell a story in the 1860s—and one of the exteriors would show a telephone wire! The early American films would fall down badly when they produced stories set in England. They got their titles wrong. They made a man go to Ascot in a soft collar and a morning coat. They put an Imperial crown over an earl's visiting card.

Those titles don't—those things mustn't happen today.

So my tramp stuff needs a lot of research.

When I made *Blackmail,* I learned from Scotland Yard detectives the exact procedures when a man was arrested, charged, identified, fingerprinted, and so forth.

In the new picture, I have to get the exact procedure when a tramp spends a night in a casual ward.

I have been thinking seriously—this is not a joke: it is quite true—of doing it myself so that I shall *know* what happens at first-hand.

I should have to grow my beard for a few days. I should have to dress the part and almost make-up for it as though I were an actor. I should have to learn the right phrases to apply for admission.

I doubt if I shall be able to do it myself, though. They'd probably think I was too well fed! And I doubt if I could get thin enough in the time.

The Woman
Who Knows Too Much

The day I proposed marriage to Alma she was lying in an upper
bunk of a ship's cabin. The ship was floundering in a most desper-
ate way and so was Alma, who was seasick. (We were returning to
London from Germany, where I had just finished directing a movie.
Alma was my employee.) I couldn't risk being flowery for fear that
in her wretched state she would think I was discussing a movie
script. As it was, she groaned, nodded her head and burped. It was
one of my greatest scenes—a little weak on dialogue, perhaps, but
beautifully staged and not overplayed.

Alma's acceptance stood for complete triumph. I had wanted to
become, first, a movie director and, second, Alma's husband—not
in order of emotional preference, to be sure, but because I felt the
bargaining power implicit in the first was necessary in obtaining the
second. I had met her a few years before at the Paramount studios
in London when I was only an editorial errand boy told by everybody to keep out of the way. She was already a cutter and producer's assistant and seemed a trifle snooty to me. I couldn't notice Alma without resenting her, and I couldn't help noticing her.
We honeymooned in St. Moritz, Switzerland.

When David Selznick invited me to the United States to do *Rebecca*, we brought with us our little girl Patricia, a maid, cook,
cocker spaniel, and a Sealyham dog. We had indifferent luck with
the group: the maid got homesick and returned to England; the

"The Woman Who Knows Too Much" was published in *McCall's* 83 (March 1956):
12, 14.

cook left us to become a chiropractor; and it was only through clever ruses that we persuaded the dogs to stay on.

The cook's departure from our cast prompted Alma to try out for the part. With only cookbooks for a script, she memorized and executed my dishes to such perfection that there's been no need since to hire more than an understudy for the role.

We're both fond of French cooking and Alma duplicates my own eating habits. When I go on a diet, which I often do, Alma faithfully loses weight with me, although she's not quite five feet and weighs less than a hundred pounds. Contrary to what one would think from my measurements, I'm not a heavy eater. I'm simply one of those unfortunates who can accidentally swallow a cashew nut and put on thirty pounds right away.

I would pit Alma against a chef in any of the finest restaurants. She can prepare a meal perfectly and completely—except trample the grapes for the wine, and I'd rather she didn't do that, really. The French need the business.

Alma is most extraordinary in that she's normal. Normality is becoming so unnormal these days. She has a consistency of presence, a lively personality, a never-clouded expression and she keeps her mouth shut except in magnanimously helpful ways. She's aware that I become paralyzed with fear at the sight of a cop, but rather than try to analyze me, a method through which more wives than one have demolished otherwise honorable husbands, Alma cheerfully offers to do most of the driving.

Alma knows much—too much—about me. But Alma isn't talking. She knows that for a thriller-movie-making ogre, I'm hopelessly plebeian and placid. She knows that instead of reading mysteries at home I'm usually designing a built-in cupboard for the house; that I wear conservative clothes and solid-color ties; that I prefer talkative colors to somber ones in a room, properly introduced through flowers or fine paintings. She knows I share her tastes for modest living, but that my tendency to utter terrible puns makes me a trial to live with. She knows how relieved we were, in a way, when our daughter settled her movie career for one part in *Strangers on a Train,* then decided that being a mother of sticky-fingered children required all her creative attention.

Next to policemen, I dread being alone. Alma knows that too. I simply like the woman's presence about, even if I'm reading. She puts up with a lot from me. I dare say any man who names his dog Phillip of Magnesia, as I did, is hard to live with. Alma won't say.

It isn't my fault, really, that Alma has stayed so much out of sight of the public, although I suspect I'm accused a lot of over-shadowing her. She does read for me and I rely on her opinion. She helped work out on paper the chase scene in *To Catch a Thief*. She tries to be on the set the first day we begin shooting a film, sometimes goes to rushes, and always gives me her criticisms. They're invariably sound. She still knows the business well, which proved handy again when I began to produce my Sunday television show for C.B.S.

Alma thinks it's a shame I've been typed as a mere maker of suspense and murder movies. But I'm afraid to risk too "offbeat" a movie; people wouldn't like it because I did it. "It wasn't good Hitchcock," the critics would say.

In many ways it's a nuisance having a wife who knows all this but won't talk. The inherent danger is that the husband will never be talked about in public. It, in fact, eventually imposes upon him the egoistic need to write about himself. I'm sure I prefer it that way. I suspect Alma knows that too.

After-Dinner Speech at the Screen Producers Guild Dinner

They say that when a man drowns, his entire life flashes before his eyes. I am indeed fortunate, for I am having that same experience without even getting my feet wet.

First of all I wish to express my deep appreciation for this honor. It makes me feel very proud indeed. It is especially meaningful because it is presented by my fellow dealers in celluloid. After all, when a man is found guilty of murder and condemned to death, it always makes him feel much better to know that it was done by a jury of his friends and neighbors.

The wording of this award is highly complimentary, but just a little disturbing. Being given a plaque for "historic contributions" makes one want to pinch himself to be sure it isn't being awarded posthumously. I am indeed touched—and I want to thank you very much.

Here on the dais I see men who have been good friends and business associates—a difficult combination. I have good news for one of these gentlemen. I came to these shores 26 years ago to

A transcription of Hitchcock's talk, delivered at the Screen Producers Guild dinner on March 7, 1965, honoring him with their twelfth Milestone Award, appears in two columns by Herb Stein, in the *Morning Telegraph,* March 12 and 13, 1965, the first titled "Award-Winner Hitchcock Performs Brilliantly" and the second titled "Witty Alfred Hitchcock Slays Audience with Barbed Tongue." This was evidently a speech that Hitchcock gave repeatedly. Parts of it, for example, were printed in "The Real Me (The Thin One)," *Daily Express,* August 9, 1966, the day after speaking at a luncheon hosted by Michael Balcon where he was honored by the Association of Cinematograph, Television, and Allied Technicians (see Spoto, *The Dark Side of Genius,* 523). And his address to the Film Society of Lincoln Center, delivered April 29, 1974, printed in *Film Comment* 10, no. 4 (July–August 1974): 34–35, includes much of the same material.

make a picture for David Selznick. Naturally upon my arrival Mr. Selznick sent me one of his interoffice memos. I completed reading that memo yesterday. I shall act upon it at my earliest opportunity. Actually, it wasn't bad reading. In fact, I may make it into a picture. I intend to call it "The Longest Story Ever Told."

The condemned man, having eaten a hearty meal, is now permitted to say a few words in his behalf. During the next few minutes . . . I shall probably make quite a number of references to myself and my pictures. I trust that, because of the circumstances of this dinner, you will excuse this immediately.

I have labored in this bizarre trade for 40 years. There have been ups and downs; battles won and lost. I shall recall only one of the latter. In *North by Northwest* during the scene on Mount Rushmore I wanted Cary Grant to hide in Lincoln's nostril and then have a fit of sneezing. The Parks Commission of the Department of Interior was rather upset at this thought. I argued until one of their number asked me how I would like it if they had Lincoln play the scene in Cary Grant's nose. I saw their point at once.

In my years in the business I have survived the silent films, talkies, the narrow screen, the wide screen, 3-D, the drive-in movie, the in-flight movie, television, smellovision, bank night, and butterless popcorn. The subject of concern at the moment seems to be runaway production. I think I can speak with some authority on this subject. After all, in England I am regarded as a runaway production. How would I stop runaway production? By urging American producers to be faithful to their wives.

I began as a writer, then became, successively, stage setter, art director, director, and now, the climax of my career: after-dinner speaker.

I think I shall avail myself of the time given me to acquaint you with the person to whom you have given this award. Who is this man? Who is the real Alfred Hitchcock? I shall begin by correcting several misconceptions about myself which have grown up over the years. It is high time I set the record straight.

First of all, there seems to be a widespread impression that I am stout. I can see you share my amusement at this obvious distortion of the truth. Of course I may loom a little large just now, but you must remember, this is before taxes.

I am certain that you are wondering how such a story got started. It began nearly 40 years ago. As you know, I make a brief appearance in each of my pictures. One of the earliest of these was *The Lodger,* the story of Jack the Ripper. My appearance called for me to walk up the stairs of the rooming house. Since my walk-ons in subsequent pictures would be equally strenuous—boarding buses, playing chess, etc.—I asked for a stunt man. Casting, with an unusual lack of perception, hired this fat man! The rest is history. HE became the public image of Hitchcock. Changing the image was impossible. Therefore I had to conform to the image. It was not easy. But proof of my success is that no one has ever noticed the difference.

Our cherubic friend had a tragic ending. It was during the 1940s while he was trying desperately to make an appearance in a picture. Unfortunately Tallulah Bankhead wouldn't allow him to climb into the lifeboat. She was afraid he'd sink it. It was rather sad watching him go down. Of course, we could have saved him, but it would have meant ruining the take. He did receive an appropriate funeral. We recovered the body, and after it had dried out, we had him buried at sea.

You may be sure that in securing an actor for my next picture I was more careful. I gave casting an accurate and detailed description of my true self. Casting did an expert job. The result: Cary Grant in *Notorious.*

As you know, I still remain a prisoner of the old image. They say that inside every fat man is a thin man trying desperately to get out. Now you know that the thin man is the real Alfred Hitchcock.

There is a dreadful story that I hate actors. Imagine anyone hating Jimmy Stewart . . . or Jack Warner. I can't imagine how such a rumor began. Of course it may possibly be because I was once quoted as saying that actors are cattle. My actor friends know I would never be capable of such a thoughtless, rude, and unfeeling remark; that I would never call them cattle. . . . What I probably said was that actors should be *treated* like cattle.

I will admit that I have, from time to time, hoped that technology would devise a machine to replace the actor. And I have made some progress of my own in that direction. In *Foreign Correspondent* Joel McCrea played a scene with a windmill and in *North by Northwest* Cary Grant's *vis-à-vis* was a crop-dusting airplane. I believe the airplane had real star quality, for it drew an amazing amount of fan mail. However, when I attempted to sign it up for my next picture, it was already asking too much money.

This leads to the next logical step when I reduced the human element still further in *The Birds*. Now *there* are some actors I would call cattle! You have heard of actors who insist that their names be above the title; these demanded that they *be* the title! As a result I am definitely in favor of human actors. As far as I am concerned birds are "strictly for the birds"—or for Walt Disney.

On the subject of actors I should like to add this footnote. I find it delightful that the stars have been placed on the Hollywood sidewalks so we can walk all over them. It is an encouraging demonstration that the city's Chamber of Commerce not only has an eye for publicity but is psychologically oriented as well.

It has also been whispered about that I hate television commercials. Once again I plead "not guilty." I love them. Oh, I readily admit that they are noisy, nauseating, ridiculous, dull, boring, and tasteless . . . but so are many other things—including after-dinner speakers. The difference—and herein lies the reason I love commercials—the difference is that one can turn them off. This is an epoch-making breakthrough. In the entire history of sadism, the television commercial is the only instance where Man has invented a torture and then provided the victim with a means of escape. What is interesting is that so few people avail themselves of the opportunity.

Actually I find commercials fascinating. They are so exquisitely vulgar and so delightfully tasteless that they must be irresistible to everyone save the few who aren't enchanted by discussions of nasal passages and digestive tracts.

TV has been an interesting chapter in the history of screen entertainment. It was only natural that it would affect theater attendance, but I explain it this way: The invention of television can be compared to the introduction of indoor plumbing. Fundamentally it brought no change in the public's habits. It simply eliminated the necessity of leaving the house.

With the sale of features to television, many a screen producer now sits in his living room in front of his television set, his past rapidly catching up to him as he watches his turkeys come home to roost.

Television brings us to another accusation I should like to refute. We often hear the criticism that there is too much violence. Screen producers need not be told that television violence is very much like an iceberg. Only a small fraction of it is visible on the screen. The public should see what goes on *behind* the scenes.

But the point is that one of television's greastest contributions is that it brought murder back into the home where it belongs. Seeing a murder on television can be good therapy. It can help work off one's antagonism. And, if you haven't any antagonisms, the commercials will give you some.

The real danger in my opinion is not violence. It is that the viewer of television murder can enjoy all the sensations without the mess. There are no stains to remove, no body to dispose of, no cement to dry. Such a situation is not good for national character. It encourages sloth and dries up creative juices. The result? Murder could someday be reduced to a mere spectator sport.

I have been making light of murder but I hope you never forget that it can be a very sordid business—especially if you don't have a good lawyer.

The public thinks I have been getting away with murder for 40 years. But am I really unscathed? I can best describe the insidious effect of murder on one's character by reading this paragraph from Thomas de Quincey's delightful essay, "Murder As One of the Fine Arts."

If once a man indulges himself in murder, very soon he comes to think little of robbing, and from robbing he comes next to drinking and Sabbathbreaking, and from that to incivility and procrastination. Once begun on this downward path you never know where you are to stop. Many a man dates his ruin from some murder or other that perhaps he thought little of at the time.

I think it is now obvious that the real Hitchcock is almost totally different from the public image. I only hope that having learned this, you do not feel you have given this award to the wrong man. I have already grown quite fond of it.

They say that a murder is committed every minute, so I don't want to waste any more of your time.

Now, will the real Alfred Hitchcock please sit down. Thank you very much.

Surviving

An Interview with John Russell Taylor

At Universal it was a mild, flat, sunny afternoon. The sort of day a crop duster might suddenly come at you out of the empty sky. I recognized the stocky white figure of Sarah, the Hitchcocks' pet Scottie, being ceremoniously walked by a secretary, signifying that the master was in residence—and Mrs. H. too, as it transpired. Regular as clockwork, whether he has some immediate project on hand or not, Hitchcock puts in a 9 to 5 day at the studio, reading properties, screening movies to check on the work of actors or technicians he might possibly be interested in using, and generally keeping a fatherly eye on the regulation of his little empire. And in any case, he has just announced a new project in the works, *The Short Night*, based on Ronald Kirkbride's novel suggested by the escape of George Blake, plus Sean Bourke's nonfiction account of the same happenings, *The Springing of George Blake*. The champion survivor, evidently, is in fine shape: the only major director of the silent cinema who is still an unshakable part of the filmmaking scene today.

In the last 50 years you have made some 53 films. What has driven you?

First and foremost, it's a case of the cobbler sticking to his last. I think you have a sort of instinct which pushes you towards what you can do best, and once you have found it, it becomes a habit to keep on doing it. And it's too late to start at the other thing I

"Surviving" was originally published in *Sight & Sound* 46 (Summer 1977): 174–176. The second part of the interview, not reproduced here, is with George Cukor.

would really have liked to do, being a criminal lawyer. I'd have really liked that—not, you know, the histrionic type like Marshall Hall or the smooth, charming type like Curtis-Bennett. But I've spent so much of my life fascinated by crime and the administration of justice. That was never really a choice, though: I left school at the age of 14, went into engineering drawing and from there by a succession of logical steps into the cinema. I was reading Buchan and Chesterton then (even as a child I never cared much for Sexton Blake and the lower orders), and all the real-life crime stories I could get a hold of, but it never occurred to me as a practical possibility that my professional life might take that turn.

Why not the theater?

When people ask me why I don't direct a play, I always answer that I wouldn't know where to begin. Until recently I've gone to the theater constantly, but I've managed to keep my innocence. I don't know how an actor projects, I don't know when he should have his back to the audience, and there's something boring to me about the idea of working within that constant fourth wall of the proscenium arch. Also, in the theater the writer is paramount, he is always there in the stalls, he is the final arbiter. In films the director has the last word.

Nearing 78, you are as busy as ever and obviously have no thought of retiring. What drives you now?

I have a contract with Universal that has to be fulfilled: two more movies. But basically, I can't help it. I need to go on. I could never retire. That seems to me the most horrible idea. What would I do? Sit at home in a corner and read? I have no outside interests, I've done all the traveling I want to do. Also, you have to remember that as well as being a creative person I am a very technical person. The actual exercise of technique is very important to me, the practical solution of technical problems. I have always needed to do things, never had much taste for philosophizing about what I do.

Has there ever been anything specific you wanted to say in your films?

Now we're back to Sam Goldwyn, aren't we?—messages are for Western Union. Of course in each specific subject there is something I want to say, in the sense that there is something which attracts my interest, and I want to bring that out in my treatment of the subject. It may be something technical, as in *Family Plot,* where it was the structural image of those two separate plots and separate groups of characters coming gradually, inevitably together, and how to do that and to make it seem completely natural. In *The Short Night* it's a situation that fascinates me: the man falls in love with the wife of man he's waiting to kill. It's like a French farce turned inside-out. If he sees a boat coming across the bay with the husband on it, he can't hop out of the back window, he has to wait and do what he has to do. And of course he can't take the wife, who loves him, into his confidence. And so the whole romance is overshadowed by this secret, which gives it a special flavor and atmosphere. That's what I want to convey.

Tell me more about The Short Night.

I read a review of the novel somewhere, and was struck by this idea. The central action takes place on an island off the coast of Finland, near where Sibelius was born. It's where Blake's wife with their two children waited for him to come and collect them once he'd got out of England, and take them into Russia with him. That's where the man who is stalking him comes also in Ronald Kirkbride's novel, and where he and the wife fall in love while they are waiting. The end of the film is a big traditional chase: the wife won't go with the spy, so he kidnaps his children and gets on the train for Russia from Helsinki, and the other man has to pursue the train, get on it somehow, and get the children away from him as well as kill him if he can before they reach the border.

The beginning comes from the nonfiction book by Sean Bourke, who actually engineered Blake's escape. The details of that are incredible: they sound as though they came straight out of a movie. Bourke and Blake communicated by a walkie-talkie that had been smuggled into the prison. Hammersmith hospital is right next to the prison, and Bourke used to stand outside it on visiting days with a bunch of flowers wired for sound, into which he would talk to Blake. They finally got him over the wall one night when there was a film show in the prison, with all kinds of delays, and then hid him three minutes away until the fuss had died down. But the main thing is the love story. I went to look at the island. It has a few low scrubby trees, very bleak and windswept, but there are lots of reeds in shallow water all round. I thought what an interesting image it would be to shoot a chase there from slightly above, so that you can't see the men at all, just the movements of the reeds as they almost converge, then get further apart, neither knowing where the other is . . .

Do you ever fear the competition of your own past?

Inevitably, sometimes. But probably less the longer you're at it. Look at that young man Spielberg, making the biggest money-maker ever so early in his career. How was he going to top that? I find the thing to do is to concentrate entirely on the film in hand; and say to yourself, it's only a movie.

Are there purely practical problems about continuing in Hollywood much after the age of 60—insurance, for instance?

I suppose so, but luckily I haven't encountered them. My health is pretty good, despite a few arthritic aches and pains. I have a heart-pacer, but that works more reliably than nature. And my films are sufficiently successful for other people to want me to go on working, which is a lot of the battle.

Is there anything you regret not having done?

Being a criminal lawyer, maybe. And some movie ideas that I haven't yet been able to incorporate into a workable screenplay. And *Mary Rose,* which I really wanted to do, but they didn't want to let me. Do you know, it's written specifically into my present contract that I cannot do *Mary Rose?*

To survive in the film business it would seem you have to be tough. Are you tough?

I don't know. In a business sense, I don't think so, particularly. Instead of being tough, I have usually been devious. Present people with a *fait accompli,* or if I want to turn down their ideas come up with a valid alternative right away, so that it is not a head-on collision. I think the only area where I am tough is in the preparation stage of my films: I never give up until things are right. It takes so long, and so much work, to achieve simplicity. And I've always felt that if you're tough with yourself, in the strictly professional sphere, the rest takes care of itself.

And after The Short Night, *what?*

Good heavens, I don't know. I have lots of ideas that I've never yet managed to get on the screen, and something always comes up, some new story that excites me. I warn you, I mean to go on for ever!

Actors, Actresses, Stars

Introduction

Hitchcock is frequently thought of and highly regarded as a unique and innovative formalist, interested primarily in exploring film structure and technique, and as a fantasist, centering his films around eruptions of the extraordinary. But he seems to have always thought of himself as a "realist," a notoriously slippery and ambiguous term, but one that conveys his awareness of various forces that restricted his autonomy: he worked within a studio system; filmmaking is a commercial as well as an artistic enterprise; and the audience is in some ways as much of a director as the filmmaker, demanding vivid, lifelike characters and at least a touch of reality in their entertainments. As early as the 1930s, the period from which all but one of the essays in this section are drawn, Hitchcock was shrewdly commenting on a complex of associated topics, related to the above issues, that have become major points of interest in contemporary film criticism more than fifty years later: the star system, women on screen and in the audience, and the economic and market determinants of cinematic expression.

Hitchcock had a simple answer for the question "Are stars necessary?"—of course they are!—but in his brief essay of that title, he carefully notes that this answer is dictated to film producers by the public. He defends "star worship" with a quick glance at audience psychology—"it fills some inherent need of which I see no reason why the public should be deprived"—but he stresses, first and foremost, that stars are an economic necessity, the "magnets" that draw people to the box office. Even the astonishingly large amount of money paid to such stars as Maurice Chevalier is not unreasonable: stars more than pay their own way by filling the house day after day.

At various points in his life, Hitchcock complained about the star system: as he told Truffaut, he was not happy when stars were forced on him for unsuitable roles, and especially later in his career, when he was a producer of and profit sharer in his films, he was upset by the increasingly large proportion of money that went to stars' salaries. Perhaps Hitchcock is describing his own wistful dreams when at the beginning of "Are Stars Necessary?" he says, "There are idealists who consider films as an art pure and simple, and who say that all actors should be subordinate to the film." Still, Hitchcock was a "realist" and accommodated himself to the system, although not without resistance: his defense of the star system here is less memorable than his persistent statements elsewhere about treating actors like cattle and children and his admiration for Walt Disney's control over his stars, who could easily be redrawn or erased; and he was certainly one of those who tried to establish that even apart from famous actors and actresses, the director could be a star and box office magnet. But perhaps more important than his resistance is his creative adaptation, his ability to use stars for his own purposes. As he notes in another essay of the 1930s, "If I Were Head of a Production Company," included in the Film Production section below, stars can be used as camouflage, as the "jam round the pill," pleasing and entertaining the audience, but thereby allowing the director to experiment with new techniques that might not otherwise be acceptable in a commercial medium.

Some of Hitchcock's most interesting comments in these essays revolve around his descriptions of his particular use of stars and his understanding of what the shape of their careers should be. In "Crime Doesn't Pay," he notes that while menacing roles provide a good entry into films, an actor should move rather quickly from villain to straight actor to comedian. His rationale is basically economic: audiences typically do not sympathize with and, more important, do not pay to see the "heavy," so a long and successful career cannot be based on such roles. There is, to be sure, some simplistic advice in this essay, but perhaps we may read between the lines to see Hitchcock beginning to conceptualize the complicated villains he is usually associated with: sympathetic, attractive, comic, and in almost all ways a captivating screen presence. He notes in passing that the "Continental" model is much different from the Hollywood model: on the Continent, for example, Peter Lorre (whom he had in fact already worked with in several films and praised for his fine acting and humorous villainy) is tremendously popular, because of rather than in spite of "the macabre *M.*" Hitchcock's attraction to this model is apparent, even in an essay that seems to recommend another, and one senses that what he outlines for an actor as the stages of a successful career soon becomes what he demands from an actor in the course of one Hitchcock film—that he be simultaneously a menacing villain, skilled straight actor, and entertaining comedian, indeed, Hitchcock notes with great satisfaction, as Lorre was in *Secret Agent*.

Modern critics often emphasize the relationship of the star system to industrial modes of production, suggesting that stars help satisfy consumer demands for readily identifiable and predictable as well as high-quality commodities. We know what we are buying, for example, when we pay to see a Cary Grant film. Hitchcock, though, is particularly intrigued by using actors and actresses "against the grain," in unpredictable and unconventional ways. In "What I'd Do to the Stars," written just as he was about to leave England for Hollywood to work with David Selznick, Hitchcock looks forward to "working under new conditions with an entirely fresh crowd of people," partly to take advantage of the well-established skills of a new cast of characters but also to stretch and modify their talents. He knows and appreciates the characteristic strengths of many Hollywood stars: William Powell, for example, is so trustworthy and skillful in both melodrama and comedy that Hitchcock could let himself go completely while working with him, and Gary Cooper is a perfect illustration of Hitchcock's often-repeated description of the ideal actor, capable of doing nothing and doing it extremely well. But he criticizes the Hollywood system for "the way it allows its stars to get into a groove" (for further comments on this topic, see Hitchcock's nearly contemporary essay "Old Ruts Are New Ruts," included in the Film Production section) and says boldly, "There is scarcely a star in Hollywood whose appeal I would not try to alter or develop."

As much as Hitchcock is ostensibly commenting on the star system, though, there seems to be much more going on barely beneath the surface when he turns his comments toward what he does and would do to the female stars who come under his control. By this time in his career, as his interviewer in "What I'd Do to the Stars" notes, Hitchcock had already "developed a reputation as a misogynist," a charge that Hitchcock does not so much deny as rationalize. He finds British actresses far too dignified and takes delight in "debunking" them, imagining Marlene Dietrich "sucking a toffee-apple" and Claudette Colbert playing "a beautiful mannequin who, having risen from the gutter, has to keep up a good appearance but who is, in her soul, lazy, good-natured, irresponsible, and slightly sluttish." He repeatedly notes that women should not be glamorized, because, as he explains in "How I Choose My Heroines," the primary film audience is composed of women who are not particularly interested in the physical sex appeal of the female characters and also, as he explains in "Women Are a Nuisance," because "reality," not artificial beauty, is "the most important factor in the making of a successful film." But this does not account for his evident glee in deglamorizing women in his films—the fine line between "humanizing" and "humiliating" women may be overstepped when he confesses "Nothing pleases me more than to knock the ladylikeness out of chorus girls!"—and his attentiveness to, as he puts it, "whether my potential heroine is sensitive to direction. In other words, whether she is the kind of girl I can mold into the heroine of my imagination."

"Nova Grows Up" is Hitchcock's most extensive commentary on molding one of his actresses, and it is both remarkably candid and telling. The essay is shot through with critical comments about what he describes as Nova's early unwillingness to be directed by him. His final praise for her quick development into an experienced actress is lavish and genuine but by no means unalloyed: she grows up from her early, somewhat annoying "self-confidence" to a maturity characterized by compliance and unassuming willingness to take direction. Derrick de Marney, the male lead in *Young and Innocent,* reported that Hitchcock was generally sharp-tongued but "deferential" and kind only to Nova on the set (quoted in Spoto, 180). But in "Nova Grows Up," Hitchcock admits that he teased her, and even though his phrases may simply be loose overstatements, his description of "threatening" her to the point where she was "terrified" is not altogether innocuous. He talks adoringly about using her in his next picture, but this was not to be. Spoto says a film titled *Empty World,* to be directed by

Hitchcock, was announced but then never heard of again (195). He notes that Nova was mentioned as signed for *The Lady Vanishes,* but Margaret Lockwood got the role. And Leonard Leff documents how vehemently Hitchcock argued against Selznick's wishes to use Nova as the female lead in *Rebecca* (49–51). Hitchcock's attraction to Nova was thus by no means simple or uncomplicated.

While we should not overanalyze such essays, we should nevertheless not miss the clear signs that the prospect of a young woman growing up in front of him both charms and disturbs Hitchcock. Barely beneath the surface we see what may well be a characteristic mixture of adoration, desire, jealousy (fantasizing about the "tragedy" of getting her "into the hands of Hollywood makeup men"), manipulation, and active hostility. What at first glance seems to be a superficial piece of publicity writing for his current film turns out to give a great deal of insight into the perennially intriguing problem of Hitchcock's conception of and relationship with women, on the screen and on the set.

Nearly twenty-five years later he was still pondering over his "conception of femininity" in "Elegance Above Sex," and he was still giving evidence that this subject remained mysterious and problematic. He has little interest in the obvious sexuality of a "big, bosomy blonde" but confesses himself particularly interested in elegant ladies, like Grace Kelly, who "blossom out for me splendidly." Written at the time when he was just introducing Tippi Hedren, who Spoto envisions as the most egregiously manipulated of all Hitchcock's leading ladies, these sentiments are more than a little troubling. Hitchcock concludes by saying that "a woman of elegance . . . will never cease to surprise you," but it may well be that the director generates just as many surprises in his complex treatment and representation of women.

How I Choose My Heroines

The chief point I keep in mind when selecting my heroine is that she must be fashioned to please women rather than men, for the reason that women form three-quarters of the average cinema audience. Therefore, no actress can be a good commercial proposition as a film heroine unless she pleases her own sex. Screen aspirants please note!

My contention will probably be challenged by the supporters of the "physical" school of screen art who assert that sex appeal is the most important quality which can be possessed by any screen actress, but ignore the fact that the woman stars whose popularity has been long-lasting, such as Mary Pickford, Lillian Gish, Betty Balfour, Pauline Frederick, and Norma Talmadge, have no sex appeal, as the phrase is used in the jargon of today. They owe their success not only to their natural talent and charm, but to the fact that they invariably appear in roles which, in respect of suggestion and ultimate achievement, appeal to the best in human nature.

The Fallacy of Sex Appeal

Cynics may sneer at this, but they cannot deny it, any more than they can deny that it is true to say of every artist who has been "boosted" on account of alleged superabundance of sex appeal that, in the words of old Omar Khayyám, "he abode his little hour and

"How I Choose My Heroines" was originally published in Langford Reed and Hetty Spiers, *Who's Who in Filmland* (London: Chapman and Hall, 1931), xxi–xxiii.

went his way." In using the masculine pronoun for correctness of quotation, I embrace actresses also. Metaphorically, as always, for, as a producer, the more fascinating business privileges enjoyed by the actor are, alas! denied me.

To regain my customary gravity, as befits the serious subject under discussion, I believe that the vast majority of women, in all ranks of life, are idealists. They may not live up to their own ideals, often they cannot do so, but they do like to see them personified by their favorite film heroines, and I have heard of a good many cases, particularly in humble life, in which mothers have attempted to model the conduct and sentiments of their young daughters on those supposedly identified with their favorite women stars, and in instances where there has already existed a slight physical or psychological resemblance have proudly declared, "Isn't our Nelly like—? The same look in the eyes, the same curl in the hair, the same high spirits and love for animals!" or words very much to the same effect.

Women may tolerate vulgarity on the screen, but not when displayed by their own sex, for they are so constituted, bless 'em! that they cannot help feeling that such an exhibition is lowering to women generally.

A Thoroughly Nice Girl

Physically as well as mentally the screen heroine of today must not only be a thoroughly nice girl, but must possess vitality, both in looks and in the quality of her voice. The reign of the purely pictorial heroine is over.

Choosing a heroine for the screen is much more difficult than choosing one for the stage. In both cases, of course, she must be able to act and have a good speaking voice, but there the essential requirements diverge. The appeal of the stage is necessarily an artificial one, materially assisted by the distance of the audience from the players. Thus a middle-aged actress of moderately good looks can often contrive to look young and beautiful. But the screen has no "distance to lend enchantment to the view," for the events it portrays are usually brought so close to the audience that, in effect, the face of the heroine is but a few feet away, even from those in the back row of the gallery. Therefore she must have real beauty and real youth; imitations of them would be instantly detected. So that the film heroine's professional career rarely outlives a dozen years, and in the case of those whose qualities do not approximate to those possessed by the ladies mentioned in the early part of this article, seldom exceeds three or four.

Five-Foot Heroines

In addition to the qualities I have enumerated, a screen heroine should not be above medium height; indeed, smallness is a definite asset. A little actress not only photographs better, particularly in close-up scenes, than one who "rears her form to stately height," but is more pleasing to the audience, who like to see the heroine's curly head nestling against the hero's manly breast. If it is a foot higher, she is apt to make him look insignificant. That is why practically every actress who has attained success on the screen in romantic or emotional roles has been on the short side. Should would-be screen débutantes of more than average height doubt this, I feel sure they have only to examine the pages of this most authoritative and inclusive work of reference to find my statement endorsed.

And last, but by no means least, I have to consider whether my potential heroine is sensitive to direction. In other words, whether she is the kind of girl I can mold into the heroine of my imagination.

With such a rare combination of qualities required, is it any wonder that first-class screen heroines are almost as rare as the proverbial dodo, or that film producers occasionally wear a worried look?

Are Stars Necessary?

Ever since the birth of films, I suppose, producers have been asking themselves this question, and with ever-growing insistence the public have answered "yes."

There are idealists who consider films as an art pure and simple, and who say that all actors should be subordinate to the film.

As a film producer, I *know* that art must first of all be commercially popular to be successful, and that one of the greatest factors which make a film commercially successful is the popularity of the stars in it.

Whichever way one looks at it, the "star" question is there, because examination of every successful play or film reveals that some strong drawing-power was responsible for the box office receipts, and that if it was not the leading player, then it was the author, or the producer, or the title, or even the effect of efficient exploitation of the production.

A production which is sufficiently startling and magnificent to justify the banging of the publicity drums, could easily be the "star" attraction, and so also could a title which is a household word.

A title, for example, like "On the Dole" would probably have box office appeal in itself. By all this, I am only trying to prove that to succeed in films, or even in the theater, you must have a "star," and that if the magnet is not human, then there must be a substitute.

I believe in the star system, because filmmaking is a business, and

"Are Stars Necessary?" was originally published in *Picturegoer,* December 16, 1933, 13.

as a director I cannot afford to lose the money I am putting into my business.

The world may complain that film stars are paid money which makes cabinet ministers' salaries look like pocket money, but, believe me, every penny he or she is paid is worth it to the producer, otherwise the producer would not pay it.

Stars are paid according to what they bring into the box office, and if they bring in £20,000, then no one can blame them that they are paid accordingly.

Maurice Chevalier once had a three-year contract signed at £500 a week the first year, £750 the second, and £1,000 a week the third. So successful was he, however, that halfway through the contract his salary was raised from £750 a week to £2,500 a week, and he was worth every penny.

At one theater it was reckoned that "if full" the theater would hold £900 a performance. When Chevalier played there they played twelve performances a week, and every performance was packed. The theater thus gained £10,000 a week, out of which Chevalier was paid £5,000 as his share.

It is all really a question of supply and demand. The pubic demand their stars and the films supply them. When the public cease to demand, then the films will cease to supply, but I do not think this will happen yet, and after all why should it?

There is a very good psychological reason for "star worship": it fills some inherent need of which I see no reason why the public should be deprived. I know it is cynically labeled "sob stuff," but does anybody really care what it is labeled?

After all, is not sheer artistic emotion something to be proud of and not ashamed? There is little enough glamour in the drab business world of many of the audiences: why then should they be blamed for wanting it in their relaxation?

Moreover, aren't we forgetting one rather important fact: that a star only attains stardom because he or she has proved his or her worth and ability on the screen or stage.

The critics who argue that "the play's the thing" and "it's good acting and not names that count," seem to forget that a star's "name" still has some connection with his or her acting.

The public which says, "Let's go and see So-and-So's film tonight," say that because they know that "so-and-so's" film and acting is always worth seeing, and the same applies to the stage.

Those names that you see in electric light over the theaters and

cinemas are all names who have proved their salt to both the producer and the public.

And if the public had seen, as I have done, the reverse of the
picture, those bitter struggles to stardom—the disappointments,
the sheer hard work, the poverty often coupled with starvation at
the beginning, the courage and pluck and determination to win
through—I do not think they would grudge them the electric
lights.

Stardom is not won easily. I know people whisper about the
power of the publicity drum, but no amount of publicity can create something which is not there, and a star who is only a child of
publicity will not last.

And I do not think that anyone can say the "star system" means
that the production as a whole is neglected. If they do, then let
them spend a day, or two days, on the sets and see the infinite
trouble, labor, and patience that is expended on one single shot. I
have known a producer throw £40,000 of work away and start
production again from a fresh angle!

You cannot destroy the star system, because at rock bottom it is
the public who create and acclaim the stars.

Women Are a Nuisance

An Interview with Barbara J. Buchanan

I asked Alfred Hitchcock point-blank: "Why do you hate women?"

"I don't exactly hate them," he protested. "But I certainly don't think they are as good actors as men."

I had gone out to Shepherd's Bush to get to the bottom of Hitch's brutal disregard for glamour, love-interest, sex-appeal, and all the other feminine attributes which the American director considers indispensable.

In *The 39 Steps* (as in other films with other actresses) Hitch deliberately deprived Madeleine Carroll, one of our best actresses, of her dignity and glamour.

It seems that if he must have women in his films, at least he's not going to allow them to look beautiful or be "glamorous." He is quite unrepentant and fully intends to do the same with Madeleine in her next film for him, *Secret Agent*.

"Glamour," he told me defiantly, "has nothing to do with reality, and I maintain that reality is the most important factor in the making of a successful film. The very beautiful woman who just walks around avoiding the furniture, wearing fluffy negligees and looking very seductive, may be an attractive ornament, but she doesn't help the film any."

"Women Are a Nuisance" was originally published in *Film Weekly*, September 20, 1935, 10. The full heading is "Alfred Hitchcock Tells a Woman that Women Are a Nuisance."

Where Beauty Helps

"I wouldn't be so foolish as to say that beauty doesn't help an actress. It is a very different quality from mere artificial glamour. A really beautiful woman starting a film career is lucky because, for a time, audiences will overlook her lack of acting ability. She may become a star overnight and learn her acting afterwards, as Jean Harlow did. But it is the dumb kind of glamour that I detest."

Hitch twinkled in his fat, cherubic way.

"If I were directing Claudette Colbert (whom I consider one of the loveliest women in American films)," he said, "I should first show her as a mannequin. She would slink through the showroom in her elegant, French way, wearing gorgeous gowns as only such a woman can. She would be perfectly coiffured, perfectly made-up. Then I should show her backstage. As she disappeared through the curtains, I'd make her suck down a piece of toffee or chewing gum which she had kept in her mouth all the time she was looking so beautiful—you see what I mean? That touch of realism would make her infinitely more human."

Those Ladylike Girls

"But what about this accusation that women can't act?" I demanded.

"With English actresses, at any rate," said Hitchcock, "it's partly their love of being a lady and partly that they divide their interest (as, of course, do many of the men) between the stage and films.

"Let's deal with these things one at a time. First, many of the American stars have come from the poorest of homes. They have had the common touch, and they have never lost it. Most of our English film actresses come from some school of acting or from the stage. It is always their desire to appear a lady and, in doing so, they become cold and lifeless. Nothing pleases me more than to knock the ladylikeness out of chorus girls!

"The second thing is that you cannot successfully combine a stage and screen career. One of them has to go. Too many stage actresses still make films merely to get together some easy money. Such an attitude is bound to show in their work—they are too busy thinking of the nice, fat check to give a sensitive performance.

"But the main disadvantage women have is undoubtedly the lady pose. I have never had any difficulty in finding men stars—perhaps because that sort of superficiality does not bother them. And I shall continue to keep the atmosphere of my films largely masculine.

"I don't ask much of an actress—I have no wish for her to be able to play a whole list of character roles, but she *must* be a real, human person.

"Any success that I may have had with *The 39 Steps* I attribute to this accent on reality. When I set out to make that film I was determined to show every angle of each situation. It may have been tragic or it may have been dramatic, but, looked at in another way, it was comic—so I put in many comedy touches. Any real-life situation, you will find, is like that. The comedy is always there.

"Comedy, too, does, paradoxically, make a film more dramatic. A play gives you intervals for reflection. These intervals have to be supplied in a film by contrast—and if the film is dramatic or tragic, the obvious contrast is comedy."

Relieving the Tension

"So, in all my films, about two-thirds of the way through, I try to supply a definite contrast. I take a dramatic situation up and up and up to its peak of excitement and then, before it has time to start the downward curve, I introduce comedy to relieve the tension. After that, I feel safe with the climax. If the film petered to an end without any contrast, the climax would probably turn into an anti-climax. Which heaven forbid!

"You see, just as I try to make a woman human by making her appear in awkward and comic situations and taking away her glamour, so I try to keep the whole film on a human level, with emotions mixed in the incongruous way they are in real life. I shall always attempt to portray the real psychology of my characters—the women as well as the men."

Nova Grows Up

Four years or so ago, I directed Nova Pilbeam in *The Man Who Knew Too Much*. And I have recently finished working with her for a second time on *Young and Innocent*.

It is well known that girls change tremendously between the ages of fourteen and eighteen. Nova Pilbeam is no exception to the rule.

The girl I have just directed might be an entirely different person from the child who appeared in *The Man Who Knew Too Much*. She has changed tremendously, both physically and mentally.

Let me say right away that the Nova of today is altogether more charming, likeable, intelligent, and talented than the girl I first knew.

When she worked for me in *The Man Who Knew Too Much*, she had just completed *Little Friend*. To filmgoers, she was still unknown. But, having just played a leading part, I sensed that she felt she was condescending to play the smaller role that she had in my picture.

Full of Confidence

I found her to be amazingly full of self-confidence, and she was inclined to tell me how scenes should be played. She had to be handled diplomatically.

"Nova Grows Up" was originally published in *Film Weekly*, February 5, 1938, 9.

I persuaded her to do several scenes which I was not certain that she really wanted to do, scenes which, as it happened, remained in audience's memories, such as at the end of the film when she was reunited with her parents. I made her so terrified by the ordeal that she had been through that she shrank from them.

Nova was undoubtedly sincere in her beliefs, and she had a surprising amount of common sense for a girl of her age. But, naturally, she lacked experience. Her ideas were not always suitable.

The greatest difference between the Nova of yesterday and today is that she now has the modesty of a true artist—and, in consequence, is more professional. She has had a great deal of stage experience besides her screen work. She has acquired more balance and camera sense.

She no longer airs her views so freely, and doesn't want to do everything her own way.

In fact, of all the people I have handled during my career as a director, I can honestly say that she is the most unassuming and willing.

I have had more understanding with her than with nine out of ten of the other stars with whom I have worked.

Unique Personality

She has grown into a entirely natural young person, and the figure she is today should have a great appeal to women.

She is not strikingly beautiful, but her features are warm and alive. She reproduces an English type which is devoid of any suggestion of artificiality.

There is no fake glamour about her—but she is not by any means dull. On the contrary, she has a bright freshness.

Her personality will make her unique on the screen. There is nobody in films in the least like her. And the greatest point of all is that she is so completely English.

The worst thing that could happen to Nova would be for her to get into the hands of Hollywood makeup men, and to have a mask fitted to her face. All I can hope is that this will never happen. It will be a tragedy if it does.

I don't think it will. Nova is a sensible young woman, tremendously ambitious, and with no particular yearning to go to Hollywood.

As an actress, there is no question that she is technically very much improved since I first worked with her. She has proved that she is not just a flash in the pan as a child actress. Hers is a difficult age. It is not easy to find suitable stories for her. But I feel that her character in *Young and Innocent* will help her to graduate into more matured roles than she has had before.

It affords her the opportunity for the first time to go in for naturalistic acting, as opposed to the more or less stylized acting in *Tudor Rose*. She has to drive an old car around; to mother four brothers, and there is a suggestion of romance.

In developing from a child into adolescence, she has to play scenes which she has never done before on the screen. Personally, I am very satisfied with the results.

She has improved tremendously from a photographic point of view since *The Man Who Knew Too Much*. She no longer has that childish roundness of the face. Her features have developed.

"Wimbledon" Accent

Her voice, too, has improved out of all knowledge. As one of her greatest qualities is her self-criticism, I shall not be offending her by saying that it used to have very much of a "Wimbledon" strain about it, and her lines were apt to sound as if she were memorizing them.

She herself has always been conscious of this weakness. I used to tease her by threatening her not to retake those scenes in which she hated her own voice so much. She was terrified at the idea of some of those scenes remaining in the finished picture.

Thanks mainly to her own efforts, plus her stage experience, she has now practically overcome this flaw in her technical makeup. Her voice records well and she has a very much wider range than before.

I am hoping to be able to make a third picture with her, and it is probable that it will be my next one. We have a story in preparation.

Nova's Next Picture

It is another of the type that will help her to bridge the gap between child parts and more mature roles.

Her part will be that of the head girl of a convent. Her parents are dead, and she is kept at the convent by her stepfather.

She leaves to go to him, believing him to be an impresario. Unknown to her, however, he is a crook. The two get to like each other a lot.

He gets involved in a murder, and, without telling her what for, he asks her to give an alibi for him. She does so, and roughly speaking, the rest of the story is concerned with the efforts of Scotland Yard to break down a schoolgirl's word of honor.

There are a great many dramatic scenes for her, and the age of the girl is just right—eighteen.

At the present, no title has been chosen. But I can tell you that I am looking forward to making the picture—and that is eloquent evidence of what I think of Nova.

Crime Doesn't Pay

When I directed Peter Lorre in *The Secret Agent,* I tried an experiment. Although the menace, he was also the comedy relief. In fact, he was far more humorous than villainous.

It was breaking all the rules, of course, but I think the experiment was a success. It permitted filmgoers to see the other side of Lorre's personality. He was known as a heavy. Since, he has become a straight actor, and you have probably seen him as "Mr. Moto" two or three times.

Lorre is undoubtedly one of the screen's most expert villains. But I think he is wise in getting away from this type of character. On the screen, crime doesn't pay—except as very valuable groundwork for an actor.

Very few heavies succeed in staying the course if they don't change their styles. This is why you'll find that most screen villains reform, unless they are content to remain in small parts. Among the straight and comedy stars of today, there are a good many who began their film careers as bad men.

The best example, of course, is William Powell, who was once a very suave villain indeed. He is typical of the development of a heavy.

The process is: villain; straight actor; comedian.

It is easiest to be a villain; less easy to be a straight actor; considerably more difficult to be a comedian.

As a rule, the development from villain to straight actor is grad-

"Crime Doesn't Pay" was originally published in *Film Weekly,* April 30, 1938, 9.

ual, and it is largely due to an attractive personality breaking through the label of "heavy." Thus William Powell's likeable qualities slowly but surely dominated his screen characterizations.

From straight actor to comedian is equally gradual, though not so frequent. It is done more or less by the player himself taking over the comedy relief instead of leaving this to small-part actors, and then developing into a full-blown comedian.

Homolka's Progress

William Powell did this. Adolphe Menjou is another. Lionel Barrymore, with certain reservations, has also done so—the reservations being that, humorous though he is, he is not a full-blown comedian (though John Barrymore has now stepped from straight work to comedy).

I shouldn't be surprised to see Oscar Homolka doing it. He has gone from heavies to straight character parts.

I found it interesting to compare his performance in my picture, *Sabotage,* with the one he gives in *Ebb Tide.* His sense of humor breaks through strongly at times in the latter.

Wallace Beery has, in some ways, reversed the process. In his early screen days, he was a deep-dyed villain. He changed to comedy before becoming a character actor. His comedy, however, was of the very broad variety. The more subtle humor came later, after he had developed his sense of drama.

On the feminine side, you have Myrna Loy—voluptuous vamp; straight leading lady; then comedienne.

And Garbo began as a vamp; became a dramatic actress; and is now said to be thinking of comedy.

Not all reformed villains, of course, develop into comedians. That is the ultimate only for those who have ability in this particular direction.

At the same time, there is no reason in the world why those who have developed that far should be typed as comedians. In fact, all of those I have mentioned play straight parts just as often as humorous ones.

I can't think of any prominent villain who has remained faithful to villainy. Those who have tried it have found that their futures were not looking too hopeful. Of necessity, the life of a prominent villain is a short one.

The reason is simple to find. A heavy doesn't get audience sympathy. And that means everything. Much as a filmgoer may admire a screen villain's performance, he is not the one who is talked about afterwards.

Hissing Doesn't Hurt

Development from menace roles has nothing whatever to do with the personal feelings of the actor. Most players will tell you that there is a great deal of enjoyment to be had from appearing as a heavy, and the fact that they are hissed doesn't hurt their feelings at all. They regard this as a compliment to their acting. But villains don't draw people into cinemas, however much they are admired. And as film players get paid in relation to their box office value, a long life of screen villainy hasn't overmuch appeal, anyway.

On the Continent, things are different. Most Continental pictures are psychological. Peter Lorre enjoyed tremendous popularity, and the picture for which he was mostly admired was the macabre *M*.

Conrad Veidt was also a big star, though most of the roles he played on the Continent would have been called "menace" here or in Hollywood.

Exceptional Rathbone

Such pictures are few and far between in England and America. *Night Must Fall* was one, and it offered Robert Montgomery a magnificent acting opportunity, which he took.

But, though it did him a lot of good as an actor, it would be useless to deny that a series of such roles would soon kill him as a box office star.

The British picture, *Love from a Stranger*, is another rare example of this type of English-speaking film—and, incidentally, Basil Rathbone is one of the very few exceptions to the short-life-for-prominent-villains rule. But he, too, tempers villainy with sympathy more frequently these days.

Conrad Veidt has left heavy roles right behind him. He made the change a long time ago, and it is interesting to note that one of his most widely popular pictures was *The Passing of the Third*

Floor Back. His saintly character in that was as far removed from his early menacing roles as one can possibly imagine.

I think Humphrey Bogart will make the change. He is such an excellent actor, and is too good to remain typed. He has already made the switch once or twice, and has shown his sympathetic capability, as, for instance, in his role of the attorney in the Bette Davis picture, *Marked Woman*.

It Pays to Reform

He is an outstandingly good character actor, and he has a big following; but that following is not anything like so big as it will be when he is recognized as a straight actor instead of a villain.

Brian Donlevy is another who, I am convinced, will eventually leave heavies right behind him. He has a great capactiy for sympathy, which is already creeping into his roles. I believe his part in the new Gracie Fields picture, *We're Going to be Rich,* is one of them.

Lloyd Nolan has also been seen as a straight actor, but he is not in the same category as most screen villains. Like Akim Tamiroff, he is never conventional, and he is a first-rate character actor.

And, as you are well aware, George Raft has left his sleek villains a long way behind him.

I'm not so sure that villainy isn't one of the best ways of breaking into films. There are always openings for heavies, and such parts undoubtedly pave the way to bigger things. Screen crime may not pay if you keep to it; but it pays if you care to reform!

What I'd Do to the Stars

An Interview with J. Danvers Williams

Any day now our most celebrated director, Alfred Hitchcock, will be off to Hollywood.

All his life, so far, Hitchcock has remained rigidly faithful to the British film industry. Now he is greatly looking forward to a change of environment.

Two pictures are definitely scheduled for him in Hollywood: *Titanic* and the Daphne du Maurier subject, *Rebecca*. He tells me that if the opportunities arise he will remain there and make several more pictures.

"Working under new conditions with an entirely fresh crowd of people will be like a tonic," Hitchcock told me. "I am itching to get my hands on some of those American stars."

"Why so?" I inquired.

"Some of them are so efficient," Hitchcock explained, "that it'll be a pleasure to direct them; and there are others I should very much like to debunk. I should like to humanize Luise Rainer and show Dietrich sucking a toffee-apple. I should like to cast Clark Gable in a much more penetrating characterization than he has yet played, and I should like to put Myrna Loy into the type of part that Edna Best had in *The Man Who Knew Too Much*.

"What a boon William Powell would be, in a fast-moving comedy thriller! He is the only actor I know who can really put across a far-fetched piece of slapstick with absolute conviction.

"What I'd Do to the Stars" was originally published in *Film Weekly*, March 4, 1939, 12–13.

"Usually when I prepare a script, I tend to hold myself back a bit because I have the constant fear that my actors will not be able to go as far as my own imagination.

"If I were going to direct Powell I should let myself go completely, both in the melodramatic and the comedy sequences, convinced that no matter how fanciful it became he would be able to bring it to life."

"Of course," Hitch continued, "I should like to direct Gary Cooper. He, too, is an actor well suited to the type of film I like to make.

"There are people who say that Cooper cannot act at all and that he owes his appeal to a long line of good directors. This is sheer nonsense.

"Cooper has that rare faculty of being able to rivet the attention of an audience while he does nothing. In this respect he is very much like the late Gerald du Maurier, who could walk on a stage, flick a speck of dust off his shoulder, study his fingernails for a whole five minutes, and do it all so dramatically and with such accurate timing that he held an audience spellbound."

Cooper and Colman

"Gary can do exactly the same thing on the screen. I have seen him perform a long sequence without once changing the expression on his face, yet screwing the audience up to a tremendous pitch of expectancy.

"I would, if I had him to direct, cast him in a film as an honest and ingenuous Middle-Wester who achieves fame in Hollywood.

"I would have him mixed up in a big studio swindle in which thugs and professional strikers are brought in by one big producer to sabotage the property of another—or something on those lines. Another actor for whom I have the utmost respect is Ronald Colman. His technique is not unlike Cooper's, but where Cooper is at his best in a fairly light part, Colman has, in my opinion, a real flair for a much more poignant theme.

"Colman can even make a role like François Villon come to life. But I, personally, should never cast him in a part of this sort. I should find him a subject like *Arrowsmith*, but my picture would have more humor than that and be considerably less static."

Uninhibited Lombard

"There are quite a number of feminine stars I should like to direct," Hitchcock continued. "Carole Lombard, for instance."

This was interesting. In this country Hitch has developed a reputation as a misogynist. Critics have often said that he treats his feminine characters unsympathetically.

"It is true," Hitch admitted, "that in certain of my British films I have concentrated largely on the development of the male characters at the expense of the female ones. But this is because I have always found it extremely difficult to get British actresses to respond naturally to a human situation.

"Plunge an English actress into a bath of cold water and she still comes to the top trying to look aloof and dignified.

"Her whole concern is not how best to express her emotions but how best to bottle them up. I do not imagine that American stars suffer from this inhibition to anything like the same extent. No girl could arrive at the pitch of efficiency achieved by Carole Lombard if her one consideration were how best to appear 'society.'

"I should like to cast Lombard not in the type of superficial comedy which she so often plays but in a much more meaty comedy-drama, giving her plenty of scope for characterization. I believe that, imaginatively treated, Lombard is capable of giving a performance equal to that of any of the best male actors, like Muni and Leslie Howard."

Vulgarizing Claudette

"Claudette Colbert is another actress I should like to have in a picture. I have often visualized her in the role of a beautiful mannequin who, having risen from the gutter, has to keep up a good appearance but who is, in her soul, lazy, good-natured, irresponsible, and slightly sluttish. This part would be rather on the lines of the one played by Jean Harlow in *Dinner at Eight,* though not quite so blatantly vulgar.

"Or I might even give her a blonde wig and cast her as the generous, promiscuous Rosie in Somerset Maugham's 'Cakes and Ale.' Claudette would be grand in such a part.

"Then, of course, there is Garbo. I expect that every director would like to have her in a picture, if only for the experience.

"Garbo, it is said, works by intuition. I am fully prepared to believe this, for at times she is magnificent. But I have also seen her make mistakes that Lombard could never have made.

"Intuitive actors, like Garbo, Laughton, and Jannings, need very special treatment. They frequently have off-days when nothing will go right, but when they are really on form they can achieve things that no mere technician could ever achieve.

"I would not undertake to direct Garbo to any given schedule. I know that to try and force her into a particular mood when she didn't feel like it would be rather like trying to force a woman to fall in love with you.

"For Garbo I shouldn't bother to construct my usual involved plot. I should choose some very simple story about life and love and should 'direct' the picture as little as possible, using my camera merely as a vehicle for her characterization. The greater the artist, the less directorial ingenuity is necessary.

"Muni I should love to have in a film, but on no account should it be a biography.

"It seems a pity to me that when a star develops a great reputation as a character actor the tendency should be to make him portray characters of which he has only a secondhand knowledge.

"I should cast Muni in a modern American subject, more in keeping with *Scarface* and *Hi, Nellie*. Probably I should cast him as a Jew in some subject dealing with the problems of his race.

"If I had Hepburn to direct I should put her in a part reminiscent of the one she played in *Morning Glory*. I do not mean by this that I should try and repeat this film, but I should try and develop in Hepburn the characteristics which she displayed in this picture.

"The strident, harsh-voiced girl of *Morning Glory* was the real Hepburn. How splendid she would be in a Eugene O'Neill role— as Lavinia, say, in *Mourning Becomes Electra*; passionate, inhibited, violent."

Getting Out of Grooves

"I do not know whether it would be feasible to put this play on the screen as it stands. All I mean is that I would cast Hepburn in some such roles, though my picture would necessarily be lightened with more movement and humor than one finds in an O'Neill play.

"There is scarcely a star in Hollywood whose appeal I would not try to alter or develop, according to the part they were playing.

"One of Hollywood's greatest failings is the way it allows its stars to get into a groove. When an actor achieves fame in some particular type of part the tendency is to grind out all his future roles in the same pattern.

"When Robert Young came to England to work for me in *Secret Agent* he had never appeared in a film as anything more than himself. In this picture I gave him a chance to give a genuine characterization, with the result that, in the final sequences of the picture, he developed a power and a conviction that would have done credit to Spencer Tracy.

"That is what I would like to do with all the stars who come under my control in Hollywood."

Elegance Above Sex

A national magazine editor once asked me to give him a few words about my conception of femininity. After devoting a lot of thought to the subject I was forced to give him even fewer words than he expected.

"Not being a woman," I said, "I don't know what femininity is."

I do think I know, however, what kind of woman is most fascinating, and therefore most feminine, to men. I am not speaking of the kind of woman at whom men are prone to gawk on the street. We have all seen women who exaggerate their physical attributes to a point where they can hardly be ignored. Men may stop and stare at such women. They may even show a lively interest in meeting them. But a man who does manage this kind of meeting may be disappointed to learn that his new friend has very little mystery left about her, once he knows her name.

As for myself, I prefer a woman who does not display all of her sex at once—one whose attractions are not falling out in front of her. I like women who are also ladies, who hold enough of themselves in reserve to keep a man intrigued. On the screen, for example, if an actress wants to convey a sexy quality, she ought to maintain a slightly mysterious air. When a man approaches her, the audience should be led to wonder whether she intends to shrink from him or tear off his clothes.

I seem to have developed a reputation for preferring blonde

"Elegance Above Sex" was originally published in *Hollywood Reporter* 172, no. 39 (November 20, 1962, 32nd Anniversary Issue).

leading ladies in my films. It is true that I have directed several actresses who happen to be blonde—Grace Kelly, Eva Marie Saint, Joan Fontaine, Madeleine Carroll, to name a few. And now, in *The Birds*, I am introducing another young lady who happens to be blonde, Miss Tippi Hedren. But I am happy to say she is not the spectacular type of blonde who flaunts her sex. It is important to distinguish between the big, bosomy blonde and the ladylike blonde with the touch of elegance, whose sex must be discovered. Remember Grace Kelly in *High Noon?* She was rather mousy. But in *Dial M for Murder* she blossomed out for me splendidly, because the touch of elegance had always been there.

Perhaps this is the essential reason I prefer ladylike women. As a movie director I have found that an actress with the quality of elegance can easily go down the scale to portray less exalted roles. But an actress without elegance, however competent she may be, can hardly go up the scale to portray, let us say, ambassador's wife. She lacks the range as an actress because she lacks the range as a person. A woman of elegance, on the other hand, will never cease to surprise you.

Thrills, Suspense,
the Audience

Introduction

Hitchcock's first published writing was "Gas," written for an in-house magazine put out by the firm he worked for at the time, the Henley Telegraph and Cable Company. It is a lurid, somewhat overheated tale, perhaps rightly described by Spoto as like an "undergraduate's imitation of a Poe short story" (46)—I prefer to think of it as a vision of Poe as filmed by D. W. Griffith—but in any event it is uncanny how this brief story prefigures so much of Hitchcock's later work. Spoto points out that "Gas" "shows the young Hitchcock's instinctive grasp of the mechanics of reader manipulation and the evocation of fear" (46). Maurice Yacowar in *Hitchcock's British Films,* notes how it sketches what will later turn out to be Hitchcock's recurrent fascination with "affrighted purity," false refuges, bondage, fantasies of horror "tenuously attached to a normal situation," and the problematic role of the creative artist who, like the dentist in the story, both induces and redeems the experience of terror (15–17). (In this context, the struggle for the dentist's chair in the 1934 version of *The Man Who Knew Too Much* perhaps takes on added resonance.) To this we might add that "Gas" also features a dramatic chase, treads the fine line between the horrific and the unacceptably horrible, and ends with at least some kind of release from the surrounding dangers: the protagonist pays a half crown at the end, but neither she nor the reader of the tale pays the price of suffering the full consequences of what is threatened. All these above-mentioned themes not only recur in Hitchcock's films but also figure prominently in the essays

99

in this section, written by Hitchcock in part to explain the relationship between the psychological dynamics of fear and his particular
cinematic method and intentions.

In all these essays he acknowledges his position as a genre artist
and energetically analyzes and also somewhat defensively pleads
the case for the genre of the thriller, with which he was inevitably,
sometimes begrudgingly, associated. In "Let 'Em Play God," for
example, he emphatically announces that he is "not at all" bothered by being "typed as a mystery maker" and goes on to talk
proudly and seriously about his trademark style, "the result of
growth and patient experimentation with the materials of the
trade." He makes even bolder claims in "Why 'Thrillers' Thrive"
and "The Enjoyment of Fear," where he takes the characteristic
aspects of his chosen genre and turns them into defining marks of
all "good cinema." (He does this as well in "Core of the Movie—
The Chase," where nearly all kinds of dramatic action turn out to
be some sort of chase.) The purpose of film-going in general, he
says, is to see things "we don't experience ourselves," consisting
of "emotional disturbances." These thrills or "shake-ups" keep us
from becoming "sluggish and jellified," which would otherwise be
the result of leading a typically modern "sheltered" life. Wood's
well-known emphasis on the therapeutic function of Hitchcock's
art, on the healing and enlivening dramas that envelop the protagonists and the spectators as well, is thus supported by Hitchcock's
own descriptions of the structure and function of his thrillers.

Hitchcock praises cinema, an artistic experience far more immediate and participatory than the theater, as a powerful way of
obtaining these shocks, but he carefully sets limits. The introductory blurb to "Why 'Thrillers' Thrive" notes that it is "a valuable
contribution to the current discussion on the vexed question of
'horror' films." Whether or not he specifically had in mind the
popularity of such recently released films as *Dracula* (1931),
Frankenstein (1931), *Freaks* (1932), *King Kong* (1933), and *The
Bride of Frankenstein* (1935), Hitchcock emphatically distinguishes
between the therapeutic shocks of well-made "horrific" films and
the "*unnatural* excitement" derived from the "sadism, perversion,
bestiality, and deformity" of horror films. Later in his career he
continually upped the ante of his thrills, so much so that he was
often accused of making the latter kind of horror films. But in the

mid-1930s he took great pride in announcing that he did not over-step the "dividing line which is apparent to all thinking people."

Perhaps the most important limit on the shock effect of his films, though, is established by what he imagines to be the implicit arrangement between filmmaker and audience, described in charming detail in "The Enjoyment of Fear." Fear is a vital principle of life, but it is enjoyable only if we are simultaneously, although perhaps only subconsciously, aware that the price of the dangers that quicken our sensations "need not be paid." As in life, so in film: threats must be experienced as real but in one way or another understood as imaginary and inconsequential. An "invisible cloak" covers characters we sympathize with, protecting them from ever being cut in half by the menacing buzz saw or run over by the approaching train and thereby freeing us to be aesthetically and emotionally entertained by dramas that would otherwise overwhelmingly disturb us. And even when sympathetic characters die, "there is no harm, because in our subconscious we are aware that we are safe, sitting in a comfortable armchair, watching a screen."

Despite his confident assertion of the duties of a responsible artist, perhaps Hitchcock was as aware as we are that if he had followed those principles rigidly he would never have achieved very much as a filmmaker. He goes on in this essay, as in many other essays and interviews, compulsively to chastise himself for breaking what he has set out as a fundamental rule of filmmaking by actually letting the bomb go off in *Sabotage*, killing innocent little Stevie. But regardless of his apologies—which are in any event qualified by a barely concealed delight in his capacity to "shake up" and outrage critics and audiences—this type of episode is common, not only in his later films, such as *Psycho, The Birds,* and *Frenzy,* where sympathetic characters pay a fearful price, but even in early works such as *The 39 Steps,* where the innocent crofter's wife is physically abused and presumably doomed to a lifetime of further mistreatment, and *Secret Agent,* where a likable little man is mistakenly assassinated.

What is characteristic about such essays as "The Enjoyment of Fear," then, is that they set out principles and formulas that Hitchcock's films both elaborate and challenge. This dynamic aspect of his art is immediately apparent in "Master of Suspense," a telling bit of "self-analysis," as the subtitle suggests, that reviews some of the key techniques he is identified with in order to suggest how they can—and must—be modified. The major metaphor he adopts here is that of "turning the tables," and he acknowledges that his intention in doing so is "sinister" and unsettling. For example, he speaks about his famous cameo appearances in his films as a kind of humbling of himself, a momentary opportunity for him to be subjected to—in fact, "shot" and "hit" by—the cinematic weapons he usually wields, and this is a comic but also startling reminder of the hostility and aggression that are intimately bound up with filmmaking (indeed, with all acts of photography, as Susan Sontag suggests in *On Photography*). A certain amount of free-flowing aggression is also evident in his fantasy about "try[ing] the same trick" with press people by torturing them with interviews and disturbing the security of his audience by making them suspicious of everyone.

Throughout "Master of Suspense," the erstwhile fixed points of Hitchcock's method become, to use the modern term, interrogated. Instead of simply trotting out once again his familiar definitions of "suspense," contrasting the bomb that suddenly goes off with the one we anxiously know is ticking away, and the "MacGuffin," telling us of the lions that are not in the Scottish highlands, Hitchcock stresses that these devices have to change with the times. His desire is to "smoke" the suspense drama "out of its old haunts," to turn it away from the trappings of espionage, secret papers, and codes and toward "more personal sorts of menace" and "the big problem of the glamorous villain." In obvious ways, this brief essay prefigures such films as *North by Northwest*, which salvages some of the "old tradition" of the thriller but also moves it into "frontier territory." In less obvious ways, it looks forward to innovative works such as *Rear Window* and *Psycho*, two of his most detailed representations of, as he says here, "a brave new world in which we are becoming conditioned to suspect our neighbors and expecting the worst." The effort to describe but also to rethink and revise his characteristic artistic techniques and relationship with his chosen genre, evident in this essay and others, is an important prelude to the achievement of the next ten to fifteen years of Hitchcock's career, which can legitimately be called his major phase.

The final articles in the section perhaps tend to portray a recognizable rather than revisionary Hitchcock, but this makes them no less interesting. "Core of the Movie" contains Hitchcock's most focused and extended discussion of the chase, obviously a central element in many of his films. While it is useful to overhear Hitchcock's broad technical definition of the chase, which comes to include basically all goal-oriented action, and his distinction between suspense and the chase, he is more subtle and interesting when discussing the rhythm of various chase sequences in his films, the dynamics of identification, tension, and release created by a chase, and the various landscapes of the chase, some external and others internal. Hitchcock's chases are indebted, as he acknowledges, to Griffith's, but they are far more complex, and his wonderful description of allowing his audience to "run with the hares and hunt with the hounds" applies not only to the double chase structure he frequently uses but also to the whole range of mixed pleasures, equivocal attachments, and moral complications that characterize his films.

"Murder—With English on It" was published at a time when Hitchcock's persona and voice were becoming increasingly familiar via his appearances as the host of his weekly television program. This polished, belletristic essay effectively captures much of Hitchcock's carefully crafted manner and "philosophy," especially his droll treatment of gruesome events, use of polite and literate euphemisms for the unspeakable, and confident knowledge that his audience shares with him a deep attraction to violence that exists side by side with our everyday, presumably high moral character. The major distinction he draws between English and American attitudes toward murder is explored in the form of a kind of witty academic or rhetorical exercise, complete with references to some of his favorite murder cases and some sociological ruminations about how taste is at least in part a product of geography, social habits, and legal customs. Perhaps somewhere behind the argument lies his disappointment over *The Trouble with Harry,* his most "British" comedy and one of his few acknowledged failures in America. And there is at least a hint of resentment that film audiences are not as astute as British aficionados of criminal trials, whose fascination for murderers does not depend on a "rooting interest" in a sympathetic character, a cinematic convention that Hitchcock challenged throughout his entire career. But beyond these fine critical comments and distinctions, Hitchcock celebrates, in his typically wry manner, the shared taste for what he calls the "juice" of murder cases, exported by the English (he no doubt has one particular transplanted Englishman in mind) and avidly imported and consumed by the Americans.

"Would You Like to Know Your Future?" is particularly intriguing because it discusses fear and suspense in a metaphysical rather than psychological and fictional context. It is one of Hitchcock's rare direct commentaries on a theme that has fascinated many critics: his conception of the role of God in human life. He uses a story about the early fate of his film *The Lodger,* first shelved and nearly abandoned, then serendipitously released to great popular success, to underscore the point that even a director who occasionally seems to have godlike qualities is by no means in control of fate. We know from other sources, especially Ivor Montagu, that the history of *The Lodger* is somewhat more complicated: it was indeed considered to be unreleasable and shelved, but then it was radically reedited, with many of the intertitles cut out, and steered to its eventual successful release by Michael Balcon, who effectively countered the resistance of the distributor, C. M. Woolf (Spoto, 97–99, summarizes these events nicely). Hitchcock's version of the story, written for the inspirational magazine edited by Norman Vincent Peale, emphasizes the inscrutable divine control of human affairs rather than the efficacy of human labor and thus credits the power of prayer and God rather than Montagu and Balcon. God is the director *extraordinaire* and, interestingly enough, works in Hitchcock's genre. After years of strenuous debate about the role of suspense in films, Hitchcock caps his argument by noting that God too says "that things would be very dull without suspense."

The penultimate essay in this section circles back on the first: the effect of Poe on Hitchcock, so palpable in "Gas," is acknowledged in "Why I Am Afraid of the Dark." Hitchcock is usually reticent about influences on him, but he states directly, "It's because I liked Edgar Allan Poe's stories so much that I began to make suspense films." He is particularly attracted to Poe's "hallucinatory logic," fantastic and precisely realistic adventures, and personal sense of loneliness and unhappiness and deeply impressed not only by Poe's stories but also by his cinematic legacy, the films of Buñuel, Clair, Epstein, and Cocteau. Hitchcock carefully distinguishes himself from Poe in some respects, but his surprising general statement "I don't think that there exists a real resemblance between Edgar Allan Poe and myself " is, if not disingenuous, then at least not entirely persuasive. Hitchcock and Poe are both profound realists and surrealists, adventurers in the linked realms of imagination and terror, and, as Hitchcock ruefully admits, prisoners of as well as experts in their genre. Hitchcock labels himself a "commercial filmmaker" and Poe a "poéte maudit," but they join arms as, in Dali's knowing phrase, "chevaliers de la mort."

The "*Redbook* Dialogue" that concludes this section not only summarizes many of the themes of the earlier articles but also shows Hitchcock's mastery of the art of the interview. If there were no such real figure as Dr. Fredric Wertham, Hitchcock might have invented him—and perhaps he did in fact invent him, in the character of the psychiatrist at the end of *Psycho,* whose glib and pompous analysis only confirms our sense of the impenetrability of Norman Bates. I do not want to be unfair to Dr. Wertham, who was a responsible spokesperson for institutional psychiatry and, as the introductory note to this dialogue explains, "an outspoken critic of violence in comic books, films, and television programs," a vigorous participant in the ongoing debate in the early 1960s about the apparently pernicious effects of mass media on children. His book *The Seduction of the Innocent* was widely read and often used as an authoritative study by those denouncing popular culture. But he is a perfect philistine foil for Hitchcock here, unable to fathom cinematic stylization, irony, and the subtleties of audience manipulation that Hitchcock patiently explains. It is Hitchcock who comes across as the master psychologist. Wertham's literal and simplistic model of human behavior and relationship to representation on film and television—for example, "a child's mind is like a bank—whatever you put in, you get back in ten years, with interest"—is in striking contrast to Hitchcock's subtle awareness of the complexity of our enjoyment of fear, even a child's ability to distinguish between fiction and reality while still being shocked by fiction, and the rhythm of fear and laughter that is integral to many experiences of the horrific. Wertham is rightly concerned about the possibility of becoming desensitized by media violence, but much like Bruno Bettelheim in *The Uses of Enchantment,* Hitchcock talks knowledgeably and wisely about how we may be educated to "awfulness" by fairy tales and other frightening fictions, presumably like his own.

Gas

She had never been in this part of Paris before—only reading of it in the novels of Duvain, or seeing it at the Grand Guignol. So this was the Montmarte? That horror where danger lurked under cover of night; where innocent souls perished without warning—where doom confronted the unwary—where the Apache reveled.

She moved cautiously in the shadow of the high wall, looking furtively backward for the hidden menace that might be dogging her steps. Suddenly she darted into an alley way, little heeding where it led . . . groping her way on in the inky blackness, the one thought of eluding the pursuit firmly fixed in her mind . . . on she went . . . Oh! when would it end? . . . Then a doorway from which a light streamed lent itself to her vision. . . . In here . . . anywhere, she thought.

The door stood at the head of a flight of stairs . . . stairs that creaked with age as she endeavored to creep down . . . then she heard the sound of drunken laughter and shuddered—surely this was—No, not that. Anything but that! She reached the foot of the stairs and saw an evil-smelling wine bar, with wrecks of what were once men and women indulging in a drunken orgy . . . then they saw her, a vision of affrighted purity. Half a dozen men rushed towards her amid the encouraging shouts of the rest. She was seized. She screamed with terror . . . better had she been caught by her

"Gas" was originally published in *The Henley: Social Club Magazine of the Henley Company, Ltd.* I, no. 1 (June 1919): I. It is reprinted in Spoto, *The Dark Side of Genius* (45–46) and, with minor variations, in Yacowar, *Hitchcock's British Films* (15–17).

pursuer was her one fleeting thought as they dragged her roughly across the room. The fiends lost no time in settling her fate. They would share her belongings . . . and she . . . Why! Was this not the heart of Montmarte? She should go—the rats should feast. Then they bound her and carried her down the dark passage, up a flight of stairs to the riverside. The water rats should feast, they said. And then . . . swinging her bound body to and fro, dropped her with a splash into the dark, swirling waters. Down she went, down, down. Conscious only of a choking sensation, this was death . . . then . . . "It's out, Madam," said the dentist. "Half a crown, please."

Why "Thrillers" Thrive

Why do we go to the pictures? To see life reflected on the screen, certainly—but what kind of life?

Obviously, the kind we don't experience ourselves—or the same life but with a difference; and the difference consists of emotional disturbances which, for convenience, we call "thrills."

Our nature is such that we must have these "shake-ups," or we grow sluggish and jellified; but, on the other hand, our civilization has so screened and sheltered us that it isn't practicable to experience sufficient thrills at firsthand.

So we have to experience them artificially, and the screen is the best medium for this.

In the theater we can see things happening on a stage, remote, impersonal, detached from ourselves. We are safe, secure, sitting in an armchair and looking at the struggle and turmoil of life through a window, as it were.

In order to appreciate what the characters on the stage are going through, we have to project ourselves into their consciousness; we have to receive our thrills vicariously, which is not the most effective method.

Watching a well-made film, we don't sit by as spectators; we participate.

Take a case in point, which a great many *Picturegoer* readers are

"Why 'Thrillers' Thrive" was originally published in *Picturegoer,* January 18, 1936, 15.

likely to have seen—the scene in *Hell's Angels,* in which the British pilot decides to crash his plane into the envelope of the Zeppelin to destroy it, even though this means inevitable death to himself.

We see his face—grim, tense, even horror-stricken—as his plane swoops down. Then we are transferred to the pilot's seat, and it is we who are hurtling to death at ninety miles an hour; and at the moment of impact—and blackout—a palpable shuddering runs through the audience.

That is good cinema.

In this there is no harm, because in our subconscious we are aware that we are safe, sitting in a comfortable armchair, watching a screen.

Let me illustrate this. Some years ago there was an exhibition sideshow promising thrills, in which people were admitted (a handful at a time) to sit facing a curtain between two columns.

They naturally expected the curtain to be drawn—but instead, with a loud cracking sound, one of the pillars began to topple over on them.

Just before it reached them, and before they even had time to leap from their seats, its fall was arrested and it hung suspended above them.

That provided a thrill, certainly, but not the kind to please the public. There were so many complaints that the sideshow was closed down—because the public's basic feeling of security was undermined.

The cinema can leave the spectator with a subconscious assurance of absolute safety, and yet surprise his imagination into playing tricks on him.

Secondary to the type of thrill in which the audience seems to participate is the type in which some character who has won the audience's sympathy is involved in danger; and here again the screen can be far more effective than the stage, because the screen can produce an impression of great danger where no danger is.

It would take several complete issues of the *Picturegoer* to list the number of ways in which this can be done, and anyway it doesn't do to give away too many tricks of the trade; but an example or two will show what I mean.

Supposing your hero is to throw himself over a castle rampart into a moat filled with crocodiles; on the stage you hear the other characters *say* there are crocodiles, you see the hero jump, upstage, and disappear from sight, and perhaps a little water is splashed up.

On the screen he is in no greater actual dangers, yet you look over and see for yourself what a terrible height it is; you see the reptiles swimming about; you not only see the jump, you see him fall, you see him hit the water, you watch him swimming desperately from the crocodiles—and you must believe the evidence of your own eyes. Your hero *must* be in grave peril . . . for the camera, as we know, cannot lie!

Or supposing you see a terrific shock of opposing horsemen, as in Cecil B. DeMille's *The Crusades*. I have it on very good authority that not a horse was hurt during production of that sequence. The effects were secured by the use of a few horses trained to fall, and skillful editing.

Such scenes, which set the blood pounding through the veins, are highly beneficial for indigestion, gout, rheumatism, sciatica, and premature middle age. The audience thrives on thrills, the cinema thrives on the audience, the director thrives on the cinema, and everybody is happy.

But the so-called "horror" film—that's an entirely different matter.

The term, meaning originally "extreme aversion," has been loosely applied to films which, to supply the desired emotional jolt, exploit sadism, perversion, bestiality, and deformity.

This is utterly wrong, being vicious and dangerous. It is permissible for a film to be horrific, but not horrible; and between the two there is a dividing line which is apparent to all thinking people.

The forerunner of the cycle of "horror" pictures which is now drawing to a close was the stage "Grand Guignol," and that was merely a "stunt," calculated to attract a neurotic section of the public.

There is a growing body of opinion, inside as well as outside the film industry, against such films, which are successful in direct ratio to their power to create *unnatural* excitement.

As a matter of fact, they are bound to fail, because the public is, as a rule, healthy-minded.

Producers of "horrible" films realize this, and consequently "tone down" their product to make it acceptable.

But in doing so they tacitly acknowledge its basic fallacy; imagine a man hitting you on the head with a hammer with one hand to impress you, and with the other holding it back for fear it offends you!

A "thriller" must be wholehearted—the more exciting the better. And that is why the authentic "thriller" will live and thrive, and the "horror" film will die.

Let 'Em Play God

Every maker of mystery movies aims at getting the audience on the edge of their seats. The ingredient to keep them there is called "suspense." Producers cry for it, writers cry in agony to get it, and actors cry for joy when they do get it. I've often been asked what it is.

As far as I'm concerned you have suspense when you let the audience play God.

Suppose, for instance, you have six characters involved in a mystery. A man has been murdered and all six are possible suspects but no one is sure including the audience.

One of the characters, a young man, is standing in a shadowy room with his back to the door when an unidentified character in a cloak and black hat sneaks in and slugs him into insensibility. It's a brutal act, but if the audience does not know whether the young man himself is a killer or a hero they will not know whether to cheer or weep.

If the audience does know, if they have been told all the secrets that the characters do not know, they'll work like the devil for you because they know what fate is facing the poor actors. That is what is known as "playing God." That is suspense.

For 17 years I have been making pictures described alternately as thrillers, dark mysteries, and chillers, yet I have never actually directed a whodunit or a puzzler. Offhand this may sound like

"Let 'Em Play God" was originally published in *Hollywood Reporter* 100, no. 47 (October 11, 1948, 18th Anniversary Issue).

debunking, but I do not believe that puzzling the audience is the essence of suspense.

Take, for instance, the drama I recently filmed at Warner Bros. called *Rope*. It stars James Stewart with Joan Chandler, our new discovery, in the feminine lead.

John Dall and Farley Granger strangle a young man in the opening shot. They put his body in a chest, cover the chest with a damask cloth and silver service, then serve *hors d'oeuvres* and drinks from it at a party for the victim's father, mother, sweetheart, and assorted friends. Everyone is gay and charming. When Stewart begins to suspect foul play late in the film John Dall puts a gun in his pocket in case things get too hot.

The audience knows everything from the start, the players know nothing. There is not a single detail to puzzle the audience. It certainly is not a whodunit for the simple reason that everyone out front knows who did it. No one on the screen knows except the two murderers. The fact that the audience watches actors go blithely through an atmosphere that is loaded with evil makes for real suspense.

These are the questions, now, that constantly pop up: Will the murderers break and give themselves away? When the victim does not show up for the party will his father suspect? Will Jimmy get killed before he discovers the actual crime? How long will that body lie in its wooden grave at a champagne party without being discovered? If we are successful we'll have the audience at such a pitch that they want to shout every time one of the players goes near that chest.

In order to achieve this, one of the necessary ingredients of the formula is a series of plausible situations with people that are real. When characters are unbelievable you never get real suspense, only surprise.

Just because there is a touch of murder and an air of mystery about a story it is not necessary to see transoms opening, clutching fingers, hooded creatures, and asps on the Chinese rug.

Spellbound was based on complete psychiatric truth. *Foreign Correspondent* was simply the story of a man hammering away at events with a woman who was not much help. *Notorious* concerned a woman caught in a web of world events from which she could not extricate herself and *The Paradine Case* was a love story embedded in the emotional quicksand of a murder trial.

In none of these was the house filled with shadows, the weather dull and stormy throughout, the moor windswept, and the doors creaky. In fact, it is important in a story with sinister implications to use counterpoint, great contrast between situation and background, as we did in *Rope*.

John Dall is guilty of a bestial crime which the audience sees him perform with young Granger. But throughout the film he is grace and charm itself and his apartment is gay and beautifully appointed. And when Granger plays the piano he picks a light and childish piece, a minuet. Suspense involves contrast.

The question is often asked—Do I mind being typed as a mystery maker? Not at all. Most professional men have their trademarks. You always know a piece of Frank Lloyd Wright architecture when you see one and the buildings of Sir Christopher Wren have that distinctive something which no others have. You would not expect to hear Lauritz Melchior crooning or Bing Crosby singing Wagner. And it would be a colossal surprise to go to the theater and see a farce written by Eugene O'Neill.

I do not believe it is necessary for a director to change his style in order to develop new characters and a different story in each film. Through the ages, in literature, acting, directing, and the dance, style has been the mark of the man, the element of his work which has tended to set it apart from the work of others.

Style in directing develops slowly and naturally as it does in everything else. In my case there was much dabbling about in so-called versatility before I found my niche. My titles included such varied films as *The Lodger* (the silent version with Ivor Novello), *Easy Virtue*, *The Farmer's Wife*, *Champagne*, *The Skin Game,* and *Waltzes from Vienna*. Then I began to get more and more interested in developing a suspense technique. By the time I had made *The Secret Agent*, *Sabotage,* and *The 39 Steps* I made up my mind to shoot this type of story exclusively.

Within its framework I can tell any story under the sun but on the screen it will have a definitely recognizable style. I suppose it should be remarked in passing that style, no matter what art it is concerned with, cannot be superimposed consciously on any work. It must be the result of growth and patient experimentation with the materials of the trade, the style itself emerging eventually almost unconsciously.

As it has happened to many others this same thing has happened to me. And having made my bed I'm quite content to lie in it.

The Enjoyment of Fear

I suppose the proper way to begin a piece on the enjoyment of fear would be to prove that such a thing exists. Can fear be enjoyable? Or even pleasant? I was discussing this point with an old friend not long ago.

"Fear," he said, "is the least pleasant of all emotions. I experienced it when I was a boy, and again during both wars. I never want my children to experience it. I think it entirely possible, if I have anything to say about it, that they'll live their entire lives and never know the meaning of the word."

"Oh," I said, "what a dreadful prospect!" My friend looked at me quizzically. "I mean it," I went on. "The boys will never be able to ride a roller coaster, or climb a mountain, or take a midnight stroll through a graveyard. And when they're older"—my friend is a champion motorboat racer—"there'll be no speedboating for them."

"What do you mean?" he asked, obviously offended.

"Well, now, let's take the speedboat racing, for instance. Can you honestly tell me that the sensation you get when you cut close to a pylon, or rough water, with a boat riding close on one side and another skidding across in front of you, is anything but fear? Can you deny that a day on the water without fear, without that prickly sensation as the short hairs on your neck rise, would be an utter dead

"The Enjoyment of Fear" was originally published in *Good Housekeeping* 128 (February 1949): 39, 241–243.

failure? It seems to me that you pay lots of money a year for fear. Why do you want to deny it to your sons?"

"I'd never thought of it quite that way," he said. And he hadn't.

Few people have. That's why my statement, made in all sincerity, that millions of people every day pay huge sums of money and go to great hardship merely to *enjoy* fear seems paradoxical. Yet it is no exaggeration. Any carnival man will tell you the rides that attract the greatest clientele are those that inspire the greatest fear. It is self-evident that the poloist, the steeplechaser, the speedboat racer, and the fox hunter ride for the thrill that comes only from danger. The boy who walks a tightrope or tiptoes along the top of a picket fence is looking for fear, as are the auto racer, the mountain climber, and the big-game hunter.

And that is only the beginning. For every person who seeks fear in the real or personal sense, millions seek it vicariously, in the theater and in the cinema. In darkened auditoriums they identify themselves with fictitious characters who are experiencing fear, and experience, themselves, the same fear sensations (the quickened pulse, the alternately dry and damp palm, etc.), but without paying the price. That the price need not be paid—indeed, must not be paid—is the important factor. Take, for example, one of the classic fear situations: the legendary, though now sadly obsolete, circular bandsaw approaching the bound and gagged heroine. If this distressing contretemps were to exist in real life, the emotional experience of the helpless young woman as the saw approached would be anything but pleasant. Even if one merely viewed a real person thus jeopardized, it would be most displeasing. The suburban matron whose eyes all but pop out of her head with ecstatic excitement as she watches the cinematic blade approach the cinematic neck would no doubt faint dead away if she encountered a similar problem in her home. Why, then, does she enjoy it in the movies?

Precisely because the price will not be paid and she knows it. The saw will never reach its intended target. The plot may, and indeed should, indicate that the heroine's rescue is totally impossible. But deep in the subconscious mind of the spectator is the certainty, engendered by attendance at similar dramatic works, that the totally impossible will occur. The hero, though we have just been made aware that he lies unconscious at the bottom of a pit, surrounded by rattlesnakes, boiling oil, and the smell of bitter

almonds, will appear in time to reverse the action of the saw and
trap the villain. Or the saw will break down. Or it will appear that
the villain has carelessly neglected to sharpen it—or, if it is an
electric saw, to pay his electric bill. Fear and fear not, that is the
essence of melodrama. Fear: the saw may dismember the ingénue.
Fear not: it won't.

Fear in the cinema is my special field, and I have, perhaps dog-
matically, but I think with good cause, split cinematic fear into two
broad categories—terror and suspense. The difference is comparable to the difference between a buzz bomb and a V-2.

To anyone who has experienced attacks by both bombs, the distinction will be clear. The buzz bomb made a noise like an outboard motor, and its chugging in the air above served as notice of
its impending arrival. When the motor stopped, the bomb was beginning its descent and would shortly explode. The moments between the time the motor was first heard and the final explosion
were moments of *suspense*. The V-2, on the other hand, was noiseless until the moment of its explosion. Anyone who heard a V-2
explode, and lived, had experienced *terror*.

Another example, one that has been experienced by most of
us, may make the distinction more definite. Walking down a dimly
lighted street in the late hours of the night, with no other people
about, a person may find his mind playing strange tricks. The silence, the loneliness, and the gloom may set the scene for fear.

Suddenly a dark form thrusts itself before the lonely walker.
Terror. It does not matter that the form was a waving branch, a
newspaper picked up by a gust of wind, or simply an oddly shaped
shadow unexpectedly coming into view. Whatever it was, it produced its moment of terror.

The same walker, on the same dark street, might have no inclination toward fear. The sound of footsteps coming from somewhere behind might cause the late stroller to become curious, then
uneasy, then fearful. The walker stops, the footsteps are not heard;
the pace is increased, so also the tempo of the thin sounds coming
out of the night. *Suspense*. The echo of his own steps? Probably.
But suspense.

On the screen, terror is induced by surprise; suspense, by forewarning. Let us suppose, to make all this clear, that our plot is
concerned with a married woman residing in Manhattan and engaged in amorous dalliance with a young cad.

The young cad learns that his inamorata's husband is in Detroit on business and immediately proceeds to the lady's apartment. The two are there engaged in activity as compromising as the censors will permit. Suddenly the door is flung open. There stands the enraged spouse, gun in hand. Net result: terror. There is no suspense whatsoever in the sequence, for the possibility that the husband might be in the vicinity was never hinted by the lovers, and the audience, identifying itself with them, must share their shock at the husband's entrance.

Now, how could we play that incident if we wished to create, not terror, but suspense? Remember our rule: terror by surprise, suspense by forewarning. Very well, we begin with the two lovers in the hotel room. The husband, we learn from the less personal fragments of their conversation, is presumed by them to be in Detroit. Then we see the husband alighting from an airplane. But what is this? This is not Detroit, but New York! For the benefit of those who are not familiar with the two airports, we incorporate a significant glance at an identifying sign at the airport or, perhaps better, at the license plate of the cab as the husband gives the address of the hotel.

Now back to the two lovers. Note that, in this telling, the audience cannot identify itself with the lovers, because the audience knows what the lovers do not, that the husband is on his way and may trap them. But the audience cannot identify itself with the husband either, for the audience knows what he, poor fellow, only suspects: his wife is unfaithful. Now we go back and forth between the lovers and the husband. They continue their lovemaking. The husband alights from his cab. The cad straightens his tie and prepares to depart. The husband begins to mount the stairs. Will he arrive in time? Will the cad make good his escape? What will happen if he does not? These are the questions that the audience asks itself, and whether or not the husband arrives in time, a suspenseful situation has been created.

It is obvious from the above that suspense and terror cannot coexist. To the extent that the audience is aware of the menace or danger to the people it is watching—that is, to the extent that suspense is created—so is its surprise (or terror) at the eventual materialization of the indicated danger diminished. This poses a pretty problem for the director and for the writer of a motion picture. Shall the terror be diminished to enhance the suspense; or shall all suspense be eliminated by making the surprise complete and the terror as shocking to the audience as to the fictional participants?

The terror-suspense dilemma is normally resolved by compromise. There are several situations in a motion picture; the ordinary, and I think best, practice is to play most of the situations for suspense and a few for terror. Suspense is more enjoyable than terror, actually, because it is a continuing experience and attains a peak crescendo fashion; while terror, to be truly effective, must come all at once, like a bolt of lightning, and is more difficult, therefore, to savor.

However, one conflict in making pictures in which fear is a major element cannot be compromised. That is the conflict between the validity of the plot and situations and the implied guarantee given the audience that it shall not "pay the price" for its fear. To the roller-coaster operator that is a simple problem; it means that, although in appearance the ride must be as terrifying as possible, it must, in reality, be completely safe. The pleasant fear sensation experienced by a roller-coaster rider as the car approached a sharp curve would cease to exist if he seriously thought for one moment that the car might really fail to negotiate the curve. The audience at a motion picture is, of course, entirely safe from that point of view. Though knives and guns may be used on the screen, the audience is aware that no one out front is going to be shot or stabbed. But the audience must also be aware that the characters in the picture, with whom they strongly identify themselves, are not to pay the price of fear. This awareness must be entirely subconscious; the spectator must *know* that the spy ring will never succeed in pitching Madeleine Carroll off London Bridge, and the spectator must be induced to *forget* what he knows. If he didn't *know*, he would be genuinely worried; if he didn't *forget*, he would be bored.

What all this amounts to is this: as the audience sympathy for a character is built up, the audience assumes that a sort of invisible cloak to protect the wearer from harm is being fitted. Once the sympathies are fully established and the cloak is finished, it is not—in the audience opinion, and in the opinion of many critics—fair play to violate the cloak and bring its wearer to a disastrous end. I did it once, in a picture called *Sabotage*. One of the characters was a small boy, with whom the audience was encouraged to fall in love. I sent the boy wandering about London with what he supposed was a can of film under his arm, but what the audience knew full well contained a time bomb. Under this set of circumstance, the lad is protected by his cloak from premature explosion of the bomb. I blew him up anyway, along with several other passengers on a bus he happened to be riding.

Now, that episode in *Sabotage* was a direct negation of the invisible cloak of protection worn by sympathetic characters in motion pictures. In addition, because the audience knew the film can contained a bomb and the boy did not, to permit the bomb to explode was a violation of the rule forbidding a direct combination of suspense and terror, or forewarning and surprise. Had the audience not been informed of the real contents of the can, the explosion would have come as a complete surprise. As a result of a sort of emotional numbness induced by a shock of this kind, I believe their sensibilities might not have been so thoroughly outraged. As it was, the audiences—and the critics, too—were unanimously of the opinion that I should have been riding in the seat next to the lad, preferably the seat he set the bomb on.

Master of Suspense
Being a Self-Analysis by Alfred Hitchcock

Directors of motion pictures, ever since the leather puttee era, have been permitted at least one eccentricity per capita, and my habit of appearing in my own pictures has generally been regarded as exercise of the directorial prerogative. In *Stage Fright* I have been told that my performance is quite juicy. I have been told this with a certain air of tolerance, implying that I have now achieved the maximum limits of directorial ham in the movie sandwich.

It just isn't true. There may have been a "MacGuffin" in my film appearance, but not a ham. My motives have always been more devious, or, if you prefer a more devious word, sinister. I have wormed my way into my own pictures as a spy. A director should see how the other half lives. I manage that by shifting to the front side of the camera and letting my company shoot me, so I can see what it is like to be shot by my company.

Big Moment

I find that my actors are kept on their toes that way. Everyone is anxious to get his work done quickly, before I take it into my head to get in his particular scene. The technicians work gaily in anticipation of the fateful moment when I will be at their mercy. And then the moment comes. I step before the cameras. The actors call for retakes. The makeup man splashes his pet concoctions on my

"Master of Suspense: Being a Self-Analysis by Alfred Hitchcock" was originally published in the *New York Times,* June 4, 1950, II, 4.

face, the wardrobe department tells me how to dress. The electricians and the cameraman joyfully "hit" me with the lights. The still photographer tells me how to look, for his photographs.

I find myself tempted to try the same trick with some of the press people, when they come for a full-dress interview. I have a secret yen to interview them, to pose them for still pictures. I would like to focus a press camera on some photographer and ask him to "express menace and suspense, please." I would also like to write a review of some of the newspaper stories.

Purely Sinister

My purpose is, as I have indicated, purely sinister. I find that the easiest way to worry people is to turn the tables on them. Make the most innocent member of the cast the murderer; make the next-door neighbor a dangerous spy. Keep your characters stepping out of character and into the other fellow's boots.

I should like, for example, to make a thriller about the United Nations, in which the delegate of one nation is denounced by another delegate for falling asleep in the middle of an important international speech. They go to wake the sleeping delegate, only to find that he is dead, with a dagger in his back. That would be the beginning of my story—except for one thing. It is too close to un-amusing reality. Which delegate will be the corpse? What tangled international threads will be caught in the skein? How do we avoid making a weighty political document instead of a suspense story?

To my way of thinking, the best suspense drama is that which weaves commonplace people in what appears to be a routine situation, until it is revealed (and fairly early in the game) as a glamorously dangerous charade. The spy stories of pre-war days fit these specifications perfectly. Today, however, there is nothing very glamorous about spying—there is only one sort of secret to be stolen and there is too much at stake for people to play charades over it.

I believe that the suspense drama is being smoked out of its old haunts. I think that we must forget about espionage and rediscover more personal sorts of menace. I think that a suspense story in the old tradition can be made today about an international crime ring, with its agents in high places, much more easily than a film about the missing papers.

The "MacGuffin"

The "MacGuffin"—my own term for the key element of any suspense story—has obviously got to change. It can no longer be the
idea of preventing the foreign agent from stealing the papers. It
can no longer be the business of breaking a code. And yet these
very same elements, disguised to fit the times, must still be there.

One of the ways in which the suspense-drama must change is in
its setting. The Orient Express, for example, has had its day as a
scene for spy melodrama. I think the same may be said of narrow
stairways in high towers, subways, and the like. Personally, I rather
lean toward Alaska as the setting for the next thriller. It is logical—
as one of the last targets of international espionage—and it has the
color of a frontier territory. (I could wear a beard for my own bit
role.) And there is such a nice air about the title "Eskimo Spy."

But the big problem of the glamorous villain—whether in Alaska
or Times Square—remains a riddle, just one minor heritage of a
brave new world in which we are becoming conditioned to suspect-
ing our neighbors and expecting the worst.

Core of the Movie—The Chase

An Interview with David Brady

Q. First, Mr. Hitchcock, I wonder if you would tell us why you consider the chase so important in films?

A. Well, for one thing, the chase seems to me the final expression of the motion picture medium. Where but on the screen can automobiles be shown careening around corners after each other? Then, too, the movie is the natural vessel for the chase story because the basic film shape is continuous. Once a movie starts it goes right on. You don't stop it for scene changes, or to go out and have a cigarette.

Q. You think, then, that the chase may be the best way to exploit the possibilities of the camera?

A. I do, yes. I would say the chase is almost indigenous to movie technique as a whole.

Q. Before we go on, maybe it would be a good idea for you to define the term "chase."

A. Well, essentially, the chase is someone running toward a goal, often with the antiphonal motion of someone fleeing a pursuer. Probably the fox hunt would be the simplest form of the chase.

"Core of the Movie—The Chase" was originally published in the *New York Times Magazine,* October 29, 1950, 22–23, 44–46. A typescript of the full transcript of the recording on which this piece was based is in the Hitchcock Collection at the Margaret Herrick Library.

Now if you substitute a girl for the fox, and put a boy in place of the hunters, you have the boy-chases-girl variation. Or substituting again, the police chasing a criminal. So long as a plot has either flight or pursuit, it may be considered a form of the chase. In many ways the chase makes up about 60 percent of the construction of all movie plots.

Q. Would you say, for instance, that Hamlet *is a chase?*

A. I'd say there's certainly a chase in *Hamlet* because Hamlet is a detective.

Q. If you broaden the term enough, perhaps the dramatic form itself is a chase?

A. I think perhaps it is.

Q. Would Macbeth *be a chase, Macbeth being the evil-doer who is pursued by fate?*

A. Well, yes, but the moment you make fate the pursuer you're getting a little abstract.

Q. Then you wouldn't take it that far?

A. No, I wouldn't. But I think any aim, any goal in a movie story to be reached, would come under the heading of the chase.

Q. Now what about the dramatic form which is a race rather than a chase, that is, where two people at two different places are converging on getting there first?

A. That is a race, you're right. But you could call it an individual chase to get to a certain point. Actually, it's a chase against time.

Q. In Sabotage, *you remember, the situation was the planting of a bomb at a certain hour and the journey of a young boy carrying the bomb. You gave the audience a time factor to observe and the constant showing of clocks toward that time deadline while the innocent victim carries the bomb. Was that a chase against time?*

A. Well, I'm not certain you would call that a chase because the boy himself had no goal. But in your mind, I suppose, you were chasing time in the sense that you were chasing the hour of one o'clock when the boy would relinquish the bomb and leave it at a particular spot. That is really almost a kind of extreme suspense.

Q. There's some doubt in my mind as to the exact distinction between suspense and chase. Can you have suspense without a chase?

A. Oh, yes. In *The Lady Vanishes,* for example, the scene where the hero and heroine are served drugged drinks is pure suspense. Incidentally, instead of creating suspense in the usual way by having the hero half raise the glass to his lips and lower it again and never quite get down to drinking it, I did it by cinematic means. I had the glasses served and left on the table while the two go on with their conversation. But I still had to make the audience ask "When are those glasses going to be picked up?" So I photographed the whole dialogue through the two glasses in the foreground.

Q. Well, if the audience, instead of merely waiting for the blow to fall, were also waiting for somebody to intervene, to stop their being drugged, wouldn't you have even more suspense?

A. Yes, but then you would also have a chase. If someone at the far end of the train, in which the two were drinking, knew they were going to be drugged and were trying to get there before they took the drinks, then you've got a chase because there's a time factor in movement. It's the time factor in movement that makes the chase, as against the time factor that is static which makes only suspense. That's the difference. But, of course, suspense provides one of the most important elements in any chase.

Q. What other elements would you say are found in a good chase?

A. Well, in the best chase plots there are usually several chases going on at once, for one thing, which eventually run into and influence each other. Then the good chase will also reveal character, and use psychology to build up tension. For example, the first chase I ever filmed, the chase after Jack the Ripper in *The Lodger.* You remember it? Well, it started with the public and police chasing the Ripper, building up information about him before showing the man himself. So by the time you got to the end of the first reel, you knew that he killed only fair-haired girls, that he did it every Tuesday, and that he's done in so many. And you also knew how it affected different people. Brunettes, they didn't care very much, but blondes were very worried about it, you know.

Q. But when did the chase begin? Not with the start of the film?

A. Yes, right from the beginning. In that particular movie you just started with the people who were doing the chasing instead of with the man being chased. The chase was in the mind of the onlooker seeing the picture, you might say. Then I got down to the case of an individual girl. The young Scotland Yard man who loves the girl is also after the Ripper. The Ripper, in turn, has become attracted to the girl who, the audience assumes, will be his next victim.

Q. You have a double chase then?

A. Yes.

Q. But when does the Ripper actually start running, physically?

A. Well, while the Ripper is how shall we say it always on the run psychologically, he really goes on the run in the last reel. That's when the whole thing is crystallized into the final physical chase. The twist at the end is that the pursued man turns out to be, not the Ripper, but the demented brother of one of the Ripper's victims.

Q. That business of crystallizing the whole thing, would you explain just what it means?

A. You see, as the picture approaches the climax of the tension, everything should begin to move faster. The threads of the plot become tauter and I even change the style of acting, broaden it. The tension is then released into the final physical chase, which must be short and breathtaking, to avoid the error of anticlimax.

Q. That seems an important thing to understand. Don't most people think of the chase only in terms of the final action, where it becomes a physical reality?

A. Oh, no, that is only part of a good chase. The more action and movement throughout, the better. In *Strangers on a Train*, the picture I am working on now, we are really exploiting the dramatic possibilities of movement. The hero plays a championship tennis match, knowing all the while that the villain is moving deliberately toward the execution of a piece of dirty work which will leave the hero hopelessly incriminated. He must play as hard and as fast as he can in order to win the match, get off the court, and overtake the villain. The villain, meantime, confident that his victim is tied to the tennis court, is taking his time and being very methodical. The camera, cutting alternately from the frenzied hurry of the tennis player to the slow operation of his enemy, creates a kind of counterpoint between two kinds of movement. Finally, the tennis player gets away after the villain, with the police after the tennis player, and the wide open chase begins, which winds up in a whirling finale.

Q. *Going back for a moment—you said characterization was one of the essentials of a good chase. Can you have much characterization when everybody is on the run?*

A. Well, when you have a chase plot with several chases intersecting and knit together, you do have the disadvantage of having little time for careful character analysis or psychological study. A picture has to emphasize one thing or another. *The 39 Steps,* my film of John Buchan's novel, for example, emphasized a close-knit chase structure. You remember, it has a double chase pattern—the police are after the hero who is after a spy ring and at the climax the police close in on him at the moment he is exposing the spies. But *The Lodger* and *The Man Who Knew Too Much* specialize more in psychology and character. In the ideal chase structure, however, the tempo and complexity of the chase will be an accurate reflection of the intensity of the relations between the characters. But I have found that even in the final physical chase, touches of characterization will embellish it.

Q. *But wouldn't the final chase be almost purely pictorial in any event?*

A. In the main, yes. But a little odd comment reflecting the feelings of the people at that moment can be illuminating. For example, in the climax of *The Man Who Knew Too Much,* the police lay siege to a house and take up various vantage points within as they advance from room to room. In one room they turn a girl out of her bed to get her mattress for a shield, and make cracks about it. At the moment one man is telling another that his wife may hear about it, he's shot dead. When they take over another room and use the piano as a barricade, a little man watches them in distress, but the only thing he wants to protect is his aspidistra plant on the top.

Q. Now, let's see, are there any other elements of the chase? What about comedy in a chase?

A. Yes, sometimes I do inject a little comic relief into a chase. But you can't have broad comedy of the kind that Mack Sennett used to do in his chases. In a serious chase while you might have your hero suddenly fall into a ditch, he couldn't come out covered with mud. He can get dirty, of course, but he mustn't look foolish.

Q. What about a situation where he is walking through a dark, deserted place, say, and something frightens him very much and it turns out to be a cat?

A. That you can have, because you get your relief laughs from the fact that the hero, too, is relieved—that it was a cat instead of a stalking foot. In your serious chase, when you have comic relief, it's important that the hero as well as the audience be relieved. Incidentally, in respect to audiences, I have found that there are certain things we can always count on the audience to feel so long as they can count on us, too. In *Sabotage,* for example, I played a kind of dirty trick on the audience.

Q. How was that?

A. Well, I broke the rule that the hero is always rescued from danger at the last minute. I had the bomb which the young boy was carrying go off, after all, and kill him. Anyway, he had to be killed for purposes of the story. But there were yowls of protest from everybody, especially from mothers. It's always been a mystery to me that audiences get apprehensive when the circular saw begins to reach the hero's neck. So far as I know, it never has yet in all the history of melodrama.

Q. But doesn't that explain one of the great attractions of the chase, that an audience is always ready to enter into it?

A. Yes, that's true. But many times you have the problem of determining on which side to enlist audience sympathy. In some chases I have felt that perhaps the audience would really prefer to sympathize with the fugitive. That is why I'm partial to the double chase. There the audience can run with the hare and hunt with the hounds. As the camera cuts from police to hero to real criminal, the audience has the opportunity to identify itself with both the chaser and

the chased in the person of the hero without suffering the frustra-
tion of a divided allegiance.

Q. Modesty aside, now, what is the best chase you have ever seen?

A. I don't know . . . I suppose, really, the ice floe scene in D. W.
Griffith's *Way Down East*. There was the heroine on a block of ice,
and the hero leaping to her from block to block and then back
again with her in his arms while all the time the camera was cutting
to a big waterfall beyond. Griffith was the first to exploit the possibilities of the physical chase. In *Birth of a Nation* there was the
ride of the hooded men, in *Intolerance* the chase to save a man
from the gallows, and in *Tale of Two Cities* [*Orphans of the Storm*]
Danton's gallop to the guillotine to save the Gish girl.

Q. Did you yourself derive anything from Griffith?

A. Only, I would say, the suspense of the chase. Griffith's chase
was fairly elementary. It didn't include any mental action, any characterization. But it was very clearly stated and you had no difficulty
following it.

*Q. Well, aside from Griffith, have you been influenced by any other
filmmakers?*

A. I have derived more from novelists like John Buchan, J. B.
Priestley, John Galsworthy, and Mrs. Belloc Lowndes than from
the movies. I like them because they use multiple chases and a lot
of psychology. My chases are the result of using all the resources of
modern film techniques to combine what I got from those novelists with what I got from Griffith.

*Q. One thing more, have you ever made a picture in which there
wasn't a chase?*

A. Oh, yes, several. Some time ago I directed a comedy called *Mr.
and Mrs. Smith* with the late Carole Lombard. It was a pretty successful picture commercially, but it wasn't considered a Hitchcock
picture because it had no chase. *Lifeboat* was another. *Under Capricorn* wasn't really a Hitchcock picture either—that was Bergman.
About *Under Capricorn* there were comments like "we had to wait
a hundred and fourteen minutes before any thrill came." If I seem
doomed to make only one type of picture, the movie audience is

responsible. People go to one of my films expecting a thriller, and they aren't satisfied until the thrill turns up.

Q. Can you think of anything else we might have missed?

A. No, I think now that I've given away all the tricks of the trade. Treat them with respect.

Murder—With English On It

A neighbor interrupted a rose-bush-pruning reverie of mine the other morning to exclaim with gusto: "Well, I see you've got another juicy murder case on your hands over there!"

I glanced hastily around to see if by chance I had overlooked a body somewhere in my matutinal peregrinations.

But it quickly developed that by "you" my friend meant not me personally but my native England; and that by "juicy murder case" he was referring to what I dare say some English newspaper by now has cited as "The Unfortunate Occurrences at Eastbourne." These involved, you may recall, what is alleged to be a rather phenomenal succession of demises of elderly, moneyed patients of a single doctor, and his subsequent arrest on charges of having unduly sped the parting clients.

But the part of my neighbor's utterance that interested me particularly was the single word "another."

"What do you mean, 'another'?" I asked, defensively. "It was my impression there were occasional homicides in the United States, too."

"Oh, sure," he conceded. "But you know—they aren't like those cases of *yours* . . ."

I winced again at the personal pronoun. But I sensed what he was driving at. Crime in England often does seem to have a specially fascinating aura.

"Murder—With English on It" was originally published in the *New York Times Magazine,* March 3, 1957, 17, 42.

As one to whom crime, in fictitious pictorial forms, is by way of being a livelihood, I have often been asked, and consequently have done some pondering, about why this difference exists. Why should infraction of the law—particularly of the Sixth Commandment—be more intriguing in Bedfordshire than Boise, Idaho? How had England, with less than one-third the population of the United States and a relative handful of homicides annually—the comparison is something like 7,000 to less than 300—managed to contribute so spectacularly to the literature of crime which occupies (without chauvinistic distinction) a half-dozen shelves of my library?

It seems to me there are two basic reasons:

(1) English crimes—and I am thinking particularly of murder—tend to be intrinsically more dramatic.

(2) When they do occur, perhaps because of their relative rarity, more is made of them—more juice is squeezed out, as it were; that juice is one of England's invisible exports to the United States.

There are, of course, a number of basic sociological differences between Britain and the United States which savants have long noted as a basis for differences in the form which the lamentable practice of murder takes.

England, Scotland, Wales, and Northern Ireland together are smaller than a number of individual states over here. If one commits a murder in Hollywood, for instance, he has within a couple of hours drive an expanse of desert bigger than the whole United Kingdom in which to dispose tastefully of the remains. In England, a murderer is faced with such stringent alternatives as the cellar or a trunk. If he chooses the latter, he then checks it at a railway station. Right away you have "The Waterloo Station Trunk Murder," pregnant with drama.

England's small expanse necessitates many people living close together. Down the centuries, this has brought about an inordinate regard for personal privacy. If Mr. Jones' wife suddenly disappears, instead of its being a subject of back-fence talk the next morning, it may be months before someone says: "Err, don't mean to pry at all, old boy, but it seems a deuced long time since we've had the pleasure of Mrs. Jones' presence . . ."

Dr. Crippen's famous disposal of his wife (a classic case, of which more later) came to light less because of her absence than because her jewelry was observed adorning another woman—a circumstance even an English woman could not resist calling attention to. In the

Eastbourne affair, it apparently was years before anyone had the temerity to suggest that the doctor's therapeutic batting average seemed to be slipping badly.

This regard for personal privacy is one of the facets of what *Punch* has illuminated humorously as "The British Character" which I think underlies the criminological disparities between opposite sides of the Atlantic.

Racial diversity in other parts of the world has produced various attitudes toward the law and the taking of human life. Among the so-called "hot-blooded" people, homicides often are spur-of-the-moment matters with few subtleties to dwell on. England's population is quite homogeneously composed of people renowned for their reserve. Emotions and urges to which other peoples give ready vent are by tradition and habit bottled up. When they emerge, the manifestation is likely to be accordingly more bizarre.

I am thinking, for instance, of the Adelaide Bartlett case around the turn of the century. An aging shopkeeper married a young girl, who soon found the attentions of the local parson more exciting than her husband's—with, it was testified, the husband's sanction; he liked to watch them neck. Still, the old fellow became obtrusive, and was dispatched with chloroform, which "burned the lining of the stomach as he lay in a recumbent position." Mrs. Bartlett and her lover were acquitted because the jury, while avowedly "suspicious," could not discover how chloroform could be introduced into a person's stomach without his cooperation. The medical profession later appealed to the principals, in the name of science, to explain how it was done—but got no answer.

Some of the more celebrated American murders—such as the Lizzie Borden, Hall-Mills, and Snyder-Gray cases—it will be observed, have an English flavor in their implications of long-suppressed passions, released in devious and tortuous ways.

But with something like twenty homicides occurring in the United States for every one in England, it still is curious that England should seem to out-produce this country in intriguing crimes.

I would attribute this in part to the British capacity for "making do" with what they have, and also to an ingrained racial sense of drama which, despite its concealment behind impassive visages, has appeared intermittently in history all the way from Shakespeare to Shaw.

Drama—particularly the melodrama of crime—involves contrast.

In films, I like to take a lurid situation and counterpoint it with understatement. A man is carrying a bomb in a satchel; a checkroom clerk refuses it—not because it has a bomb in it but because it is all greasy.

This same sort of understatement is an occupational tradition of English police. With the most atrocious criminals, they never bluster up and say, "O.K.—we gotcha!" They say: "I beg your pardon, but it seems that someone has been boiled in oil. We wondered if you'd mind answering a few questions about it. . . ."

The Crippen case was fraught with understatement, restraint, and characteristic British relish for drama.

Dr. Crippen was a quack dentist—from Detroit, incidentally—who opened an office in London, became enamored of his petite secretary, Ethel LeNeve, and relegated his wife to a grave under the cellar door. The appearance of the wife's jewelry on Miss LeNeve spurred inquiries about Mrs. Crippen.

After vouchsafing that she had gone to California and had died there, Dr. Crippen vanished, along with Miss LeNeve. They were on a British liner bound for Montreal, disguised as "Mr. Robinson and Master Robinson," when the first oceanic wireless alarm ever flashed for a criminal alerted the ship's captain. He quickly spotted the "boy's" disguise. He could have locked the two up forthwith. But instead he attenuated the quest in little games, such as making "Mr. Robinson" laugh so he could check distinctive features of his dentures. It was not until Inspector Dew of Scotland Yard, who had hopped a faster liner, boarded the ship in the St. Lawrence River, that the jig was formally up. Inspector Dew's salutation was: "Good morning, Dr. Crippen. . . ."

The British judicial mechanism seems timed almost with an eye for dramatic pace. There is only one court of appeal; it customarily rules on a case inside of a fortnight. British sentences by ancient tradition are supposed to be executed "within three clear Sundays." The possibility of swift doom endows a case with far more tension than the usual prospect in this country of a series of appeals that may go on for years until everybody is quite tired of it.

The rigid British libel laws contribute to the dramatic impact even of cases which intrinsically may have no more excitement than many in the United States. Newspapers are precluded from much discussion of a case before trial. Once the trial begins, every detail is seized and savored. Justice has a ritualistic vocabulary of provocative euphemism. Victims of sexual attacks, for instance, have been "interfered with." In the recent trial of John Haigh, who disposed of three women in barrels of sulphuric acid, there was repeated resort to the ominous word "sludge."

There is a group of intellectuals in London called Our Society which meets periodically in a private room at some London restaurant to "postmortem" interesting criminal trials. Counsel for both sides attend and let their hair down, off the record. Often even the judge in the case attends and the exhibits are shown. The auditors may include journalists, novelists, playwrights, and even actors. (Sir Henry Irving, incidentally, was an avid attender of major trials.) Interest of this sort tends to make cases, if only retrospectively, *causes célèbres,* thus creating an atmosphere of anticipation for the next one.

The question arises why, if English murder cases are so fraught with drama, more are not used as the basis for motion pictures. (Of the dozens of films I have made, none has been based on an actual case.)

The answer is a technical one. In real-life crime, public interest is focused on the identification and conviction of the murderer. He is not a "sympathetic" figure of the sort films customarily have as their protagonists, and his fate is already known. This vitiates the vital element the trade calls "rooting interest." In *Suspicion,* the story of a wife who suspects her husband of being a homicidal maniac, I had to make the suspicion ultimately a figment of her imagination. The consensus was that audiences would not want to be told in the last few frames of film that as popular a personality as Cary Grant was a murderer, doomed to exposure.

And now, if you will excuse me, I shall get back to my rose bushes—with the lingering thought, from the shock of my neighbor's salutation, that there still may be a body somewhere on the premises. That is one situation, I readily concede, which would be more pregnant with drama than any body in England.

Would You Like
to Know Your Future?

Would you like to be able to predict the future? A movie director can, you know. In making a film, he takes an imitation slice of life in his hands and arranges it just the way he wants it. He knows, in the first scene, just what is going to happen in the last.

Now, this is a godlike quality. It gives the director a great sense of power. But there's just one small trouble with it. The stuff the movie director is working with isn't real. It's synthetic. It's not life itself. It's only an imitation of life.

In real life, we can plan, and take precautions, and hope that things will happen in a certain way. But we can never be sure. And I sometimes wonder why it is that, if we try *too* hard to control the future, we get a rude shock.

I ran up against this hard fact quite early in my movie career. It was back in London when I was still in my twenties, young, unknown, but very knowing—or so I thought. I'd entered the movies through the back door, first designing titles, then as a cutter, scriptwriter, set designer, production man, and finally as a director of a few minor films. When I got the opportunity to pick my own story and direct it for one of the major British studios, I was certain I had the future, in the film and out of it, right in my hand.

The story I chose was *The Lodger*, a quiet yarn in which one of

"Would You Like to Know Your Future?" was originally published in *Guideposts Magazine* 14, no. 8 (October 1959): 1–4.

the occupants of a rooming house is suspected of having a secret hobby—homicide.

Films were still silent in those days, and I used every trick I could think of to build the suspense visually and hide the outcome. It was full of innovations; I was very proud of the result.

When the day came for the bigwigs at the studio to see it, my wife, Alma, and I remained at home, excited, but unworried. We knew they'd like it. Like it? They'd love it!

We timed our arrival at the studio to coincide with the ending of the screening. When Alma and I walked in, we knew instantly we hadn't convinced anyone of the superlative merits of Alfred Hitchcock, director.

"It could be patched up," one of the executives said hopefully.

"No," I said stubbornly.

"There's a lot of money tied up in this," another executive said.

"No," I persisted.

Then the big boss uttered the final doom: "It's unshowable. We'll shelve it."

It was a kind of day of judgment. Alma and I stumbled out of the studio. We walked. And we prayed. For what? For another chance.

This had been my first real chance at directing. Once a director in the movies, it's impossible to go back to a lesser job, like title or set designing. I was like a new captain given his first ship and running it on the rocks. Finished.

For months the film sat in a can on the studio's library shelves. But one day one of the executives, the one who said there was an awful lot of money tied up in it, suggested that it be shown quietly to a few distributors, with the explanation—and apology—that the studio didn't think much of it, just wanted expert reaction.

The few distributors watched it, and that magic ingredient, unpredictability, began working. They liked it. The studio decided to release it. All the distributors wanted it. *The Lodger* became a great movie hit from the very start.

But I was not elated. No. I had to find a rational explanation for the strange events that made it a failure at the beginning and an enormous success at its end.

In the film story, the synthetic future was certain. I controlled it. When I completed the movie, I was arrogantly certain of its real future too. I was sure that everyone would love it. When they didn't, I walked about in desperation, praying for another chance.

There it was: I had been grasping at the real future, wanting it in my own hand. It was almost as if God deliberately delayed success to show me that my efforts at controlling the future was not in His scheme of things.

This was an amazing thought. But over the years I've been forced to the conclusion that a blind future is one of God's most strictly enforced rules and that scientific effort to see into the future is also doomed to failure. There are two main reasons.

The first reason is simple. In life, if we knew the outcome of everything, most of the zest would go out of living. What fun would it be to go to a baseball game if you knew which team was going to win? Why go fishing if you knew that you would (or wouldn't) catch fish? The unknown has its appeal precisely because it is mysterious. Take the concept of heaven, for instance—wouldn't we tend to lose some of our interest in it if we knew exactly what it was like?

So when God keeps the future hidden, He is saying that things would be very dull without suspense.

But I think He has a deeper reason than that when he hides the future. I think He is also being merciful. Because, if life would be dull knowing about tomorrow, it would also be terrible.

Do you remember the story of the king who befriended a wizard and was granted two wishes? His first wish was to see the future completely. But when the king saw the pain, the misery, the death, along with the beautiful things ahead, he immediately asked for his second wish: that the future be hidden again.

"I did not know that I already had the greatest gift of all," he explained. "The gift of a blind future."

And so, I've come to believe that a hidden future is one of God's most merciful and exciting gifts. Without it there would be nothing to wait for, worse, nothing to hope for. In any case, whether we like it or not, we have to live with it.

How we live with it is up to us. We can live in a state of constant anxiety about the future, always afraid that in the long run the bad guy wins, injustice triumphs, and mankind will destroy itself.

Or we can use the gift creatively; help men of goodwill to win, justice to triumph, and believe that the drama of man must end in happiness.

In other words, we can live in a state of chronic despair, or we can live with faith in the future, even though it is hidden from us.

Yes, the best thing about the future is that it comes one day at a time. And I thank Heaven daily that tomorrow does not belong to any man. It belongs to God.

Why I Am Afraid of the Dark

It's been several years that people have called me "the king of suspense." Was I influenced by Edgar Allan Poe? To be frank, I couldn't affirm it with certainty. Of course, subconsciously, we are always influenced by the books that we've read. The novels, the painting, the music, and all the works of art, in general, form our intellectual culture from which we can't get away. Even if we want to!

First of all, I have to confess that I'm easily frightened. I realized this when I was four or five years old. I remember that night when I woke up with a start. The house was plunged into darkness and completely silent. I sat up and I began calling my mother. No one responded because no one was there. I trembled with fear. However, I was able to find enough courage to get up, in the completely empty house, I might add. I came to the kitchen which was illuminated in a sinister fashion. I trembled more and more. At the same time, I was hungry. I opened the kitchen buffet, in which I

"Why I Am Afraid of the Dark" ("Pourquoi J'ai Peur la Nuit") was originally published in *Arts: Lettres, Spectacles,* no. 777, June 1–7, 1960, 1, 7. It is translated for the present volume by Claire Marrone. (Some of it is translated and included in Spoto, 40–42.)

Jane Sloan, in *Alfred Hitchcock: A Guide to References and Resources* (382), notes that it was used as a preface to a French edition of suspense stories, *Histoires abominables de Hitchcock* (Paris: Laffont, 1960). But the headnote to the original simply says that Hitchcock will write the preface to a French edition of Poe's tales, even though a French edition of *Histoires abominable* has just come out. It goes on to say that *Arts* is happy to present Hitchcock's ideas on Poe but does not specify that this piece is a preface to any other volume.

found some cold meat, and I began eating and crying. I couldn't calm down until my parents came back. They explained to me that they had gone for a walk because they thought I was asleep. Since that day, there are two things that I can't take: being alone when it's dark and eating cold meat!

At that time, I hadn't, of course, ever heard of Edgar Allan Poe. It was only when I was sixteen that I discovered his work. I read first, at random, his biography, and the sadness of his life made a great impression on me. I felt an immense pity for him because, in spite of his talent, he had always been unhappy.

When I would come back from the office where I worked, I would hurry to my room, take a cheap edition of his *Tales of the Grotesque and Arabesque,* and begin reading. I still remember my feelings when I finished "The Murders in the Rue Morgue." I was afraid, but this fear made me in fact discover something that I haven't since forgotten.

Fear, you see, is a feeling that people like to feel when they are certain of being in safety. When one is tranquilly seated at one's home and one is reading a gruesome story, one feels nevertheless secure. Naturally one trembles, but as one finds oneself in a familiar surrounding, and when one realizes that it's only imagination which is responsible for the fear, one is invaded by an extraordinary happiness. A happiness comparable to that which one feels when one drinks after having been very thirsty. A happiness which makes one appreciate the sweet warmth which the friendly lamp diffuses, under its lampshade, and the soft armchair in which one is comfortably seated.

In my opinion, the reader is exactly in the same situation as the cinema spectator. And, very probably, it's because I liked Edgar Allan Poe's stories so much that I began to make suspense films. Without wanting to seem immodest, I can't help but compare what I try to put in my films with what Poe put in his stories: a perfectly unbelievable story recounted to readers with such a hallucinatory logic that one has the impression that this same story can happen to you tomorrow. And that's the rule of the game if one wants the reader or the spectator to subconsciously substitute himself for the hero, because, in truth, people are only interested in themselves or in stories which could affect them.

Myself, I'm not an exception to this rule. If "The Gold Bug" fascinated me and fascinates me still, it's because I always loved adventure, voyages, and the impression of homesickness. When I was a child, to satisfy my passion for boats, I had an immense map in my room on which I indicated, with the help of little flags, the exact place of the navigating buildings on the seas and the oceans of the world. It was enough for me to look at it to believe myself captain on a long cruise! This story of treasure, which one finds thanks to a mysterious beetle, corresponds to my love of the fantastic and of precision.

I think that Edgar Allan Poe has a very particular place in the world of literature. He's at the same time, without the shadow of a doubt, a romantic and a precursor of modern literature. He couldn't escape romanticism, because no one can escape the tendency of the era in which he lives. One mustn't forget that Edgar Allan Poe went to school in England in 1818, when Goethe had already published *Faust* and when the first stories by Hoffmann had just come out. This romanticism is perhaps even more apparent in the translation done by Baudelaire, which is the one you use. In my opinion, these two authors are very close to one another and I would go as far as to say that one could name Baudelaire the French Poe.

And surrealism? Wasn't it born as much from the work of Poe as from that of Lautréamont? This literary school certainly had a great influence on cinema, especially around 1925–1930, when surrealism was transposed onto the screen by Buñuel with *L'Age d'or* and *Un Chien Andalou,* by René Clair with *Entr'acte,* by Jean Epstein with *The Fall of the House of Usher,* and by your French academician Jean Cocteau with *The Blood of a Poet.* An influence that I experienced myself, if only in the dream sequences and the sequences of the unreal in a certain number of my films.

However, because of the difference in means of expression and the difference in era, I don't think that there exists a real resemblance between Edgar Allan Poe and myself. Poe is a *poéte maudit* and I am a commercial filmmaker. He liked to make people shiver. Me too. But he didn't really have a sense of humor. And for me, "suspense" doesn't have any value if it's not balanced by humor.

In cinematographic style, "suspense" consists in inciting a breathless curiosity and in establishing a complicity between the director and the spectator, who knows what is going to happen. In a book, however, the reader must never guess what is going to happen and must not know the unraveling of the intrigue before getting to the end.

But Edgar Allan Poe and I certainly have a common point. We are both prisoners of a genre: "suspense." You know the story that one has recounted many, many times: if I was making "Cinderella," everyone would look for the corpse. And if Edgar Allan Poe had written "Sleeping Beauty," one would look for the murderer.

A *Redbook* Dialogue
Alfred Hitchcock and Dr. Fredric Wertham

DR. WERTHAM: I didn't see *Psycho,* I'm sorry to say, but many people have commented on the act of violence in that movie. Was it a little stronger than you would have put in formerly—say ten or fifteen years ago?

MR. HITCHCOCK: Well, I don't know. I have *always* felt that you should do the minimum on screen to get the maximum audience effect. I believe the audience should work. Sometimes it is necessary to go into some element of violence, but I only do it if I have a strong reason. For example, in *Psycho* there was this very violent impressionistic murder in a bathroom, you see, and it was montaged by little pieces of film giving the impression of a knife stabbing a victim, and so on and so forth.

Now, once I had completed that piece of film, I had instilled in the minds of the audience enough apprehension about the existence of a murderer so that as the movie went on, I was able to reduce and eventually practically eliminate all further violence because I only wanted the threat left. Once I had given the audience that one—shall we say, sample?—I allowed them to imagine the violence, you see. I did not have to show it. Violence for the sake of violence I don't think has any effect. I don't even think the audience is moved by it. It's so obvious.

WERTHAM: But wasn't this violence stronger than your usual dose?

"A *Redbook* Dialogue: Alfred Hitchcock and Dr. Fredric Wertham" was originally published in *Redbook* 120 (April 1963): 71, 108, 110–112.

HITCHCOCK: It was.

WERTHAM: More?

HITCHCOCK: More.

WERTHAM: Then am I fair in thinking that some of this atmosphere of needing and wanting violence which exists in our society at present has rubbed off on you? Is it possible? In other words, Hitchcock would not volunteer it, but the audience demands it because they are accustomed to it and do not want to settle for less?

HITCHCOCK: I didn't do it for that purpose.

WERTHAM: Well, perhaps unconsciously?

HITCHCOCK: Well, no. Actually I would say as far as violence goes, no; the lovemaking, yes. I felt that in the portrayal of lovemaking, the ordinary embrace and the kissing on the cheek or what-have-you—I feel that young people today would laugh at that.

WERTHAM: That's right.

HITCHCOCK: They would yawn. And I was conscious of making the lovemaking scenes a little more risqué than I normally would, only because I felt that modern manners had changed, to some extent.

WERTHAM: I wonder whether an audience that would laugh or yawn at—shall we call it old-fashioned?—lovemaking isn't the same audience that would yawn at scenes of violence that didn't measure up to what they expected. But let me present the problem in another way. From a scientific point of view there is still a great question about the effect any kind of entertainment has on people psychologically. One way of trying to learn more about it—about the effect, for example, of scenes of violence on television—is to ask someone what they saw and what they thought about it. This kind of survey is supposed to be a scientific way; I don't happen to think it is. With questionnaires, you get answers you can count and use to give percentage of yeses and noes, but you mustn't look too closely to see if the answers mean anything. In this so-called scientific study I'm thinking of, they asked: "Do you or do you not believe in God?" One young boy answered: "Sometimes." And this is the kind of questionnaire they used to find out about the effect of violence in Western movies on children who watched television— the cowboys being shot and falling from their horses and nobody even stopping to look at them and so forth. And this scientific study reports that shootings and killings on TV movies don't do any harm because they are stylized. Stylized! I'm not sure what that word means. You show killing, that means killing to any child.

HITCHCOCK: Well, that is true to a point. But on the other hand, don't forget little children themselves play at being dead. A little boy holds his hands up with three fingers and one finger pointed out and he says, "Bang—you're dead." And the other little boy falls down. A minute later he's up and the two are running around again. They know what make-believe dead is. Not long ago when I was in Los Angeles, a boy came up to me—he was about nine years old—and he said, "Oh, Mr. Hitchcock, in the murder scene in *Psycho,* what did you use for blood? Chicken blood?" I said, "No, chocolate sauce." He said, "Oh . . . Okay—thank you," and went on his way.

WERTHAM: But of course there is another side to that, you see. This is what concerns me: not that violence scares children—or adults, for that matter—but precisely the fact that it doesn't. If people see too much violence on movie or television screens, why shouldn't we expect them to get used to violence? The child isn't scared any more by one person being murdered. If five get killed, or fifty, it can't make much difference.

HITCHCOCK: Well, let's look at the fairy stories. Look at the violence and—shall we coin a word?—the Grimm-ness of them.

WERTHAM (*smiling*): With two m's.

HITCHCOCK: Yes, two m's. Now, Red Riding Hood, you see— "What big teeth you have, Grandma." "All the better to eat you with, my dear." These stories, remember, are read to little tots; they grow up on them. Hansel and Gretel, for example—the old woman is pushed into the oven! And think how early this starts.

WERTHAM: Fairy tales, of course, are creations of art. But you see, there's a difference. Movies take real life as it is in the street and the house and the drawing room. Now, that's totally different from a fairy tale. I mean, who has a grandmother who's eaten by a wolf? That doesn't mean anything to a boy. That's a totally different thing than if he sees on the screen a gangster on the street who shoots from an ordinary car right there and then, you know, or in a bathroom or whatever. That is much closer to something he knows.

HITCHCOCK: Well, I'm only going back to the fairy story to show that this thing is part of a child's education and they get educated to some kind of—shall we call it awfulness?—that they don't really believe in.

WERTHAM: I want to defend fairy stories. There are many fairy stories that are not violent at all.

HITCHCOCK: But the children do not know they're fairy tales. This little boy, sitting on his mother's knee, wide-eyed, listens with awe, and he *believes*. All this, mind you, starts at such an early age. Somebody once asked me: "When did you first learn about creating fear in people?" As you know, when you tell a movie story as I do, you trade on the fear which is within everyone. When did I learn this? When I was six months old. I was in my mother's arms, and she went "Boo!" and scared the hell out of me and gave me the hiccups. And then I giggled, and she was so pleased. Now, what makes the mother take a little child six months old and go "boo" and the child gets hiccups? This could be the beginning of parental irresponsibility.

WERTHAM: May I take up the subject of parental responsibility in perhaps a more serious way? In my own experience—from seeing people and examining them and trying to find out what influenced them for good or bad—I am certain that we must make an absolute distinction between children and adults. It doesn't do any harm for a forty-year-old man to watch anything; his life is crystallized. But what a child watches must affect him, and particularly violence. Television, after all, sits in his living room, and it wouldn't be there if his parents didn't approve of it. That gives the programs he watches just so much more power over him.

HITCHCOCK: Well, naturally it boils down to parents and their control over their children looking at the set. But I think we can say this much about television as a kind of gleam of hope—I don't believe every child is corrupted by it.

WERTHAM: Of course, "corrupted" isn't the word for it, is it? The reason people aren't doing much to see to it that television improves is just this: Here, they are told, are abnormal children— these are the ones who are affected; and here are normal children who are completely immune. I have been trying to combat this notion for a long time because I don't think you can divide children like this. I believe that *all* children, including those from the best families and with the best education, can be influenced in the areas of sex, of violence, of dishonesty, of prejudice.

But I don't think parents can just sit around waiting for things to happen by themselves. Not too long ago, as you may know, I was involved in protesting the horror comic books that were flooding the country. What you may not know is that many parents in many communities joined the protest, and did what they could to prevent these things from coming into their children's hands, and in a few years twenty-four out of twenty-nine publishers stopped putting out these comics.

I think today parents have a new level of responsibility. All the answers aren't available as to how society can protect children, and parents cannot afford to wait. They have to, at the very least, let their children know how they themselves feel about violence, and they have to express their criticism of what they think are really harmful programs to the sponsors of such programs.

HITCHCOCK: One point I would like to make here is that you can always create suspense without resorting to violence. The fact that a man dies, we only have to say, Well, the man died, drank a glass of milk or whatever it was—off-screen, anyway you like, you see. You can get an audience worried terribly without any violence. It's not necessary.

WERTHAM: I have always referred to your film *Rebecca* as a movie about violence without violence, which I think is a marvelous achievement.

HITCHCOCK: But in producing the movies that I do, I find it would be impossible without a sense of humor. I play with people's emotions, it's true. I know how to prepare them, how to give them a laugh at the right moment, and I know how to make them react by clutching their seats with fear, almost screaming—because I know that they will finally go out giggling. These are the same people who scream on the roller coaster when it goes off on the deep dive, you see, and then when it levels off at the end, they're laughing.

For some reason they enjoy this fear. As I've said before, they love to put their toe into the cold water of fear to find out what it feels like. If you take the average fairground midway, you will find people paying money to be frightened—the haunted house, for example, where the floorboards move up and down, skeletons pop up, spiders drop down—and it's all done on a basis of humor.

WERTHAM: This is part of the science of psychoanalysis. To fight the biggest fears, people try a sample of their little fears. A little at a time.

HITCHCOCK: Little children go on a swing. They go higher and higher—and then they scare themselves and stop at the crucial point. And after they get off the swing, they're laughing.

WERTHAM: Humor, yes. But you know, movies have one thing in common, most of them—they have no sense of humor at all. They don't have the safety valve of humor. But a question I want to ask you now is totally different. It's this: I have been preoccupied for quite some time now, and so have many other people, with the fact that we are technologically so advanced that we don't make old-fashioned wars any more, with guns and so on, but it is perfected now, like—well, like agriculture. We can simply exterminate.

HITCHCOCK: Yes.

WERTHAM: We can exterminate people the way we exterminate pests. And I am preoccupied with the fact that psychologically people are getting more and more ready to accept this. Now, the question is this: Can the mass media, can they do something to bring home to people that something quite serious could happen, and if it happens, it's their own fault, not the fault of two or three people sitting pressing buttons? Can you do something about this threat of violence?

HITCHCOCK: I don't think they would accept it.

WERTHAM: I'm afraid I agree with you.

HITCHCOCK: No, they wouldn't believe it. The concept is so vast, you see, and after all, they've seen so many times the mushroom cloud. They've seen it in newsreels, and they haven't any conception still as to what it means. And then I think it's so far beyond their imagination, the average person's imagination. Of course, they see Hiroshima, pictures of that, you know, and so forth, but that's very remote from them.

WERTHAM: But shouldn't it be possible for people like you who are interested in communication and are masters of entertainment to see if you can reach them about that too?

HITCHCOCK: I don't think so, because I belong to fictions. It would be like science fiction. They wouldn't believe it anyway. I still prefer to play on their emotions my way.

WERTHAM: Aren't they also being shaped and educated and conditioned?

HITCHCOCK: No, because I'm not conditioning them. I'm using their natural instincts to help them enjoy fear. That's what I trade on. I know those people can all be scared. I play them like an organ. I know exactly when to stop, to relieve them at the right moment, otherwise they'll laugh in the wrong places.

WERTHAM: I have admired very much a number of movies you

have made—*Rear Window,* for example. And I have wondered: Quite apart from your professional plans and professional abilities, how do you become interested in the themes that recur in your movies? To be more blunt, can it have any connection with your own life?

HITCHCOCK: No. Strangely enough, Doctor, my life is a very simple one. It's the direct antithesis of what I do on the screen. Women often regard me as an ogre or a monster until they get to know me, and then they find I'm just the opposite. My wife and I have been married for thirty-six years and—but you know, Dr. Wertham, in a way, one could almost say you would be the best person to answer this. How can a simple fellow like me get involved in all these crime and murder complications which come up on that screen? Because they do not reflect in any way whatsoever my own private life or my own private mind.

WERTHAM: Part of the answer lies in the very word you have given me. You say your movies are the *antithesis* of your life. In my experience it is often true that an artist does not live the kind of life he describes best. But we psychiatrists [*smiling*] are annoying people. We assume and generally can demonstrate that some submerged connection does link the creator to what he creates. So I would expect there must be a little connection between the psychology of these movies and your own feelings about them.

HITCHCOCK [*slowly*]: Well, let's examine the—I'm English by birth, you see, and the fact happens to be that many great English literary figures have always interested themselves in crime. Consider, for example, a trial at the Old Bailey, which as you must know is England's chief criminal court. Behind the bewigged counsel are long leather seats for privileged guests, and you'll find the people who go there when an important trial is on include the most important writers of the day. The whole thing is examined on a very high plane. Now, this is indigenous, it seems to me, to the English.

WERTHAM: It is true that if a crime is studied properly—which it rarely is—but if it *is* examined thoroughly, it can suddenly illuminate a whole community—even, perhaps, a whole nation. When it comes to revealing reality, I don't think there is anything that is more revealing than a crime, particularly a murder. We can pretend a lot about how we feel in our social lives, but once a murder has been committed, we are forced to look reality in the face. The pretending is over. This man may have said he loved his wife, but all that is certain is that he murdered her. Why? What really was in his heart and mind? And in hers? I was in England shortly after the Dr. Crippen case, and there is a murder case that tells you as much about England at the time as any history book.

HITCHCOCK: Well, therefore—you see there is a connection between me and this whole approach to crime. The English have always been interested in crime. Now, I had a friend whose name was Mrs. Belloc Lowndes; her brother was the well-known English writer Hilaire Belloc, you know. Well, now, Mrs. Lowndes, God rest her soul, was like a little housewife. But she used to write these more or less horrific novels. I made a movie—it was one of my first exercises in this genre—based on a novel by Mrs. Lowndes. We called it *The Lodger.*

WERTHAM: Oh, yes, that's a famous one. It was based on a real case, wasn't it?

HITCHCOCK: Yes, Jack the Ripper. That was the third picture I directed but my first in England—I had made two earlier ones in Germany. Now, *The Lodger* was full of suspenseful devices which in those days, the silent-picture days, we had to show visually. I remember the opening of the picture—ten minutes on a London afternoon, with the news of the latest Ripper murder, and I showed how the news was spread through all media. I showed all the details of newspaper production, but each time I gave away some more information about Jack the Ripper—that he only did it on Tuesdays; he only did it to blonde girls—murdered them—what he looked like, and so forth. I waited a whole reel before I introduced him. I followed one girl home to her mother and father at night, and while they're talking about the Ripper, the lights go down slowly—gas lamps, you know—and as it gets dark the mother says: "Dad, put a shilling in the gas meter; the gas is going down." So the father goes off to the meter with a shilling. Mother gets up to answer a knock at the door, and as she opens it, by quick cross-cutting, you see the shilling put into the meter and then Mother opens the door, the lights come up, and there is Jack the Ripper with a black coat, a black hat and a black bag, standing there, you see.

WERTHAM: The trouble with so much of the crime writing in this country is that—well, first of all it isn't so carefully done. Much of it is pretty shabbily written. Then what happens here is that it gets mixed up with what I shall call social reform. Now, that would be very good—there is always the example of Dickens, you know—but this isn't really aimed at opening people's eyes to the reality around them. It's halfhearted. If it touches the Puerto Rican problem in New York, for example, it touches it gingerly and then pulls back. Social reform is just another ingredient to throw into the murder-story stew.

Another trouble is that crime writers here are mixed up with some kind of Viennese jargon of psychoanalysis. And I feel obliged to say that they often misuse psychiatry and psychoanalysis. It's not too difficult to write about sex and sadism and violence in nice sensational detail as long as you pretend that you're really proceeding on safe psychiatric ground—which generally isn't the case.

Finally there is the fact that Americans, unlike the English, have made a cult of violence. Take a Los Angeles television station I know about. In one week's time, on programs appearing before nine P.M., mind you, they showed three hundred and thirty-four completed or attempted killings. And all that violence was displayed for children to see. This is a dangerous and vicious circle because a child's mind is like a bank—whatever you put in, you get back in ten years, with interest.

HITCHCOCK: Yes, but what about the so-called influences that are just afterthoughts? For example, there was a case in Los Angeles. I don't know whether the man is still in Death Row or not, but he committed—killed a woman and he said he did it after seeing *Psycho*. He had killed two other women before, so when the press called and asked if I had any comment, I said, "Yes. I want to know the names of the movies he saw before he killed the other two, or did he kill the first one after drinking a glass of milk?"

WERTHAM: Well, of course there are all kinds of theories to explain such killings. But I have one question. The other day a boy of four killed a girl of five with a .22-caliber rifle. He had loaded it himself. How does a boy of four learn to load and handle a rifle?

Violence, guns, killings, they are all around us. And you know, Mr. Hitchcock, this affects your audience. All this exposure to violence desensitizes them. They want stronger and stronger stuff. *The Lodger*, I think, wouldn't be enough for them today.

Film Production

Introduction

Hitchcock is recognized as one of the great auteurs, and he frequently praises the model of what he calls "one-man pictures," films that bear the signature of a strong producer-director, knowledgeable in all areas of cinematic technique, construction, and economics. The essays and interviews in this section, though, show Hitchcock's deep awareness that an auteur by no means operates independently but rather in the context of stylistic conventions, production routines, and institutional pressures that set up the horizon of filmmaking (a highly charged term for a director who often identifies his ideal sight as a clear horizon). Describing these circumstances helps Hitchcock analyze why films turn out as they do—that is to say, why films are often unexciting, "stodgy," and without a soul—and how this might be remedied. He offers not only critical comments and idealistic suggestions but also his own production method as one possible way out of the "old ruts." Despite his enthusiasm for reform, though, the underlying tone here is often somber, born of the knowledge that film is as much, if not more, an art of unequal negotiation as it is an art of imagination.

"Films We Could Make," for example, might well be subtitled "And Why We Can't Make Them." An important background for his essay is what Tom Ryall calls "the quest for national cinematic identity" (*Alfred Hitchcock and the British Cinema*, 61) in the mid-1920s, an attempt to strengthen the confidence and economic base of the British film industry and decrease reliance on imported films, especially from America. (This movement culminated in the

Cinematograph Films Act of 1927, which had the unfortunate effect of creating not quality pictures but "quota quickies," made to satisfy the mandate that a certain percentage of films had to be British productions.) Hitchcock participates in this quest not only by enthusiastically calling for films about British village boys, rural dramas, and sea stories but by making such a film himself: *The Manxman*, one of his finest silent films, which went into production not long after this essay was written, incorporates all these elements.

But a change in subject matter is only one of Hitchcock's wishes—and somewhat easier to accomplish than his desire to make films that live up to the medium's full artistic potential. British cinema is a capital-intensive commercial enterprise, and in a situation where the financiers demand profits, the "average film-goer misses little points which were apparently too subtle," and the aesthetically interested and sophisticated audience is a small minority, directors do not have the freedom to experiment with films of "rhythmic movement and light and shade" or "studies of cubes and circles . . . like a Cubist painting in motion." Such elements, however, can be integrated into commercial films. Hitchcock was obviously aware of but does not, for example, make an entire film comparable to Marcel Duchamp's *Anaemic Cinema* (1926) or Fernand Léger's *Ballet Mecanique* (shown at the London Film Society in March 1926). He does, though, use such avant-garde images and techniques as swirling circles and dreamlike, disordered, kaleidoscopic perspectives to good effect in a number of early films such as *Blackmail* and *Murder!* The making of fully satisfying and successful films is for Hitchcock always a matter of balancing "arty" elements with commercial considerations, a balancing act that he mastered. (At this time I suspect that the film *Variety* [1925]—echoed repeatedly in *Murder!* and later listed as one of his ten favorite films—was a particularly influential model for him of how one could effectively harmonize experimentation and mass entertainment.) But especially early in his career, one occasionally senses Hiitchcock's regret that a creative compromise is still a compromise.

Although he resigns himself to working within the system, he does not hesitate to shake things up a bit. " 'Stodgy' British Pictures," for example, begins from unexceptional premises—films, he says, must be entertaining and realistic to create sympathetic attachment to the main characters—but generates a manifestolike urgency. Like Truffaut many years later in "A Certain Tendency of the French Cinema," which shows more than a trace of the Master's influence on the young critic and theoretician, Hitchcock energetically calls for films to be fresh and unusual, atmospheric and cinematically varied rather than literary and predictable. Conventional films are "stodgy" not because they are theatrical but because they fail to learn the lesson of the best plays: drama on stage and on screen should be based on contrast, light and shade, and a comic touch that adds both a sugar coating and a bang to the action. (Hitchcock so typically emphasizes suspense that we should pay careful attention to places where he notes the importance of "complete unexpectedness.") And, following the example of American films, he notes that British films need to get out more: "Why must we always stick to our middle-class drawing rooms and our middle-class characters?" He elaborates on this argument in "More Cabbages, Fewer Kings," a plea for British films to stop ignoring "the dramatic coloring to be picked out in the existence of the ordinary people." Here he describes these people somewhat loosely as "middle class," but it is clear that he has in mind not the drawing room crowd but the more "colorful belt" of working people, "the men who leap on buses, the girls who pack into the Tube," and so on. "I am trying to get this stratum of England on the screen," he says, but it is a difficult battle: filmmakers are restricted by "a hard enemy" of complacent audiences and recalcitrant tastemakers, arbiters of conventionality.

He shrewdly analyzes what might be called these anticinematic forces throughout the pieces collected in this section. Some of the most pressing director's problems, as he notes in his essay of that title, are economic. After calculating what must be paid for studio rent, equipment, setting, salaries for actors and actresses, film stock, script preparation, technicians' and director's fees, and insurance, he concludes that the high cost of making a film is a "Moloch that engulfs everything." The immediate casualty is cinematic art: "When you are working with those figures there does not seem much hope of experimenting with new ideas." Ironically, the innate power of cinema to appeal to a universal audience "automatically" imprisons it in an antiaesthetic of common simple stories with happy endings that, he concludes, "has pretty well gone a long way to destroy it as an art."

In struggling to define and salvage cinema as an art, Hitchcock realizes that he has to do battle with more than mundane audiences, profit-hungry executives, and market conditions. As if this is not enough, there was still much resistance among highbrow critics to the idea that film should be taken seriously as a form of cultural and artistic expression. The specific background of Hitchcock's essay "Much Ado About Nothing?" is an attack by the arch-Shakespearean critic and man of the theater Harley Granville-Barker on recent films of Shakespearean plays. Why should Hitchcock get involved in this debate? Nearly ten years later he announced plans to make a film of *Hamlet* with Cary Grant, an unrealized project that he spent more time on in court (defending against a legal action brought by a disgruntled writer who claimed that his rights were being infringed by the proposed film) than in preproduction work, but in the late 1930s Hitchcock had no particular stake in Shakespearean films. It was undoubtedly Granville-Barker's implicit more than his explicit arguments, though, that exercised Hitchcock, and he energetically and effectively defends the legitimacy of visual expression, the independence of cinema from literature, and the role of cinema as not only a mediator of high culture, bringing Shakespeare to the people, but also as a valuable cultural product in its own right.

Far more formidable an adversary for Hitchcock than Granville-Barker is the institutionalized pressure of the censor. As both Annette Kuhn, in *Cinema, Censorship and Sexuality 1909–1925,* and James C. Robertson, in *The Hidden Cinema: British Film Censorship in Action, 1913–1975,* have recently analyzed in great detail, various censorship boards and unwritten as well as written codes exerted a great deal of influence on filmmakers and exhibitors in England during the 1920s and 1930s, and Hitchcock was a frequent contributor to and focal point of the ongoing debate about censorship in film magazines and newspapers. (See, for example, "*The 39 Steps*: An Appreciation of the New Hitchcock Film, with a Word on Censorship," *New York Times,* September 22, 1935, sec. 10, p. 5; the editorial "Hitchcock vs. the Censor," *Film Weekly,* May 16, 1936, 3, noted by Sloan, 352; and W. H. Modaine, "Films that Hollywood Dare Not Make," *Film Weekly,* August 4, 1938.) Hitchcock notes matter-of-factly in "Director's Problems" that "There are dozens of films I want to do" but cannot, including one about "a prison governor who revolts against his job of hanging a man." This would not be allowed: "Capital punishment is part of our law, and we mustn't propagate against it." In "The Censor and Sydney Street," he says that he "would like to make a film showing the balance of justice in English courts" (the legal system is a recurrent topic whenever he discusses films he would like to make). This is understandably another example of a subject that would cause "difficulties with the censor": we know from the films Hitchcock did make that he was both fascinated by the law and deeply critical of its mechanisms and operations.

Hitchcock's most interesting observations on censorship come in "The Censor Wouldn't Pass it," in which part of his defense against the claim that his typical film formula is beginning to wear "just a little thin" is his complaint that his options are very restricted. Those who think of Hitchcock as primarily and intentionally a formalist and "nonpolitical" artist may be surprised to hear him explain, "Circumstances have forced me into the realms of fiction. I have always wanted to make films with some sociological importance—but I have never been allowed to do so." His most startling statement is that he wanted to make a film about the General Strike of 1926, showing "fistfights between strikers and undergraduates, pickets, and all the authentic drama of the situation," but this was "immediately vetoed" by the British Board of Film censors. Even one of his current film projects, *Titanic,* he says, is encountering political opposition because cruise operators do not want anyone to be reminded of the horror of the sinking of the *Titanic* and the incompetence that may have precipitated it.

"The Censor Wouldn't Pass It" thus helps revise our understanding of Hitchcock in two important ways. First, it at least partially explains why his films do not focus directly on certain political topics that he otherwise was interested in. "Do not blame me for ignoring such subjects," he concludes. "Blame Whitehall." Second, it reminds us that these political interests are not always ignored but often obliquely reflected in his films. He did, after all, manage to get a Sydney Street siege scene into *The Man Who Knew Too Much* (1934). And although he never made his film on the General Strike, he did not drop the subject completely: *The Manxman,* for example, is set during a time of economic distress and labor protest and subtly announces its political subthemes by stylistic allusions to Eisenstein. Politics is no mere MacGuffin for Hitchcock, and much more work needs to be done on the often very subtle political dimensions and intentions of his films, as he himself alerts us in his writings.

Hitchcock's analysis of the many pressures and restrictions imposed on filmmakers led him to an inevitable conclusion: "Directors are dead," he announced, in his characteristically outrageous manner. This is not a statement of capitulation or despair but a sensible acknowledgment of current conditions and the beginning of a call for change. For Hitchcock, filmmaking, like politics, is an art of the possible, and many of his writings illustrate how skillfully he maneuvered within the cinematic establishment, carving out a creative space for himself. But we also catch glimpses of Hitchcock attempting to seize as much control of the system as possible. "Directors are dead" is only the first part of his proposition, which ends implicitly with a hopeful cry, "Long live the producer-director."

If films are to improve, the material and managerial conditions of filmmaking must change, and Hitchcock fantasizes about how he might like this to happen in "If I Were Head of a Production Company." Unlike the Americans, who have a well-supplied but mechanical production system that creates films without a "soul," he wants an experimental but integrated system, wherein "one guiding mind is behind the whole production." Filmmakers need physical space, and in this respect he wants to follow the model of American and German studios, with their extensive capital resources, including state-of-the-art equipment and solid, permanent sets that are cost-efficient and add high production values to their films. But even more important is "mental elbow-room," rarely a characteristic of a system in which directors are "functionaries" in an assembly-line process, there "only to direct." The ideal director for Hitchcock is a director-writer-producer, well versed in everything from camera setups to market research but whose primary commitment is to working out all details "in terms of cinema."

Hitchcock's vision is more than a fantasy. In "Directors Are Dead," he notes that the film industry is indeed beginning to move away both from old-style producers who were merely moneymen and ruined pictures by thoughtless cost-cutting and from old-style directors who ruined many pictures by their lack of restraint and careless, unprofessional work habits. The new age Hitchcock foresees will be one of strong producers, overseeing and supporting strong directors (if, indeed, they are not also directors themselves), and he gives the names of many who are leading the way, including David Selznick, Victor Saville, Alexander Korda, Michael Balcon, Pandro S. Berman, Ernst Lubitsch, and Frank Capra.

Conspicuous by its absence on this list is Hitchcock's own name, but it is clear that he is not only surveying the current state of filmmaking but charting his own future as a director-producer and both forging and describing his approach to film. He turns more directly to his own practice in such essays as "Production Methods Compared" and "Film Production" but still with an eye toward situating himself against the background of conventional filmmaking. In "Production Methods Compared," for example, he not only offers many specific comments on what goes into the making of a good Hitchcock film—flexibility, efficient pictorial storytelling, careful preplanning, and harmony, that is, the integration of all shots into a cinematic whole—but also seems to be trying to position himself as a filmmaker somewhere between the careless hacks who have only a rudimentary sense of cinematic construction and the overly sophisticated directors who have no concern for a mass audience and make films only for those few who have a "special knowledge of filmmaking." He is shy of being too "arty," but he also acknowledges that "a picture maker need not try to please everyone."

"Film Production" is his longest essay, and it is both a survey of film history and technique and a deeply personal statement of his particular methods and concerns. The latter are conveyed both directly—by inserting many of his well-known statements about suspense, the pictorial basis of cinema, acting as the ability "to do nothing—well," and so on—and obliquely, through subtle allusions to many of his own films: the discussion of the possibility of dramatic action in a phone booth recalls *Blackmail*; "murder by a babbling brook" is the basic premise of *The Trouble with Harry*; the description of how to film a boxing match echoes his technique in *The Ring*; and the example of sound used to evoke "a stream of consciousness over an unspeaking mouth" is drawn from one of the most memorable scenes in *Murder!* But the point here is not to blow his own horn. Rather, it is to continue his lifelong effort to determine and assert his place in the dynamic history of film. The concluding sections of the essay show that even after forty years in the business, he was still assessing the impact of changing modes of film production, new patterns of distribution, and the impact of new technology, especially color, the wide screen, and television.

The story of Hitchcock's career, illustrated in his writings as well as, of course, his films, is one of creative response to such challenges. All the more unfortunate, then, that the last essay in this section shows Hitchcock late in his career, without much buoyancy and resiliency. "In the Hall of Mogul Kings" is both a nostalgic look back at the days when films were hammered out under the supervision of creative talents like David Selznick and Irving Thalberg and a worried look at the current vogue of the "instant producers," no-name moneymen who are masters, not of cinema, but of the "package deal." His concern for "the future of the craft of the cinema for world entertainment" perhaps coincides with anxiety over his own position in the changing film establishment. Still, it is bracing to hear him acknowledge, however briefly, that there will be "survivors" of "the hit-and-miss era of picture making"—"purely creative people: producers-directors, writer-directors, producer-writers, etc." Hitchcock was such a survivor.

Films We Could Make

Captain Cook, when he discovered Australia, must have felt like I do when I am asked to suggest what the new British film should be or may be. How shall one lay down rules for the development of an uncharted continent?

For that is what the film is as a medium of expression. It differs from the novel, the play, music, and the ballet. Perhaps it approaches nearest to music and the ballet. It can play on the emotions and can delight the eye. But how we shall finally use the film none of us—British directors or otherwise—can tell. The stage drama has been 2,000 years in reaching its present state of perfection—or imperfection! The film show, in less than 20 years, has made much quicker strides. But it is still far from being an art in the sense that painting and writing can be art.

How far the builders of a new British film industry can remedy this state of affairs is difficult to say. The Americans have left us very few stories to film. And did not someone once say that there are only six plots in the world?

The Merchant Seamen's Drama

But there is no reason why we should not tell stories of *English* boys who leave the village and make good in the big city—why rural drama should not be found and filmed among the mountains of Wales and the moors of Yorkshire. Our history—national and imperial—provides a wonderful storehouse of film drama. And

"Films We Could Make" was originally published in the *London Evening News*, November 16, 1927.

there is the sea, our particular heritage: not only the Navy but the great business of the mercantile marine should have a place on our screens.

Perhaps our immediate opportunity lies in more careful and more intelligent treatment of film stories. The American film directors under their commercially minded employers have learnt a good deal about studio lighting, action photographs, and telling a story plainly and smoothly in moving pictures. They have learnt, as it were, to put the nouns, verbs, and adjectives of the film language together.

But even if we conceive the film going no further as an art, it is obvious that what we must strive for at once is the way to use these film nouns and verbs as cunningly as do the great novelist and the great dramatist, to achieve certain effects on an audience.

A historic example of what I mean was introduced by Charles Chaplin in his *Woman of Paris*. He crystallized a situation with subtlety and economy of time when he made his dilettante hero take a clean handkerchief from a drawer in his mistress's dressing chest and let fall an evening dress collar. You knew all you needed to know about their relationship.

We are still working on those lines of economy in pictures today. The difficulty is that our art is commercial. We have no benefactors to finance productions which only a minority of the public want to see. So we can only advance a little—a very little—faster than the public's understanding.

One is disappointed sometimes to find now the average filmgoer misses little points which were apparently too subtle. If the public will only learn to take more for granted on the screen, it stands to reason that we directors will have *more screen time* in which to deal with the big situations in a film.

Then what of the future? We must not forget that our duty is always to provide entertainment for those who pay. Ideas of entertainment vary. The man who enjoys the latest detective thrills probably hates poetry. But, luckily for the poet, books cost less to make than films—considerably less. When you have to spend £50,000 or £100,000 on a film you must make it to please a lot of people in order to get your money back.

Filming the Rain

But suppose we *could* make really artistic films for the artistically minded minority. Could we not then make as beautiful a film about rain as Debussy did a tone poem in his *"Jardins sous la pluie"*? And what a lovely film of rhythmic movement and light and shade we could make out of cloud studies—a sort of film interpretation of Shelley's "The Cloud." Such things have been attempted on the Continent, where they frequently make pictures for love rather than profit; one German producer even makes film studies of cubes and circles which change their shape as they move over the screen in rhythmic form like a Cubist painting in motion. But those things are not for the present, though they suggest how the film may become an artistic medium.

There is no reason, however, why we should not use such rhythmic pictures as moods and backgrounds for our screen stories. How many people realize, I wonder, that we *do* aim at moods in our films? We call it "tempo," and by paying careful attention to the speed with which we act our little plays we do attempt to guide the observing minds into the right mood.

One-Man Pictures

A light-hearted comedy played slowly may produce the sense of impending doom, just as a too brightly acted drama might never give an atmosphere of tragedy.

And, having decided the "tempo" of a film, we must keep to it all through or it will jerk up and down. I had to film a little scene in *The Farmer's Wife* six times the other day because the players took it too slowly to fit in with the mood of the picture.

Film directors live with their pictures while they are being made. They are their babies just as much as an author's novel is the offspring of his imagination. And that seems to make it all the more certain that when moving pictures are really artistic they will be created entirely by one man. It often happens today that the author's story is made into screen form on paper by one man, who may have been overseen by some important executive, filmed by another, cut by another, and edited by another.

Suppose novels were produced in this way!

"Stodgy" British Pictures

It is just six years since I started work on the first British all-talking picture, *Blackmail*. I am now preparing an adaptation of John Buchan's *The 39 Steps*.

In those six years the sound picture has progressed and matured enormously, but there is a danger of our British studios being content to turn out standardized types of pictures. British talkies need more variety.

It must always be remembered that the primary aim of pictures is to provide entertainment. To entertain people, one must first capture their interest.

For example, the initial problem which has confronted every film director since the invention of moving pictures has been to give a three-dimensional (realistic) effect to his two-dimensional creations. You've got to convey the impression that your characters are really alive before you can persuade an audience to take them and their problems seriously. To do that the director relies on camera movement and other technical devices which give a full-bodied effect and, what is more important, *freshness*.

Why Stop at Plays?

In the early talkie days there was a tendency to film plays just as they might have been seen from the stalls of a theater. The camera

"'Stodgy' British Pictures" was originally published in *Film Weekly,* December 14, 1934, 14.

was set up, the microphone placed in position, and the actors reeled off whole chunks of dialogue for about five hundred feet of film without a single cut. The result was intensely boring.

We have learnt our lesson since then. Now we can film a stage play in which the action takes place almost solely in one room, yet give it freshness and movement by manipulation of the camera and skillful editing.

But why stop at that? Surely a film should have freshness and life in construction as well as in the way it is photographed and edited? To get that freshness one must have contrast. One must have light and shade.

It is because of their lack of light and shade that British films have hitherto been criticized as "stodgy." They have been pitched too much on one note, and have maintained too level a style. A British film is too liable to be one solid chunk of drama or comedy and nothing else.

In this country we have overlooked the fact that a mixture of style can point a dramatic effect. *Murder at the Vanities,* to take rather an extreme instance, mixed musical-comedy and murder, so that the one acted as a foil to the other. The Americans have shown themselves adept at this trick of switching from grave to gay. Why shouldn't we do the same?

I can see no reason why every British drama should be played out in an atmosphere of unrelieved tension. It defeats its own end. By being eternally dramatic it sacrifices its opportunity of rising to a contrasted dramatic climax.

See what happens on the stage. A play like *The Last of Mrs. Cheyney* has comedy in the first act, which builds up to the drama of the second, and concludes with a third act of pure farce. The continual change from one mood to another keeps the audience interested and heightens the effect of both the comedy and the drama. But if you suggested doing that in the average British film, you would be greeted with howls of horror.

Comedy Coating

Why? Simply because people believe that a film (for some unexplained reason) should be written and acted in the same style and the same mood throughout.

Yet the masters of the modern stage—Barrie and Pinero, for

example—all laid the foundations of their plots with comic first acts. The comedy provided for one thing, the perfect coating with which to sugar the plot-planting pill. A more important consideration is this:

In a lighthearted setting, the advent of drama is made all the more effective by its unexpectedness.

That is the theory I have worked on in my latest picture, *The Man Who Knew Too Much*. I cannot tell you just *how* I have put it into practice—that would spoil the surprise. But I can promise that the entry of drama into the story will come with complete unexpectedness. It will come with a bang.

After all, that is how things happen in real life. Although a tragic event may be destined to happen some time during the afternoon, we do not go about all the morning with somber faces. We just *don't know* that the catastrophe is coming—consequently, when it does arrive, we are as likely as not to be laughing and drinking in complete lightheartedness. Certainly we shall not be sitting around with that theatrical air of foreboding that enshrouds the characters in so many British pictures.

The more happy-go-lucky the setting, the greater the kick you get from the sudden introduction of drama.

Just as we have light and shade in mood, so let us have a little variety in setting. The Americans use imaginative backgrounds. They give us pictures about telephone exchanges, icemen, newspaper reporters, police cars, repair gangs—anything and everything under the sun. They make the most of every possible setting for their stories. *Emergency Call, Looking for Trouble, It Happened One Night, The Crowd Roars, The Devil Is Driving*—all of these were set against unusual backgrounds. They all had a freshness that is lacking in our drawing room school of drama.

"Atmosphere"

Have you ever considered what an interesting film might be written round, say, the engineer of Tower Bridge who lets the bridge up and down?

If the Americans had had such material at their disposal they would have made a film about it years ago. The engineer as the central character, the river craft and docks for atmospheric background—and you can bet your life they would have managed to make their way up to Piccadilly for a little more atmosphere before the film was over! That is where they excel—in capitalizing the unusual and achieving freshness by contrast and variety.

Why don't we do the same? Why must we always stick to our middle-class drawing rooms and our middle-class characters? Why don't we go out more for variety and contrast in the telling of our stories, unusualness in the characters we present, and freshness in our choice of backgrounds?

If I Were Head
of a Production Company

It's easy and pleasant to theorize; but unsupported theory has explosive properties when exposed to the air, so I propose to confine these remarks strictly to a basis of experience.

Remember, I am speaking of the ideal conditions; true, they are realizable—but they might cost a lot of money.

Still, as I can't imagine myself becoming head of a production company that hadn't a lot of money at its disposal, that's quite legitimate.

Starting with the actual studio, I want plenty of space. There will be derisive grins here from readers who know my corpulence; but I want more space even than that demands.

I want space to build permanent sets—and I mean *permanent.* When I was working on my very first picture in Munich—*The Pleasure Garden*—there was an exterior set on the "lot," representing an Algerian village, which had been standing in all weathers for five years and did not even require painting!

The initial outlay in a case like this is very large—but it's amply justified by results, for such a set can be used over and over again.

Hollywood has proved the value of this beyond possibility of doubt; in fact, some of the streets in the studio administrative blocks have been built in various types of architecture to form a ready-made background for almost any kind of street-scene.

In British studios it too often happens that immense labor and a

"If I Were Head of a Production Company" was originally published in *Picturegoer,* January 26, 1935, 15.

great deal of money are expended on running up a quite convincing set made of plywood and scantling—which hardly even retains its conviction to the end of the picture, and would certainly be useless after another month's exposure to wind and rain; but by this time it has had to be scrapped to make room for something else—and Heaven help the poor director who wants any "retakes"!

With the cycle system in vogue, a set (such as, for instance, the London square, built at Fox Hills for *Cavalcade*) is bound to "come in handy" again and can be let out to other companies; this has been done with semi-permanent street sets at Welwyn and Sound City.

Inside the studio, too, it pays handsomely to have elbow room.

When I was directing at the B.I.P. studios at Elstree, I had an elaborate staircase constructed with rooms opening off it; it seemed a big undertaking just for a few scenes in one film; but its cost was distributed over at least a half a dozen subsequent films in which it was used.

UFA built a whole city-center for *The Last Laugh*. The expense would have been justified for that fine film alone; but the set was used for years afterwards. Furthermore (an important point), the production value gained by a cheaper film made on such a set is tremendous.

How many times in a year do the last few shots on a large set have to be scurried through because the space is needed for another!

I've known a unit to work continuously from nine one morning till three the following morning for this very reason—and you can imagine the result on the screen.

So much for physical space. Now for mental elbow-room.

The director must have latitude. Here there are two distinct schools of thought. One (the American) says the director is there only to direct; in many cases he has no knowledge of story or script until he comes up to the floor for the first day's shooting; everything is prepared for him by functionaries whose duty it is.

Consequently, though Hollywood films are slick, smart, efficient to the *nth* degree, to British audiences they are frequently lacking in what, for want of a better word, we call "soul."

To mass-produced America, this mechanical system is probably most acceptable; in Britain we still adhere more to the product of individuality, in which one guiding mind is behind the whole production.

We make mistakes; but they are experimental mistakes, and justifiable so long as we learn from them.

So for my ideal production company I should seek out and secure the services of men who are capable of taking charge of a film from the first glimmering of an idea for the original story, to the final cutting.

They would cooperate with story-writers, scenarists, dialogists, cameramen, art directors, cutters; but theirs would be the decisive guiding hand throughout, and every inch of the way would be worked out *in terms of cinema*.

That is to say, the film would exist pictorially in the director's mind from beginning to end.

Here I should find myself up against my greatest handicap, for, in my view, one of the chief disadvantages of British production is the scarcity of people with an instinct for films—who can, in fact, think pictorially.

Such instinct can hardly be taught, but it can be acquired by experience; and the problem would be to assemble the personnel most likely to acquire it.

These, and writers who know how to appeal to the popular taste, and as much polish and finesse as are consistent with clearness, are some of the outstanding needs which it would be my first care to supply.

As to stars, here is a vexed question, to which I have certainly not the space to do justice here; but I may say this: that if I were building stars I should adopt the American plan of flinging them on to the screen as often as possible—*at first*—so that their names would become familiar to the public; and then gradually I would withdraw them from the screen, so that the better known they were, the less they would be seen.

That is the way to make a Garbo.

When a producer is offering the public something which may be unwelcome or indigestible to it, stars are of the utmost value as camouflage—or, if you prefer it, as the jam round the pill; for the sake of the star, the public will accept the new lighting, or the new cutting, or the new use of sound, or whatever the producer is trying to get away with.

This film business is almost the only industry in which it is left to the retailer to gauge the public taste; that is to say, the exhibitor has the responsibility of finding out what the public require—which is obviously unfair as well as being slipshod and unmethodical.

Therefore, incorporated in my production-cum-distribution organization would be a corps of investigators who would discover and report on the trend and fluctuations of public taste and audience reaction in the key-centers of the country and of the world, to observe the comparative effectiveness of various kinds of publicity, and so on; and through these I would have my fingers on the public pulse, find out what was wanted, and make my plans accordingly.

These are just a few of the points that occur to me now at random. But if you care to ask me again, after I have been head of a production company for five years or so, I may be able to tell you quite a lot!

More Cabbages, Fewer Kings
A Believer in the Little Man

There is a certain man whose annual holiday from work causes considerable regret to the British people, for with his holiday comes the cessation of a newspaper feature that makes millions laugh. Strube, the *Daily Express* cartoonist, is the man, because through the medium of his pen-and-ink character, the "Little Man," we see our true British selves, the failings, the shortcomings, triumphs, and achievements of the middle class.

The middle classes are the essence of England, and Strube in his wisdom has chosen his "Little Man" from their ranks because that little bowler-hatted individual reflects the only genuine life and drama that exist in this country.

Cottages and Cocktail Cabinets

But who else realizes this? Certainly not the one concern which should—the British motion picture Industry. The dramas entangled in the lives of England's "little men," the dramatic coloring to be picked out in the existence of the ordinary people—these elements of first-class entertainment in film have lain dormant and ignored for years.

British film producers know only two strata of English existence, the poor and the rich. On these they base the plots of their films which

"More Cabbages, Fewer Kings: A Believer in the Little Man" was originally published in *Kinematograph Weekly,* January 14, 1937, 30. It was also published in *Kine Weekly,* April 1937, with slight changes.

go out to the cinemas of the world, conveying the impression to other audiences that the English live either in cottages or cocktail cabinets, and speak with their lips twisted or with a plum in their throats.

Totally ignored by British filmmakers is that vital central stratum of British humanity, the middle class. Forgotten are the men who leap on buses, the girls who pack into the Tube, the commercial travelers, the newspaper men, the girls who manicure your nails, the composers who write the dance numbers, the city clerk and his weekend Rugger, the stockbroker and his round of golf, the typist and her boyfriend, the cinema queues, the *palais de danse* crowds, the people in the charabanes, on the beaches, at the race courses; the fellows who love gardening, the chaps who lounge in pubs, the secretaries of clubs, the chorus girls, the doctors, the car salesmen, the speed cops, the schoolteachers.

The Real Spirit of England

In them lies the spirit of England that, for some unknown reason, is almost entirely ignored on the screen. American producers have not halted where we have stood still. They have exploited the drama of their people and made it a feature of eight out of ten of their films. If we in this country only got our education from the screen, we should know more of the life of a middle-class American than we do of the English people who fill our trains and trams at rush hours.

The higher you run your finger up the British social scale, the faster the drama dies. The veneer of civilization is so thick among the rich that individual qualities are killed. There is nothing to film, nothing worth putting on the screen. Voices are the same, expressions are *nil*, personalities are suppressed. The upper classes are too "bottled up" to be of any use as colorful screen matter, too stiffened with breeding to relax into the natural easiness and normality required by the screen.

But come downwards into that more colorful belt of beings, the middle class, and observe their unhampered attitude to life. Here is something that film producers should get their hands on—the British personality that the world should really know. Here are people who smile and mean it, girls who catch their fingers in doors and say what they feel. Here are expressions that come swiftly and naturally without restraint, here are manners and ways flowing easily, speech unaffected, emotions more free, instinct sharper. In other words, there is grand camera stuff waiting at the Industry's door.

I am trying to get this stratum of England on the screen. I am fighting against a hard enemy, the film of chromium plating, dress shirts, cocktails, and Oxford accents which is being continually made with the idea that it shows English life. Soon I hope we shall do unto America what they have done to us, and make the cheerful man and girl of our middle class as colorful and dramatic to them as their ordinary everyday citizens are to the audiences of England.

Much Ado About Nothing?

Shakespeare was an imaginative playwright—he wrote his scenes as taking place in forests and ships at sea. He had almost the scenario writer's gift for keeping the story moving from setting to setting. But, for all his flow of imagination, sixteenth-century stagecraft let him down. It could not rise to the settings of forests or ships at sea—it had not the skill to build him Macbeth's castle as a fitting background to his drama.

Shakespeare, undaunted, used another device. Perhaps inwardly he pined for scenery, but, deprived of a paint brush, he put his colors into the words of his plays. In poetic meter he called upon his actors to make up for the loss and describe the scene supposedly around them in words. A clumsy device, perhaps, but he had no other way out, and all through the years the stage has not once tried to help him. And Mr. Granville-Barker has no intention of doing so today.

The cinema has come to Shakespeare's rescue. This "baby" of artistic expression has seen stage directions in Shakespeare's poetry where decades of theatrical craftsmen have only seen words. The filmmakers have today given Shakespeare a forest where he asked for it—a courtyard where his action pleaded for it (and was denied it)—a banquet hall where Mr. Granville-Barker would have only a trestle table with three planks laid across it. Still firmly convinced that the only thing that matters about Shakespeare is the poetry,

"Much Ado About Nothing?" was originally published in *The Listener*, March 10, 1937, 448–450.

Mr. Granville-Barker ignored the pictorial side of the plays. With that trestle table still in his mind he shuddered when in *A Midsummer Night's Dream* he saw what he told you was "fantastically fine pseudo-Athenian architecture."

Shakespeare, in words alone, builds up a delicately beautiful picture of Titania, the Queen of the Fairies. The screen did justice to his words by casting Anita Louise for the role. Mr. Granville-Barker *shuddered*. She was too beautiful for him.

Then, what is a clown but a grimacing buffoon? Shakespeare's clowns were the criterion of all clowns, but Mr. Granville-Barker *winced*. . . . The clowns in the film grimaced too much. And Puck? What is an Englishman's idea of Puck—Shakespeare's idea of Puck? . . . A merry laughing little devil, chortling through the woodlands. Mr. Granville-Barker *choked*. . . . Puck on the screen laughed too much!

"Shakespeare," said Mr. Granville-Barker, speaking on behalf of Shakespeare, "does not want pictures." Speaking on behalf of pictures, I say they don't want Shakespeare. The cinema can do without Shakespeare. The stage and the screen both have their range, with the difference that the screen's range is unlimited. The stage can go so far, but beyond that it comes up against a solid wall. Its power of dramatic expression fails. In its attempt sometimes to surmount this barrier, it produced pitiful results. Stagecraft is so limited that it just can't imitate the devices of the screen.

The screen, on the other hand, can take a novel, a story, a biography, and most certainly a play—and improve it. Adaptation from the stage is an everyday occurrence. Can it be said that the stage has ever successfully adapted anything from the screen?

This great power of improvement that the screen holds is used with a certain judiciousness by filmmakers. Their territory is enormous—the subjects which they can take and produce as films on the screens of the world are legion. But they temper their enthusiasm with a certain caution, for, above all, the film must still retain its universal appeal. The general public will not be talked at, and will never allow themselves to be forcibly educated from the screen. Therefore in the world of films and film production it is the public's appetite that must first be appeased—their natural craving for romance, drama, and comedy that must be sated. This naturally handicaps experimenting with films as an art form.

The art of Shakespeare and the art of the cinema, Mr. Granville-

Barker says, are radically and fatally opposed. He is being polite. He means why the devil are the films meddling with Shakespearean art. Why don't they stick to their own art form? He forgets that the stage has had Shakespearean art for over 300 years. The juvenile film industry, in comparison, still has 300 years to go. Therefore, to draw level and in its constant search for an art of its own— its constant probing for something new in ideas—its adoption and discarding of new sources—it lighted on Shakespeare.

Novelty is the essence of a successful film, and the cinema took Shakespeare as something new to present to its millions of film-goers. It was a bold step, for to the majority of the public anything connected with Shakespeare is as dull as ditchwater. Mr. Granville-Barker will not understand this. I do not expect him to. With due credit to the playwright, the world of Shakespeare lovers (ruled by Mr. Granville-Barker) is a very little one compared with the world of the cinema enthusiasts.

What is poetry to the busy housewife but a lot of nonsense and something they teach her kid at school? To the man in the street Shakespeare is something very dull and too pregnant with classroom memories to smack of entertainment. To the modern girl *Romeo and Juliet* may certainly be the top in love stories, but she would not be able to follow the dialogue of the sixteenth century. In other words, Shakespeare spells considerable gloom to the average mind of today.

The screen, therefore, took a heavy gamble when it filmed Shakespeare. Hollywood made a projectile, as it were, to break down the barrier of public prejudice. Briefly, the cinema condescended to make Shakespeare palatable. That may be rather blunt, but it is perfectly true. It is no use adopting the rather sacred attitude of Mr. Granville-Barker towards Shakespeare when you are banking on entertaining millions of cinema-goers. With Shakespeare anathema to the man in the street, the trestle table and carefully dictioned poetry methods of Mr. Granville-Barker won't do. They would seal the fate of Stratford's playwright once and for all in the minds of the cinema-going public.

People pay their money to be entertained, and the film of *Romeo and Juliet* achieved this object. In making this play as a film, the producers sugar-coated the bitter pill of literature. They added the finer essences of romance and vigor—of vitality and pace. It livened Shakespeare—humanized him, if you prefer—and gave warmth to characters that to the average man were lifeless figures out of a schoolbook.

What has Shakespeare on the film done? Earned the undying hatred of Mr. Granville-Barker, alone on his trestle table. But the cinema has popularized Shakespeare. In one showing of *Romeo and Juliet* round the country, more people will see a work of Shakespeare than will ever attend stage Shakespeare in a year.

Mr. Granville-Barker's little world will swell with the addition of thousands of new Shakespeare lovers in a matter of weeks. Countless members of the general public will develop a new regard for Shakespeare—may become Shakespeare fans. To them the works of the playwright will assume new meanings, new comedy, romance, adventure. And what is going to popularize Shakespeare in England? I am afraid Mr. Granville-Barker will never admit it. The answer is—The Cinema.

Directors Are Dead

Filmgoers are at last beginning to realize that producers and directors are entirely different screen species. In the past, the director has received all the publicity. The producer has been a vague man-behind-the-scenes.

Apart from the late Irving Thalberg, Sam Goldwyn, and perhaps one or two others, producers used to be completely unknown by name, and most filmgoers have given the director all the credit for the success of a picture.

A lot of people have criticized my recent declaration that the director was becoming less important and that the producer was really the man on whom pictures relied.

I stick to my guns. And, let me remind you, I am still a director myself.

In the old days, it is true, the director was the man who mattered. The producer was concerned merely with the financial side of picture-making, and probably didn't know the difference between a long shot and a close-up. But this type of producer is fast going out.

You have heard, of course, numerous fantastic-sounding stories of mismanagement in film production, many of them true. All the trouble could be traced to this splitting up of authority. But it is being realized today that there must be one man at the helm.

That man should be the producer. He should see the picture through from beginning to end. He must know all sides of the business and be a complete technician.

"Directors Are Dead" was originally published in *Film Weekly,* November 20, 1937, 14.

One very prominent producer frankly says to his directors, when asking them to make a picture for them: "Do you think you could sink your individuality to suit me?" And every picture that bears his name *is* individualistic.

The Writer-Producer

The ultimate ideal is the writer-producer (and this is already happening in America), a man who creates the story with the right material around him—in his case, the studio personnel, just as the painter has his brushes and canvas. And he can follow his story through right to the cutting-room.

Many a good script results in a mediocre picture. Something goes wrong before the film reaches the screen. With the author-producer watching every point, this sort of thing is far less likely to happen.

Pending this idea, the producer must be the man in control. There is no doubt that the story has become the most important thing in film production. And control of the story must be in the hands of a person who can most objectively see the finished effort.

The producer must be the man with this flair. Consider, for instance, David Selznick. He works closely on the story end of his pictures and follows them right through.

The Great Producers

I consider Victor Saville a good example of the modern producer. His films all bear his imprint and are full of his ideas. Alexander Korda and Michael Balcon are other examples, and Samuel Goldwyn is an old-time producer who has kept pace with the times.

Many filmgoers can now discern the touch of Pandro S. Berman. He has produced all the Fred Astaire–Ginger Rogers pictures. Different directors have actually handled the films, but there has been that Pandro S. Berman shine on all of them.

Then, there are those elaborate M-G-M musicals, such as *Maytime, The Great Ziegfeld* and *Rose Marie*. All have been produced by the same man, Hunt Stromberg.

The producer may be a man with vision but without the actual ability to handle the technical task of putting a picture together. He needs a director to carry out his ideas, just as he needs the property men to build the scenery and the electricians to look after the lights.

But, in some cases, there are men who are equipped to be directors as well as producers. Thus we have such men as Ernst Lubitsch and Frank Capra. They have the right knowledge and capacity.

I shudder to think of the pictures that have gone wrong through the old-time all-powerful director, without the right flair, who was allowed to do as he liked on the floor, and chopped and changed stories about until they were completely ruined.

I shudder to think, too, of pictures that have never fulfilled their promise because of the old-time producer who cared for nothing but finance, and short-sightedly restricted production expenses quite unnecessarily, spoiling the ship for a ha'porth of tar.

What of the director? I seem to have been pretty hard on him. I want to make it clear that there are exceptions to every rule. There are a good many directors who are as important as the producer. In fact, they are almost producers themselves.

I am thinking more of the future than anything else. These brilliant directors of today are the producers of tomorrow; and the directors of tomorrow will be their stooges.

This is going to mean more opportunities for younger and ambitious people in the film business. At the moment, the would-be director has a big uphill fight which is almost sufficient to kill his initiative. Studios refuse to entrust an important picture to a new man.

So the newcomer has to start with cheap productions, the weakest of stories, the poorest of stars. It is a miracle if he can do anything with his material. It is like asking an architect to build a good house with inexperienced workmen, an insufficient number of bricks, and rubbish with which to make the finishing touches.

But the producer who is personally interested in every stage of a picture can afford to experiment with his interpreters, and younger people are going to get chances they never had.

Just because the director is no longer top dog doesn't mean that he is at all unimportant. Of course he is important. But in a different way from yesterday.

The film industry is always changing. And this is one of its very necessary and very interesting changes.

Director's Problems

There are directors and directors. There are directors who merely interpret a script. In other words, their job is largely to see that the characterization is carried out, that the story is complete and presented on the screen by their choice of shots. That is to say, each piece of film that goes to make the whole is chosen and designed by them.

The general method that is used by, I might say, the average director, is to shoot what we'd term plenty of material and then cut.

I personally don't use that method at all. I aim at getting a complete vision of my film before it goes on to the studio floor. For example, in a film I did—*Sabotage*—with Sylvia Sidney, there was a whole scene at the end where the woman kills her husband. Now, I wanted to make the murder inevitable without any blame attaching to the woman. I wanted to preserve sympathy for her, so that it was essential that she fought against something stronger than herself. So the thing was staged in this way.

It was a supper table. The man complained about the color of the greens. All I did was to show the close-up of the woman, about ordinary bust size, and the man the same. Sometimes the man from her eye-line, sometimes the woman from his eye-line. That was all we were concerned with. The most important aspect of the scene was her hand. It was essential to play up to her using the carving knife. She carved meat with it, and then found herself help-

"Director's Problems" was originally published in *The Listener*, February 2, 1938, 241–242. It also appeared in *Living Age* 354 (April 1938): 172–174.

ing him to vegetables with the carving knife. She realized what was wrong. Then I showed her hand dropping the knife, trying to get rid of it, and then having to pick it up because more meat needed carving—and dropping it with a clatter. Then immediately a close-up of the man hearing the clatter. Then the woman's hand clasping and unclasping over the handle of the carving knife. All we saw was a foreground of a table, glasses and cutlery, and her hands hovering. Then back to him. He got up, and the camera tilting up with him. He realizes his danger. I never bothered to show the room, and I allowed that man to go right past the camera towards the woman; and then again he comes to her and he looks down, and the camera goes right from him, following his thought, down to the knife and her hand still hovering over it. And then he makes a grab and she gets it first. Then the two hands: her hands win. And then all you see is two figures, and the man gives a cry and falls.

To have shot all that in a long view would have been useless. It had to be made up of these little pieces. With a first-class director the final cutting is a simple job, if he has constructed the scene in his mind in advance and knows what he wants to create.

The most valuable thing in creating a film is criticism at the time. A film is so expensive to make. After all, a play can be written and come on, run for four days, say, and be taken off at a loss of a couple of thousand pounds. But a film is so costly that there is bound to be some safeguard. The producer is the man who should watch everything and make sure that the story is right and the casting is right. He goes every day and sees the "rushes," and it is up to him to say, as a critic, how it is turned out. That is the value of a producer. In other words, his is the job of watching the film from the point of view of the audience.

The director and the producer should, of course, work hand in hand, though there are some producers who exercise too much control over the direction of a film. It is, of course, very difficult to lay down a hard and fast rule. To me the producer of the future is the writer, because I feel the control of a film should come from its original creator. Just as in the theater the author is the No. 1 man. Years ago, the author used to write something which was accepted, and that was the last he ever saw of it until it came on the screen completely unrecognizable. The producer should be a writer. Or if not, he should be able to employ writers and understand writing himself. Because that's the root of the whole business.

Money for Nothing

I think there is much less confusion than there used to be in the production of a film. But there is no doubt that odd conferences go on. A fellow told me once, a songwriter, that he had written a very successful song and on the strength of it he got a Hollywood contract. He arrived there and nobody took any notice of him. He got his weekly check, and that was all. So he decided to play golf. For fifteen weeks he played golf. One day he was out playing golf, and the message came to him that he was wanted at a conference in the afternoon. So he went, and they all sat round, and the head of the conference said, "Now, what about this music? Can't we get the chap who wrote so and so?" So this young man heard instructions given to get on to New York and try to get him out to Hollywood. Naturally, he got on the line first to New York and warned his agent to ask for double the salary he was already getting. I have even known two people from the same studio bidding for the same story. It is just this Moloch that engulfs everything. It needs so many stories, so much talent to provide these eight hundred plays. Supposing the theater attempted eight hundred plays a year, just think what a madhouse it would be. It takes a lot of brains and a lot of money to make even a bad picture.

Of the cost, I should say that a third goes in studio rent, use of equipment and settings; about another third in artists' costs. Today, in order to maintain a decent standard of acting, if we have one line which has to be said we engage a fairly competent and expensive actor to do it, because we find selecting people out of a crowd is uneconomical. They get nervous and hold everything up. In this country we have quite a number of character actors who are good; and we have paid as much as £20 for one line to be said, to make sure, because we have found in the long run it is economical to do so. In my last picture *Young and Innocent* with Nova Pilbeam we had seventy-three small parts costing a total of over £3,000. The rest of the costs are made up of film stock, electricity, labor, story-writers, and scenario work, director's fees and star, and insurance. It is very hard to get a good average English film today under forty or fifty thousand pounds.

When you are working with those figures there does not seem much hope of experimenting with new ideas. The average person thinks of the camera, the sets, and a script to work from the major items. But we have trick work to do as well. For instance, back projection. Supposing we want a close-up of two people driving a car. That means to say that we have to send a camera out on the back of a lorry, probably a distance, to take a view of the street going away from the motorcar. That is developed in the studio, projected on a large screen, and then our motorcar placed in front—with a couple of men to shake it.

Then there are things like scenes that take a long time and all day to shoot, like dogs or babies or motorboats. Motorboats are the worst things, because if you are photographing a man in a motorboat you cannot tell him when the shot is ended. He goes on for miles. Once I was shooting a scene in the Tyrol. There was a tiny figure trudging through the snow. Well, the fellow was so far away that no one could run and tell him when to stop, as their footprints would show in the snow. Then there was a scene in *Secret Agent* shot from an observatory. Two men were trudging in the snow: actually they were two little figures on cotton wool. In the studio the people who have the really delightful times are the model-makers. You can never get the scene started; they always want to add just one thing more. We have a grand time. What they love best are the tank scenes with ships, and they are very ingenious, some of the model-makers.

The best films have their material *created* for the camera. And that applies through the whole of the making of pictures, from the lighting to any other department. People must *act* for the camera to get the best results rather than have the camera try and grab what the people are doing. That's the difference between the film that is a stage play and a film that is a motion picture.

Many people feel that the fact that many of the top experts in film studios are foreigners tends to make British pictures unrepresentative, but I think there should be room for foreigners because, while we should express the English idiom, it should always have an international outlook. The American film is pretty international. And after all, the biggest stars in America are foreigners—Greta Garbo, Marlene Dietrich, and so on. I think if they have anything to contribute they should be allowed to. It's the second-raters we don't want. Another criticism of English films is that they seem slow compared with American films. This is largely idiomatic. The

American mode of life is much faster than ours, and by instinct we are bound to be a bit more labored or casual than Americans. That is why the fast American film is an entertainment to us.

I am very often against playing dramatic scenes against familiar backgrounds, for the reason that the public is saying to themselves: "That's Hyde Park Corner; I wonder where they hid the camera; they must have done it very well, because nobody seems to know they're there."

Being a filmmaker in this country we have very little violence to create drama on the screen. I know that's a very sweeping statement, but the Americans find it much easier. Look at their history, the shooting and goodness knows what in films like *The Covered Wagon*. In other words, they have comparatively modern history and modern happenings with violence; violence is good screen material, good screen fare. Here we have only got war or crime.

"Films I Want to Do"

There are dozens of films I want to do. I want to do a film about the prison governor who revolts against his job of hanging a man. It is quite a thrilling story right up to the eve of execution, but I don't think the censor would look at it. Capital punishment is part of our law, and we mustn't propagate against it. I had a good deal of trouble over putting Sydney Street in *The Man Who Knew Too Much*. I don't think films made of local rather quiet history—*The Edge of the World* sort of thing or *Turn of the Tide*—will ever be great box office, because they are what one might term grey subjects—no glitter or glamour.

Then there is the question of whether we shall have happy or unhappy endings. Unfortunately, commercially you can't shelve it by saying: "We'll have a natural ending." It is fatal from a commercial point of view to allow your audience to come out of a cinema saying: "Oh, what a shame!" "I *was* sorry. . . ." They tell their friends about such and such a picture: "Oh yes, it was all right, but . . ." The fatal word.

And here we come to the biggest problem of the cinema—that its own power is automatically its own weakness. The power of universal appeal has been the most retarding force of the motion picture as an art. In the efforts of the maker to appeal to everyone,

they have had to come down to the common simple story with
the happy ending; the moment they begin to become imaginative,
then they are segregating their audience. Until we get specialized
theaters, we shall not be able to do anything else. The Continental
films go into specialized theaters in London, and that is about all.
The cost of making a picture is so great, and there are so many
aspects of the business—world markets, American markets, and so
on—that we find it difficult to get our money back, even for a successful film with a universal appeal, let alone in films that have experimented with the story or the artist. That is the thing that has
kept the cinema back. I should say it has pretty well gone a long
way to destroy it as an art.

The Censor
and Sydney Street

An Interview with Leslie Perkoff

The film world with its play of names, sensational and unsteady in
its juggling with stars, is more sober in its treatment of craftsmen.
Griffith, Disney, Eisenstein, Duvivier—such names have solid foundations. Likewise the name Alfred Hitchcock, one of the few real
English contributions to film technique.

Unlike too many of his colleagues, Hitchcock often rejects the
Philistine insensitiveness to film problems. Thus his unequivocal
recognition of the writer as the prime factor in the substance of the
dramatic film, his prophecy of the future obsoleteness of the director unless his status and power expand to that of the producer, and
his attitude to the question of universal appeal which he considers
detrimental to film art.

He is a product of British films, yet where most British films
lack individuality, he has at least specialized in a peculiar treatment
and applied a measure of realism in portraying characters. And on
the lack of individuality in British films he says:

"I think the shortage of personnel in this country is largely to
blame. We have to consider that we're in competition with Hollywood. In the case of France this is not so marked, since only comparatively few of their talented people percolate through to Hollywood. People like Bauer remain, and although Laughton and
Donat now remain in England, their price value has gone up since

"The Censor and Sydney Street" was originally published in *World Film News* 2, no.
12 (March 1938): 4–5.

their contract with Hollywood, and this puts them out of the reach of many British producers. It is because of the language question that Hollywood has been able to draw so much on British talent.

"It is all a root problem, yet I would say that English humor has got individuality, for comedy has suited the English temper. Yet nothing is really being done to develop talent here, although I have sometimes taken on untried people. There is an absence of good technicians, particularly a lack of first-class cameramen. The whole thing mystifies me, and I would be inclined to say that the young men don't take their work seriously enough. There's too much of this knocking off at six o'clock attitude. London perhaps is too distracting. In America, you see, Hollywood succeeds as a production center where New York fails. As for places like Denham and Elstree, they are too near London."

These difficulties recognized, this should point more strongly to the need for the growth of a film movement in England, something as creative as the old German school and as individual as many of the French films of today. This is the rather diffused feeling which exists among a number of the younger film people. To bring this about a coordinated movement is necessary. Its practicability is submitted to Hitchcock.

"That, of course, is academic," he declares. "But I endorse such a movement. The interests in Wardour Street, however, are primarily concerned with the commercial aspects, therefore it would have to have finance. But there is always this drawback: the handling of star material and story. These are difficulties which are not present in the making of documentary films. I would like to make documentary films, because here you have slabs of action or movement which can be easily treated by photography and cutting. But a cataclysm in any film, for example, is akin to documentary material. It begins with the camera and goes directly to the cutting-room."

If the handling of the stars presents an obstacle to filmmaking, could not the star system itself be lessened in favor of actual story value and treatment of a film?

"The point about the star system is that it enables you to exaggerate from a story point of view. And the stars do bring the audiences into the cinemas. A star's name is like a clarion call and brings in the time factor when, for instance, a film is shown and you want people to come and see it on definite days. A film without stars would have to wait to be appreciated."

A problem which has recently given grounds for strong comment is now introduced: The clash of idioms brought about by the irruption of film people into a strange country whose language even they sometimes have not mastered.

"I had an experience bringing this up when I was directing a film called *Murder!* in English and German," Hitchcock says. "I could speak German, but I found it was a difference of idiom and not of language. You've got to live twenty years in a country before you can express its idiom."

At this juncture the paradox in Hitchcock's own work is put forward; on one hand, his feeling for and treatment of real characters, and on the other hand, the fantasy, unreality, and sometimes lack of social background that accompanies the treatment.

"Failing to get a good script, I've invariably descended or ascended to using my own resources and becoming a crime reporter. I've always found it difficult to get proper themes."

Certain criminal types are dealt with in his films, but has it occurred to him to give the psychological background to these types? For instance, the social and personal conflicts that make criminals of people?

"Of course, I've studied criminal types from many aspects. I've read many books on the subject, but it is a matter of the sugar-coated pill with films. I wanted to make an anti-capital punishment film where the prison governor revolts and refuses to hang his man. It's a stirring subject. But here there would be difficulties with the censor. America can send over things of this sort, because the attitude here is that America can do what she likes with social subjects in her own country. In England this has to be left alone. When I put the Sydney Street affair in *The Man Who Knew Too Much,* the censor's objection was that it wasn't the thing to show English policemen using arms. He was very decent about the matter though. I would like to make a film showing the balance of justice in English courts. I feel that this is a subject which has not been shown to the full."

Was he going to Hollywood, and if so did he expect to have better facilities there for expressing himself?

"I've only discussed this with David Selznick so far. The matter is still in the air. But if I do go to Hollywood, I'd only work for Selznick."

And finally there is a touch of dismay in Hitchcock's attitude to the present situation of the cinema. "Cinema as an art form doesn't really exist," he says. "So many people have brought the theater into it. It is no longer used in a technical sense, but as a proscenium."

The impression is given of fundamental problems having been touched on, but not resolved: The conflict between England and America on the question of talent; the obstacles in the way of a creative film movement in England; the compelling aura surrounding the star system; the dearth of cinematic story material and the lack of freedom in dealing with important subjects; and the stereotyped treatment of films, so that they are forced into the "proscenium." Somewhere else Hitchcock has inferred that the power of universal appeal and the need to cater for this has done much to destroy film art. Tacitly, then, the uncreative elements at work in the cinema are recognized.

One is safe in submitting that the public is not solely responsible for this, since the very nature of a society that demands that film be utilized as an anodyne must be considered. Apparently the film executives and the financial powers operating behind their movements, do not realize what a powerful yet sensitive medium they control, for they have so far underestimated and failed to understand the complex structure of the public they cater to. To reverse their logic, it is not always this incoherently defined public that dictates film demands, but rather they themselves.

The Censor
Wouldn't Pass It

An Interview with J. Danvers Williams

When I saw his latest film, *The Lady Vanishes,* it struck me that Hitchcock's famous formula of secret agents, guns, and hold-ups was wearing just a little thin.

True, as an evening's relaxation, *The Lady Vanishes* is worth anybody's shilling. Judged purely as a piece of mechanical entertainment it compares favorably with the majority of American-made pictures.

But what a pity, I couldn't help thinking, that so talented a director as Hitch should waste his knowledge of the film medium and his sense of the dramatic on such a basically trivial story.

There were sequences in *The Lady Vanishes* (as, for example, the one halfway through the picture depicting a near-slapstick fight) which seemed to me to have been included for no reason except that there is invariably one such situation in every Hitchcock film.

So many of the situations were mechanical that I began to suspect Hitchcock himself (though, perhaps, only subconsciously) of growing just a little weary of his formula.

Working Up Excitement

It heartened me considerably when I went to see him to hear that this is the last secret agent film which he will make for a very long time.

"The Censor Wouldn't Pass It" was originally published in *Film Weekly,* November 5, 1938, 6–7.

I asked Hitch why he had stuck to his formula so long—why he had never used his brilliant technique to dramatize real events in our national life.

"Because," said Hitch, "circumstances have forced me into the realms of fiction. I have always wanted to make films with some sociological importance—but I have never been allowed to do so.

"You must remember," he continued, "that my chief appeal is an ability to work people up into a state of excitement.

"I do this not by quick cutting or by incessant camera movement, but by packing every sequence with incident and small details of characterization.

"If you study one of my films closely you will find that, compared with a Russian or an American gangster film, it is visually quite slow.

"Situation follows situation at a leisurely pace, and it is only the amount of detail which I pack into each sequence that makes my films appear to move so quickly.

"Working in this way, I can create scenes of great intensity and violence. But if you suppose that I consciously evolved this technique you are quite wrong.

"It emanated naturally from my own personality. It grew up automatically from my innate love of a dramatic situation and from my desire to generate excitement in other people."

The Censor Objected

"I have never made a subtle, psychological drama on *Blue Angel* lines, not because I dislike this type of film, but for the very simple reason that my mind does not work in this way.

"Give me any subject to be turned into a motion picture and I immediately judge it from the number of dynamic situations it contains.

"No matter how good a picture it might become in the hands of another director I toss it aside unless it has the forcefulness and violence which appeals to me personally.

"Now, paradoxically, it is my love of the dynamic that has forced me into the fields of fiction.

"Soon after the General Strike in 1926 I wanted to put the whole thing into a film. I saw in this subject a magnificently dynamic motion picture.

"When I suggested the idea to my production chief he approached the British Board of Film censors, who immediately vetoed it.

"I should, no doubt, have been allowed to make a wishy-washy picture about the general strike, but in this form the subject no longer appealed to me. I wanted to show fistfights between strikers and undergraduates, pickets, and all the authentic drama of the situation.

"Much the same thing happened when I wanted to put the Sydney Street siege on the screen for *The Man Who Knew Too Much.*

"When the idea was submitted for approval to the Home Office they informed me that I mustn't show the militia being called out and the house in Sydney Street surrounded by machine guns. All that I was allowed to do was depict the policemen being handed rifles and shown how to use them."

It Mustn't Happen Here

"Again and again I have been prevented from putting on the screen authentic accounts of incidents in British life.

"Again and again I have suggested authentic ideas to my production chief, only to be told: 'Sorry, Hitch, but the censor'd never pass it.'

"In order to give utterance to the violent things which I want to express I have been forced into fiction.

"If you imply 'it can't happen here'—if you set your story in Central Europe or even make your villain a foreigner—officialdom raises no objections. But if your picture is too obviously a criticism of the social system, Whitehall shakes its head.

"Although circumstances have forced me into fiction I have always sincerely tried to draw my characters and their behavior from genuine observation.

"Given that the basic story is imaginary, the characters, I think, always behave as real people would, in a similar set of circumstances.

"Thus, in *The Lady Vanishes,* at that point in the picture where the vanished lady turns up unexpectedly in the dining car of the train, I make one of the Englishmen (Naunton Wayne) remark casually: 'Hello! the old girl's back again.'

"This, in my opinion, is exactly how the type of Englishman

which Wayne was depicting would react to that given situation. The remark told the audience a great deal about the psychology of the character."

The Cup of Tea

"Again, in *The Man Who Knew Too Much* (I merely mention this because it was so widely commented on) during the siege sequence I showed a policeman being handed a cup of tea.

"I did this because I have always found that, in a moment of crisis a person invariably does something trivial, like making a cup of tea or lighting up a cigarette. A small detail of this sort adds considerably to the dramatic tension of the situation.

"Experience has taught me that if one detail is inaccurate, one gesture or one line of dialogue illogical, a situation loses its sting.

"To illustrate the importance of credible characterization I will give you an example of a sequence which, I admit, missed the mark in *The Lady Vanishes*. It was the fight scene halfway through the picture.

"When we were preparing to make this, Michael Redgrave told me that were he doing a similar scene on the stage he would want to rehearse it for a week. There is no opportunity for doing this in a film studio where thousands of pounds are running away every day of production. To aid Redgrave I shot the action first, adding the dialogue after. Even so, the behavior of the characters was just a little bit inaccurate, with the result that you immediately picked out this sequence as being weak."

Jamaica Inn

"I do not think that a truly exciting sequence of film can be made unless every detail is true to life. Looking back at such of my pictures as *Blackmail* and *The Man Who Knew Too Much*, I believe that these made you sweat with excitement (if indeed they did) because of the credibility of the characterizations.

"*The Lady Vanishes* will be the last secret agent picture that I shall make for a very long time. My next film will be the Laughton vehicle, *Jamaica Inn*. This is the story of a Cornish squire who, besides being the local magistrate, is the head of a gang of shipwreckers and smugglers.

"Usually I do not like historical subjects (for it is very difficult making characters in costumes behave credibly), but I accepted the invitation to make this film because I felt that it offered plenty of scope for my particular technique.

"I am primarily interested in the Jekyll-Hyde mentality of the squire. I shall also get a great deal of fun out of the shipwrecking sequences, the vessels being lured on to the rocks with false lights.

"When I have finished *Jamaica Inn* I am going to America to make one or two films. I hope that the first will be based on the disaster of the *Titanic*.

"This seems to me a marvelously dramatic subject for a motion picture; the greatest liner every built ploughing through the North Atlantic on her maiden voyage; the iceberg floating ominously into her path; the band playing 'Abide With Me'; the vessel sinking with most of its passengers and crew because the wireless operator of a nearby ship had gone to bed a few minutes before."

"Blame Whitehall"

"My idea is to show that over the grave of the *Titanic* modern shipping can now pass in safety. But the old trouble has cropped up again.

"The shipping companies are trying to prevent me from making the picture. They seem to think that if I recapture all the horror and violence of the situation it will stop people going on cruises.

"The picture which I shall make as well—or instead of—*Titanic*, will be based on Daphne du Maurier's novel, *Rebecca*.

"This is really quite a new departure for me. It concerns the wife of a rich young man who feels that the house in which she lives with her husband is haunted by some malignant influence.

"Subsequently she discovers that her husband nurdered his former wife.

"I shall treat this more or less as a horror film, building up my violent situations from incidents such as one in which the young wife innocently appears at the annual fancy-dress ball given by her husband in a frock identical with the one worn by his first wife a year previously.

"When *Rebecca* is finished I may stay in Hollywood or come home—I don't know!

"I would like to come back to Britain and weave a film around a pit disaster or an incident of sabotage in the Glasgow dockyards or around the crooked financiers of the city.

"But I am afraid that such subjects, handled as I must inevitably handle them, would have great difficulty getting past the censor.

"Do not blame me for ignoring such subjects. Blame Whitehall."

Old Ruts Are New Ruts

Somebody told me that Hollywood motion pictures were in a rut; I was told that at a party a few days after I arrived here to sign a long-term contract with David O. Selznick. Well, in fifty years the movies have made a lot of ruts, but I don't imagine any of us are still in the rut that was used ten or twenty or thirty years ago.

Somebody also said, in writing this article I should talk about Hollywood ruts because I was new to Hollywood and could see the ruts.

I'll talk about that in a moment. Just now I should like to digress and say that some ship news reporters in New York took one look at my shape when I came down off the gangplank and started interviewing me on food. I told them my favorite dish was steak *à la mode*. They believed me and it made quite a story. So you see, when anybody asks me a question such as "Why don't you tell Hollywood directors what they can learn from an English director?" I am likely as not to say anything that pops into my head.

I really haven't been here long enough to discuss Hollywood with a profound assumption of authority—such a pretension would be repellent to me anyway. But when one is asked questions, it is only polite to answer them.

Hollywood has such infinite material resources for motion picture making, and such a tremendous supply of alert, keen, and thor-

"Old Ruts Are New Ruts" was originally published in the *Hollywood Reporter* 54, no. 28 (October 28, 1939, 9th Anniversary Issue).

oughly skilled technicians, that it might seem presumptuous at first to say Hollywood can learn anything from anybody.

But on second thought, the answer seems to be that Hollywood might learn from an English director about the same thing it could learn from a Swedish director, a French director, or a Russian director; it might learn to take an excursion off on a side rut that is thrilling and new to the American, but just an old rut to the foreigner. Now America is a fresh rut to me and a very exciting one at that.

A great deal has been said about factory-made pictures. This criticism is heard in England as well as America where mass production has become a fine art, so to speak. Certainly it is a fault when producers and directors get in a rut and repeat mistakes they shouldn't make more than once. Habit is a useful servant of the mind, but a vicious master.

The pioneering age is still fresh in American tradition, its virtues honored, and handsomely requited. What is vital and important to American pictures is not mere ingenuity—a large native supply happily is available—but what is necessary is a new way of looking at old things.

Tradition has begun to bind American directors. A strange thing for a tradition-bound Englishman to say! But there are signs that some American movie makers are becoming too conventional, doing things simply because such action has proved successful in the past. A director from England, or Italy, or Rumania might have his own habit patterns, but they would be different from American trends of thought, and the chance that fresh and exciting pictures might result seems worth taking.

This is one thing that Hollywood can learn from an English director, but he can learn many things from Hollywood. To the student of motion picture making, Hollywood is a vast laboratory. A scientist may make important discoveries in a shed with a leaky roof—Mme. Curie did—but the efficiency worker is improved by better chemicals and more accurate instruments of measurement. This is what we get in Hollywood—the best cinema equipment in the world.

I find I can do things with cameras and lights and the manipulation of stage props that I often longed to do in England, but found myself hindered or even thwarted by cost of operation, lack of technical skill, the obstacle of tradition—a British one this time.

I am learning to do things every day that we wouldn't even attempt in an English studio. It's great fun.

Meanwhile, of course, I'm learning all those little geographical details that an experienced traveler cherishes in a new country. I'm learning how and when to watch a California sunset—that a tree-picked orange has a flavor all its own—that American drivers use the right side of the road. I am learning by experience what I already suspected, that people are pretty much alike in Elstree and in Hollywood, and that no matter where a good picture is made—everybody will want to see it.

But there is much yet to be learned. I used to say, ironically, if you will, that the ultimate in color pictures would be a drop of blood on a daisy petal, and that the perfect subject for a color drama would be an oyster, with a touch of green to indicate the oyster was bad—that being the drama.

Now that I am associated with a studio where some of the finest color pictures ever made have been produced, I am not so flippant about color. I am convinced that with early imperfections removed, it will prove the ultimate medium of cinematographic expression.

There are many more serious infirmities of the industry than the abuse of color. Typing is the real evil. If you have the same people, you have the same story. If a picture seems stale, it is because the same people keep moving through it in the same fashion.

Actors should be permitted to act. The success of fine character actors like Leslie Howard and Laurence Olivier should indicate the basis for enduring popularity.

Production
Methods Compared

The filming of each picture is a problem in itself. The solution to such a problem is an individual thing, not the application of a mass solution to all problems.

Something I do today makes me feel that the methods I used yesterday are out of date, and yet tomorrow I may be faced with a problem which I can best solve by using yesterday's methods. That is why I try to make my first rule of direction—flexibility.

Next, I try to make it a rule that nothing should be permitted to interfere with the story. The making of a picture is nothing but the telling of a story, and the story—it goes without saying—must be a good one. I don't try to put onto the screen what is called "a slice of life" because people can get all the slices of life they want out on the pavement in front of the cinemas and they don't have to pay for them.

On the other hand, total fantasy is no good either—I'm speaking only for myself remember—because people want to connect themselves with what they see on the screen.

Those are all the restrictions I would place on the story. It must be believable, and yet not ordinary. It must be dramatic, and yet lifelike. Drama, someone once said, is life with the dull spots removed.

Now, having got our story—what next? Obviously we must

"Production Methods Compared" was originally published in *Cine-Technician* 14, no. 75 (November–December 1948): 170–174, and reprinted in *American Cinematographer* 30, no. 5 (May 1949), and in Richard Koszarski, ed., *Hollywood Directors 1941–1976* (New York: Oxford University Press, 1977), 156–161.

develop our characters and develop the plot. All right, let's say that's been done. It may be putting a year's work in a few words, but let's say it. Are we ready to go on the floor? No, because our picture is going to need editing and cutting, and the time for this work is right now. The cuts should be made in the script itself, before a camera turns, and not in the film after the cameras have stopped turning.

More important, if we shoot each scene as a separate entity out of sequence, the director is forced to concentrate on each scene as a scene. There is then a danger that one such scene may be given too great a prominence in direction and acting, and its relation with the remaining scenes is out of balance, or, again, that it hasn't been given sufficient value and when the scene becomes a part of the whole, the film is lacking in something.

You are all familiar with the "extra shots" that have to be made after the regular schedule is completed. That is because in the shooting of the scenes, story points were missed. The extra, expository shots are generally identified by an audience for what they are— artificial devices to cover what had been overlooked in the preparation of the film.

Now, how can this be avoided? I think it can best be avoided if a shooting script is edited before shooting starts. In this way, nothing extra is shot, and, most important, story points will be made naturally, within the action itself.

Let me give an example of what I mean. Let's suppose that our story calls for two scenes in a certain street, one a view of a parade going by, and the other—several days later in our plot—being an intimate conversation between two people walking along the pavement. We shoot the scenes on different days, the parade a long shot, and the conversation a close-up. Now, after we've finished our scenes, we discover that the locale of the conversation is not quite clear to the audience. We must now shoot another long shot of the street which we will tack onto the front of the conversation merely to identify the street.

That "identifying long shot," in this case, is an unnecessary one. Because it's not really needed, it's awkward. If we'd seen to it that the script had been given expert editing before the film went on the floor, we would have found some way to identify the street within the structure of the conversation itself. Or, better still, since the parade scene is a long shot, we could have tried, at least, to combine the two. In this way, the parade would serve a dual purpose, its plot purpose, and its expository one.

Another example: if we do not edit before we shoot, we may be faced, in the cutting room, with one of the nastiest of all editorial problems—the unexplained lapse of time. Our characters speak on Monday, and then speak again on the following Monday. That a week has gone by may be essential to our plot, but we may have failed to make it clear in the sequences we have shot. There was a time—long since past—when we would simply have photographed the words "One Week Later" in transparency and caused them to appear on the screen in mid-air during the second scene.

The lapse of time can easily be indicated by the simple method of shooting one scene as a day scene and the next as a night scene, or one scene with leaves on the trees and the next one with snow on the ground. These are obvious examples, but they serve to illustrate what I mean by editing before production commences.

I try never to go to the floor until I have a complete shooting script, and I have no doubt everyone else tries to do the same thing. But, for one reason or another, we often have to start with what is really an incomplete script.

The most glaring omission in the conventional script, I believe, is Camera Movement. "Jane embraces Henry," the script may read. But where is the camera while the two have their fun? This omission is of very great importance. Of course, the director may decide how he is going to film the embrace "when the time comes," as the story conference idiom has it. I think the time is before shooting. And here we come face to face once again with the fact that the tendency today is to shoot scenes and sequences and not to shoot pictures. The embrace can be shot from the front, from either side, or from above. If we are really going to be arty about the thing, it can be filmed from behind. But when we make that concession we are speaking only of the embrace by itself, and not as part of a sequence which is, itself, part of a picture which ought to be a dramatic whole. The angle from which that embrace is to be shot ought to flow logically from the preceding shot, and it ought to be so designed that it will fit smoothly into whatever follows it, and so on. Actually, if all the shooting is planned and incorporated into the script, we will never think about shooting the embrace, but merely about shooting a picture of which the embrace is a part.

I've taken a long time to get around to telling you that I favor shooting pictures in sequence. After all, the film is seen in sequence by an audience and, of course, the nearer a director gets to an audience's point of view, the more easily he will be able to satisfy an audience.

A picture maker need not try to please everyone, of course. It is important to me, before anything else is done on a picture, to decide just what audience I'm aiming at, and then to keep my eye on that target from that moment on. But it is obviously uneconomic to shoot for a small audience, and a motion picture costing some hundreds of thousands of dollars, which has taken the efforts of one hundred or perhaps two hundred men, has no more business directing its appeal toward people with a special knowledge of filmmaking than exclusively towards, say, Seventh Day Adventists, or Atomic Research scientists, or Chicago meat-packers.

Now what of the actual techniques of picture making? I happen to have a liking, for instance, for a roving camera because I believe, as do many other directors, that a moving picture should really move. And I have definite ideas about the use of cuts and fadeouts which, improperly handled, can remind the audience of the unreality of our medium and take them away from the plot. But those are personal prejudices of mine. I do not try to bend the plot to fit technique; I adapt technique to the plot. And that's the important thing. A particular camera angle may give a cameraman—or even a director—a particular satisfying effect. The question is, dramatically, is it the best way of telling whatever part of the story it's trying to tell? If not, out it goes.

The motion picture is not an arena for a display of techniques. It is, rather, a method of telling a story in which techniques, beauty, the virtuosity of the camera, everything must be sacrificed or compromised when it gets in the way of the story itself.

An audience is never going to think to itself: "what magnificent work with the boom" or "that dolly is very nicely handled"; they are interested in what the characters on the screen are doing, and it's a director's job to keep the audience interested in that. Technique that calls itself to the audience's attention is poor technique. The mark of good technique is that it is unnoticed.

Even within a single picture, techniques should vary, even though the overall method of handling the story, the style, must remain constant. It is, for instance, obvious that audience concentration is higher at the beginning of a picture than at the end. The act of sitting in one place must eventually induce a certain lassitude. In order that that lassitude should not be translated into boredom or impatience, it is often necessary to speed up things a little towards the end, particularly towards the end of a long picture.

This means more action and less talk, or, if talk is essential, speeches ought to be short, and a little louder and more forceful than they would be if the same scene were played earlier in the picture. Putting it bluntly, it's sometimes necessary to ham things up a bit. This rule was recognized very early in the picture business, and the old-timers used to say: "when in doubt, get louder and faster." They were putting it a bit crudely, but perhaps the rule still applies.

It takes a certain amount of tact, of course, to induce a good actor to overact and this is another argument in favor of shooting pictures more or less in sequence, because, once you have edged an actor into overacting, it is, sadly enough, entirely impossible to edge him back again.

Direction, of course, is a matter of decisions. If it were possible to lay down a hard and fast rule that would cover all the decisions, all directors would be out of work. I shudder to think of *that,* but fortunately, it's impossible.

The important thing is that the director makes his decisions when the need for them arises, and operates with as few rules as possible. The fewer rules you have, the fewer times you'll have to experience the unhappiness of breaking them.

Film Production

By far the greater majority of full-length films are fiction films. The fiction film is created from a screenplay, and all the resources and techniques of the cinema are directed toward the successful realization on the screen of the screenplay. Any treatment of motion picture production will naturally and logically begin, therefore, with a discussion of the screenplay.

1. THE SCREENPLAY.—The screenplay, which is sometimes known, also, as the scenario or film script, resembles the blueprint of the architect. It is the verbal design of the finished film. In studios where films are made in great numbers, and under industrial conditions, the writer prepares the screenplay under the supervision of a producer, who represents the budgetary and box office concerns of the front office, and who may be responsible for several scripts simultaneously. Under ideal conditions, the screenplay is prepared by the writer in collaboration with the director. This practice, long the custom in Europe, has become more common in the United States with the increase of independent production. Indeed, not infrequently, the writer may also be the director.

In its progress toward completion, the screenplay normally passes through certain stages; these stages have been established over the years and depend on the working habits of those engaged in writing it. The practice of these years has come to establish three main stages: (1) the outline; (2) the treatment; (3) the screenplay. The

"Film Production" was originally published in *Encyclopaedia Britannica*, vol. 15, 1965 ed., 907–911, as a section of the eight-part entry "Motion Pictures."

outline, as the term implies, gives the essence of the action or story and may present either an original idea or, more usually, one derived from a successful stage play or novel. The outline is then built up into the treatment. This is a prose narrative, written in the present tense, in greater or less detail, that reads like a description of what will finally appear on the screen. This treatment is broken down into screenplay form, which like its stage counterpart, sets out the dialogue, describes the movements and reactions of the actors, and at the same time gives the breakdown of the individual scenes, with some indication of the role, in each scene, of the camera and the sound. It likewise serves as a guide to the various technical departments: to the art department for the sets, to the casting department for the actors, to the costume department, to makeup, to the music department, and so on.

The writer, who should be as skilled in the dialogue of images as of words, must have the capacity to anticipate, visually and in detail, the finished film. The detailed screenplay, prepared ahead, not only saves time and money in production but also enables the director to hold securely to the unity of form and to the cinematic structure of the action, while leaving him free to work intimately and concentratedly with the actors.

Unlike the screenplays of today, the first scripts had no dramatic form, being merely lists of proposed scenes, and their content when filmed was strung together in the order listed. Anything that called for further explanation was covered in a title.

Step by step, as the form and scope of the film developed, the screenplay grew more and more detailed. The pioneer of these detailed screenplays was Thomas Ince, whose remarkable capacity for visualizing the finally edited film made a detailed script possible. In contrast were the talents of D. W. Griffith, who contributed more than almost any other single individual to the establishment of the technique of filmmaking, and who never used a script.

By the early 1920s, the writer was meticulously indicating every shot, whereas today, when the scenarist writes less in images and gives more attention to dialogue, leaving the choice of images to the director, the tendency is to confine the script to the master scenes, so called because they are key scenes, covering whole sections of the action, as distinct from individual camera shots. This practice also follows on the increasingly common use of the novelist to adapt his own books; he is likely to be unfamiliar with the process of detailed dramatic and cinematic development. The dramatist, on the other hand, called on to adapt his play, is usually found to be more naturally disposed to do the work effectively. However, the scenarist is faced with a more difficult task than the dramatist. While the latter is, indeed, called upon to sustain the interest of an audience for three acts, these acts are broken up by intervals during which the audience can relax. The screenwriter is faced with the task of holding the attention of the audience for an uninterrrupted two hours or longer. He must so grip their attention that they will stay on, held from scene to scene, till the climax is reached. Thus it is that, because screenwriting must build the action continuously, the stage dramatist, used to the building of successive climaxes, will tend to make a better film scenarist.

Sequences must never peter out but must carry the action forward, much as the car of a ratchet railway is carried forward, cog by cog. This is not to say that film is either theater or novel. Its nearest parallel is the short story, which is as a rule concerned to sustain one idea and ends when the action has reached the highest point of the dramatic curve. A novel may be read at intervals and with interruptions; a play has breaks between the acts; but the short story is rarely put down and in this it resembles the film, which makes a unique demand for uninterrupted attention upon its audience. This unique demand explains the need for a steady development of a plot and the creation of gripping situations arising out of the plot, all of which must be presented, above all, with visual skill. The alternative is interminable dialogue, which must inevitably send a cinema audience to sleep. The most powerful means of gripping attention is suspense. It can be either the suspense inherent in a situation or the suspense that has the audience asking, "What will happen next?" It is indeed vital that they should ask themselves this question. Suspense is created by the process of giving the audience information that the character in the scene does not have. In *The Wages of Fear*, for example, the audience knew that the truck being driven over dangerous ground contained dynamite. This moved the question from, "What will happen next?" to, "Will it happen next?" What happens next is a question concerned with the behavior of characters in given circumstances.

In the theater, the performance of the actor carries the audience along. Thus dialogue and ideas suffice. This is not so in the motion picture. The broad structural elements of the story on the screen must be cloaked in atmosphere and character and, finally, in dialogue. If it is strong enough, the basic structure, with its inherent developments, will suffice to take care of the emotions of the audience, provided the element represented by the question "What happens next?" is present. Often a successful play fails to make a successful film because this element is missing.

It is a temptation in adapting stage plays for the screen writer to use the wider resources of the cinema, that is to say, to go outside, to follow the actor offstage. On Broadway, the action of the play may take place in one room. The scenarist, however, feels free to open up the set, to go outside more often than not. This is wrong. It is better to stay with the play. The action was structurally related by the playwright to three walls and the proscenium arch. It may well be, for example, that much of his drama depends on the question, "Who is at the door?" This effect is ruined if the camera goes outside the room. It dissipates the dramatic tension. The departure from the more or less straightforward photographing of plays came with the growth of techniques proper to film, and the most significant of these occurred when Griffith took the camera and moved it in from its position at the proscenium arch, where George Méliès had placed it, to a close-up of the actor. The next step came when, improving on the earlier attempts of Edwin S. Porter and others, Griffith began to set the strips of film together in a sequence and rhythm that came to be known as montage; it took the action outside the confines of time and space, even as they apply to the theater.

The stage play provides the screenwriter with a certain basic dramatic structure that may call, in adaptation, for little more than the dividing up of its scenes into a number of shorter scenes. The novel, on the other hand, is not structurally dramatic in the sense in which the word is applied to stage or screen. Therefore, in adapting a novel that is entirely compounded of words, the screenwriter must completely forget them and ask himself what the novel is about. All else—including characters and locale—is momentarily put aside. When this basic question has been answered, the writer starts to build up the story again.

The screenwriter does not have the same leisure as the novelist to build up his characters. He must do this side by side with the unfolding of the first part of the narrative. However, by way of compensation, he has other resources not available to the novelist or the dramatist, in particular the use of things. This is one of the ingredients of true cinema. To put things together visually; to tell the story visually; to embody the action in the juxtaposition of images that have their own specific language and emotional impact—that is cinema. Thus, it is possible to be cinematic in the confined space of a telephone booth. The writer places a couple in the booth. Their hands, he reveals, are touching; their lips meet; the pressure of one against the other unhooks the receiver. Now the operator can hear what passes between them. A step forward in the unfolding of the drama has been taken. When the audience sees such things on the screen, it will derive from these images the equivalent of the words in the novel, or of the expositional dialogue of the stage. Thus the screenwriter is no more limited by the booth than is the novelist. Hence it is wrong to suppose, as is all too commonly the case, that the strength of the motion picture lies in the fact that the camera can roam abroad, can go out of the room, for example, to show a taxi arriving. This is not necessarily an advantage and it can so easily be merely dull.

Things, then, are as important as actors to the writer. They can richly illustrate character. For example, a man may hold a knife in a very strange way. If the audience is looking for a murderer, it may conclude from this that this is the man they are after, misjudging an idiosyncrasy of his character. The skilled writer will know how to make effective use of such things. He will not fall into the uncinematic habit of relying too much on dialogue. This is what happened on the appearance of sound. Filmmakers went to the other extreme. They filmed stage plays straight. Some indeed there are who believe that the day the talking picture arrived the art of the motion picture, as applied to the fiction film, died and passed to other kinds of film.

The truth is that with the triumph of dialogue, the motion picture has been stabilized as theater. The mobility of the camera does nothing to alter this fact. Even though the camera may move along the sidewalk, it is still theater. The characters sit in taxis and talk. They sit in automobiles and make love, and talk continuously. One result of this is a loss of cinematic style. Another is the loss of fantasy. Dialogue was introduced because it is realistic. The consequence was a loss of the art of reproducing life entirely in pictures. Yet the compromise arrived at, although made in the cause of realism, is not really true to life. Therefore the skilled writer will separate the two elements. If it is to be a dialogue scene, then he will make it one. If it is not, then he will make it visual, and he will always rely more on the visual than on dialogue. Sometimes he will have to decide between the two; namely, if the scene is to end with a visual statement, or with a line of dialogue. Whatever the choice made at the actual staging of the action, it must be one to hold the audience.

2. DIRECTION.—Film direction was born when for the first time a man held a motion picture camera and turning it on his friend said, "Do something." This was the first step in creating movement for the camera. To create things that move for the camera is the aim at all times of the storytelling director.

Documentary direction is different. Its directors are primarily editors or, rather, discoverers. Their material is provided beforehand by God and man, noncinema man, man who is not doing things primarily for the camera. On the other hand, pure cinema has nothing in itself to do with actual movement. Show a man looking at something, say a baby. Then show him smiling. By placing these shots in sequence—man looking, object seen, reaction to object—the director characterizes the man as a kindly person. Retain shot one (the look) and shot three (the smile) and substitute for the baby a girl in a bathing costume, and the director has changed the characterization of the man.

It was with the introduction of these techniques that film direction departed from the theater and began to come into its own. Still more is this the case when the juxtaposition of images involves a noticeable change, a striking variation in the size of the image, the effect of which is best illustrated by a parallel from music, namely in the sudden transition from a simple melody played on the piano to a sudden burst of music by the brass section of the orchestra.

The essence of good direction then is to be aware of all these possibilities and to use them to show what people are doing and thinking and, secondarily, what they are saying. Half the work of direction should be accomplished in the script, which then becomes not merely a statement of what is to be put before the camera but in addition a record of what the writer and director have already seen as completed on the screen in terms of fast-moving rhythm. This, because it is a motion picture that is visualized and not a play or novel—an adventure carried along by a central figure.

In a play, the action is moved forward in words. The film director moves his action forward with a camera—whether that action is set on a prairie or confined to a telephone booth. He always must be searching for some new way of making his statement, and above all he must make it with the greatest economy and in particular the greatest economy of cutting; that is to say, in the minimum of shots. Each shot must be as comprehensive a statement as possible, reserving cutting for dramatic purposes. The impact of the image is of the first importance in a medium that directs the concentration of the eye so that it cannot stray. In the theater, the eye wanders, while the word commands. In the cinema, the audience is led wherever the director wishes. In this, the language of the camera resembles the language of the novel. Cinema audiences and readers of novels, while they remain in the theater or continue to read, have no alternative but to accept what is set before them.

Then comes the question of how they are to see what they are shown. In a mood of relaxation? Not relaxed? It is how the director handles his images that creates the state of mind, of emotion, in the audience. That is to say, the impact of the image is directly on emotions. Sometimes the director goes quietly along in a mood of simple, normal photography, and the eye is pleased as it follows the story. Then suddenly the director wishes to hit hard. Now the pictorial presentation changes. There is a bursting impact of images, like a change in orchestration. Indeed, orchestration is perhaps the best simile for a film, even to the parallel of recurrent themes and rhythms. And the director is, as it were, the conductor.

Given the skill that permits a man to direct, skills shared in varying degrees, perhaps the most significant and individually important thing about a director is his style. This style is evidenced by both his choice of subject and his manner of directing it. Important directors are known for their style. The record speaks of Ernst Lubitsch as having a style characterized by cinematic wit, or the pictorial quip. Charlie Chaplin is spoken of as having a style, and it is interesting to notice that it was his incursion into dramatic direction in *A Woman of Paris* that seemed to crystallize this style.

On the whole, style was slower to manifest itself in U.S. pictures, always excepting the extravaganzas of C. B. DeMille and the works of Griffith and Ince. In the early 1920s the Germans gave great evidence of style. Whether or not it was something imposed by the studios, or individual to the directors, it is clearly in evidence in the work of Fritz Lang, F. W. Murnau, and many others. Some directors are more concerned with style and the treatment of the content than with securing new themes. This is to say that, for the director, as often as not, what is important is the manner of telling his tale. The more original will revolt against the traditional and the cliché. They will want to show contrast, to present melodrama in a revolutionary way, to take melodrama out of the dark into the bright day, to show murder by a babbling brook, adding a touch of blood to its limpid waters. Thus the director can impose his ideas on nature and, taking what savors of the ordinary, can, in the way he handles it, render it extraordinary. So there emerges a kind of counterpoint and sudden upheaval in the ordinary things of life.

Motion pictures would be a source of much richer enjoyment, as is the case in other arts, if the audience were aware of what is and what is not well done. The mass audience has had no education in technique of cinema, as they frequently have in art and music, from their school days. They think only of story. The film goes by them too fast. The director, then, must be aware of this and must seek to remedy it. Without the audience being aware of what he is doing, he will use his technique to create an emotion in them. Suppose he is presenting a fight—the traditional fight in the barroom or elsewhere. If he puts the camera far enough back to take in the whole episode at once, the audience will follow at a distance, and objectively, but they will not so really feel it. If the director moves his camera in and shows the details of the fight—flaying hands, rocking heads, dancing feet, put together in a montage of quick cuts—the effect will be totally different and the spectator will be writhing in his seat, as he would be at a real boxing match.

Styles in direction can be individual; they can show trends or fashions. In recent times, the Italian directors have worked in the manner or style known as neorealism. They were concerned with the hardships of World War II as currently manifested in the life of the man in the street. There was a style, too, in German films in the silent days. More recent films from Germany show little new development. The French directors are well served by their cameramen and their art directors, who have great originality and a fine understanding of the cinematic. In the United States, there has been a movement in the direction of realism, but in the key areas of photography and settings the director is still forced to work in

an atmosphere of artificiality. The plushy architecture of Hollywood militates against a pure atmosphere and destroys realism.
Only gradually is the situation changing, and it is not so long ago
that the artist was shown to be starving in an attic as large and as
luxurious as the living room of a wealthy house.

Sets, lighting, music, and the rest are of immense importance to
the director, but everything, as Ingmar Bergman has said, begins
with the actor's face. It is to the features of this face that the eye of
the spectator will be guided, and it is the organization of these oval
shapes within the rectangle of the screen, for a purpose, that exercises the director. What figure is to be shown—and how? Near to—
or at a distance? Often it is wiser for a director to save long shots
for a dramatic purpose. He may need them, for example, to express loneliness, or to make some other verbal statement. Whatever
his choice, the content of the pictorial frame must have an impact.
This is the real meaning of the word dramatic. It signifies that
which has emotional impact. So it may be said that the rectangle of
the screen must be charged with emotion.

At all times the director must be aware of his intention. What is
his purpose, and how can he effect it in the most economical way?
Not only must he provide images that add up to a language; he
must also know what it is that makes it a language.

The most apparent and, to the outsider, the main function of
the director is the actual staging of the action of the film. From a
director's point of view, this staging is best described as the mechanical process of setting up the action so that the actors can move
in and bring their emotions to bear, not spontaneously, however,
but under his strict supervision.

In the theater, albeit after long and intensive rehearsal, the actor
is finally free and on his own, so that he is able to respond to the
live audience. In the studio, he responds to the director, who is
staging the action not only piecemeal but, as often as not, out of
sequence. The director controls every movement of the screen actor, working for the most part intimately and closely upon him.

The amount of action contained within a frame should convey
neither more nor less than what the director wishes to convey.
There must be nothing extraneous. The actor, therefore, cannot
operate at will, spontaneously improvising. The restrictions that this
imposes on the actions of the body are readily seen.

Certain special considerations apply to the face. In this regard, the chief requisite for a good screen actor is the capacity to do noth-ing—well. Furthermore, the director must bear in mind that the audience is not absolutely sure of the precise significance of the ex-pression until it has seen what causes it. At the same time, this re-action must be made with the greatest measure of understatement.

In a world of images, in which both actors and things are alike capable of such significant statements, what is the role of dialogue? The answer is that the introduction of dialogue was an added touch of realism—the final touch. With dialogue, that last unreality of the silent film, the mouth that opens and says nothing audible dis-appeared. Thus, in pure cinema, dialogue is a complementary thing. In the films that for the most part occupy the screens of the world, this is not the case. As often as not, the story is told in dialogue, and the camera serves to illustrate it.

And so it is that the last infirmity of both writer and director, when invention fails, is to take refuge and perhaps relief in the thought that they can "cover it in dialogue," just as their silent predecessors "covered it with a title."

3. PRODUCTION METHODS.—*Sets and Art Direction.*—The stag-ing of the action by the director draws on all the resources of the medium. Of first importance among these are the skill and knowl-edge of the art director who plans the sets, and the dresser who furnishes them.

Originally, film sets were neither so complete nor so elaborate as they are today. Usually, they were bits and pieces constructed for single scenes and always planned as part of the scene. The sets built today are usually large and complete. The result is that the prosce-nium arch of the theater is virtually restored. The mere building of a room does not build it for the camera, and this should be the aim of all construction. The set is a kind of shorthand. It gives an impression of locale and as often as not by means of a stock shot: Washington is a view of the Capitol; New York, a skyscraper. To use an unfamiliar view would confuse the audience.

An art director must have a wide knowledge and understanding of architecture. On the other hand, he must be able to distinguish between what characterizes a type of dwelling and what individu-ates the inhabitant of that dwelling. The profession of a man may be characterized by what is on his walls. His untidiness, however, will be personal to him. Indeed, it is only the more imaginative as-pects of art direction that require the art director to depart from the letter of his research. His basic information is not the answer to the actual requirements of a character or a scene. Increasing awareness of the capacity of the camera to show reality, to set the action in real streets under real trees, created the demand for reality even in interior sets. Therefore the woodwork and the lath and plaster of sets, no matter how manifestly artificial from behind, must face the camera with all the appearance of visible reality.

With the increasing cost of materials and labor, sets become a very serious budgetary consideration. Their construction calls upon the resources of machine shops, carpenter shops, plasterer shops, the paint shop, in short, upon all the resources needed for house building, so that the audience may be given the reality it demands. One of the results of this has been the discovery, over the years, of an amazing variety of ways to circumvent this problem by the use of models of all kinds, of trick work and of various special effects, or trick shots, all of which are realistic substitutes for a reality beyond the resources, both financially and otherwise, of any studio.

The most intelligent place to be economical is at the scriptwriting stage, and the preparation of the script should be well advanced before any artwork is begun. The main factor to be borne in mind in art direction, as in other areas of filmmaking, is the complete control that can be exercised not only over what the audience sees or does not see on the screen but even over the actual movements of the eye.

Lighting.—The lighting of the sets is the concern of the photographer and not, as is commonly supposed, the concern of the designer. Originally he was referred to as the cameraman. Today he is more commonly referred to as the lighting expert, the actual working of the camera being carried out by an operator under his supervision. In addition to supervising the work of the electricians and the camera operators, he functions by adding creatively to the mood and cinematic value of the scenes. The common impression that the sets are designed for lighting is incorrect. In theory, it should be possible to plan lighting ahead, at the set construction stage, but the actual lighting of a scene is a specific and particular operation demanding a fine, on-the-spot sense of light and shade and of composition.

Camera.—All uses of the camera, whether it be used straight on or at an angle, whether it be stationary or moving, must be directed to one and only one thing, namely to the dramatic impact of pictorial images that are to be cut together to reveal the progress of an action or story. The movements of the camera come under two main headings:

1. Movement in relation to the movement of the characters. Here the camera follows a character, dollying ahead or following in profile, because the character is walking. The ideal to be aimed at here is that the audience should never be aware of the camera moving. Thus there always must be complete coordination between the movement of the camera and the movement of the character. If the two movements are out of synchronization at any time, so that the camera is moving while the character is still, the effect is not obtained.

2. Dramatic movement, movement of the camera—that is, with the character in repose, and always for a dramatic purpose. For example, the camera may dolly up to the face of the character for emphasis, or dolly away at the end of a scene to reveal a lonely figure standing by himself in the center of a room. So used, the camera may be said to make a statement. The film, like the novel, is the sum total of these statements.

Sound.—The principal adjustment that had to be made between the technique of talking pictures and that of the silent screen was in the respective roles of image and word. The written word, when brought to the moment of filming, may turn out to be redundant, the expression of the actor conveying the meaning with equal force.

Sound has many other uses, however. It can serve very effectively to denote the progress of an action. Or it may be used for a stream of consciousness over an unspeaking mouth. It is likewise of great help in expressing the mental processes of the characters. The screen shows the face of a girl. Over it comes the sound of a school bell, thus revealing that she is reminiscing. It is in its own way, then, an image maker and has been used as such from the first in a variety of ways.

Music.—Though it is entirely possible to see a silent film and become so engrossed in it as to be oblivious of the absence of sound or accompanying music, there have never been public showings of films without music. From the beginning there was at least the single piano, improvising; and later the orchestra, sometimes with specially composed scores. Sound has tended to increase the importance of music, and regularly over the years composers of the highest standing have written scores that, while serving to add a dimension of mood and atmosphere to the film, have also stood by themselves as compositions.

The presence of music, then, is perfectly in accordance with the aim of the motion picture, namely to unfold an action or to tell a story, and thereby stir the emotions.

Color.—Color, like sound, is to be used dramatically, when needed. Its values are never realistic and often are merely for embellishment or for decorative purposes. Thus, like the wide screen, its use belongs to the realm of showmanship. It can also serve an aesthetic purpose when the subject, whether the face of a woman or of a landscape, is enhanced by its use. It can likewise be used for spectacular or emotional purposes, as in battle scenes or in displays of pageantry or splendor, such as occur in historical or epic tales. Its range of uses is from the mood of décor to the clothes of a star. However, until such time as the realism of truly natural color is achieved, the use of it is primarily as an embellishment.

Wide Screen.—The development or at least the use of the wide screen in public theaters really belongs, like color, to the realm of showmanship. In its most common form, namely CinemaScope, it requires a rectangular screen. This shape, with a very low ratio of height to width, is now generally regarded as unsatisfactory, and some studios, by lopping off the ends of the screen, narrow down its excessive width.

Editing.—Editing, or, as it is sometimes called, montage, has been described as the foundation of the art of making films. Basically, it is the placing of the strips of film in the order and sequence deemed best to unfold the action or story. Initially, the strips of film were joined in a simple sequence. Even pioneers of the photodrama, such as George Méliès, made no attempt to do more than follow the story quite simply, as seen from the point of view of a camera, the position of which was fixed and central. Other pioneers, in particular the Englishman G. A. Smith and his associates in the Brighton school of filmmaking, and Edwin S. Porter, working in the U.S. for Edison, began to experiment with what were the rudiments of editing and montage. The Russian filmmakers, Eisenstein, Pudovkin, and their contemporaries, in the late 1920s developed creative editing, or montage, as they called it, by way of the juxtaposition not just of sequences but also of individual shots or frames, to illustrate character, to convey ideas or even to create motion by the juxtaposition of static objects.

Methods of editing vary according to the preference of the director. In most cases, the material is assembled as the film is in progress, by an editor working from the screenplay. The director who plans the editing at the screenplay stage makes his decision as to the coverage of the scenes and characters at that stage and then shoots as planned.

Whatever method is used, it is used with the realization that everything in cinema is a visual statement and the images are its language. Film, therefore, like any language, has its own syntax, which, as the word implies, is a lining up or ordering of images to create the maximum effect.

The Machinery of Filmmaking.—Serving the filmmakers is the machinery of production, and in treating methods of film production it is necessary to distinguish between what is needed to bring one film and what is needed to bring a hundred films to the screen. In other words, it is necessary to distinguish between individual and mass production. A single production, planned by an independent filmmaker, carries with it no overhead costs and needs space only during the time of production. It can be made anywhere that there is space to be rented, and it employs only the personnel required for the project. Equipment is also hired, as are the services of the laboratories and printing establishments that are available in any production center.

The independent producer, then, whose increasing emergence in the decade following World War II was a significant feature of the changes that have continued to overtake film production, notably in Hollywood, is, in theory, much freer to concern himself with the quality of his film. The 20 years between World Wars I and II saw Hollywood studios at the height of their productivity, under executives like Marcus Loew, Carl Laemmle, Adolph Zukor, Jesse Lasky, Louis B. Mayer, Joseph Schenck, Samuel Goldwyn, the Warner brothers (Harry M., Samuel L., Albert and Jack L.), and others who brought their organizing ability, developed in other fields, to bear on the making of motion pictures. They took over the entertainment of the people and put melodrama, comedy, and musical plays on an industrial footing. They put large sums into the improvement of techniques and encouraged the development of new devices for camera, sound, editing, the recording of music, and three-dimensional and wide screen; all were calculated to give glamour to the film on the screen, to attract back a wavering audience by the novelties and the devices of showmanship.

A basic method of production has survived from those days and begins with sending the script to the production department. There it is broken down into its physical requirements. These are estimated and a budget drawn up.

After the script is approved and the budget passed, copies are sent to all departments for each to prepare its contribution to the production against the day set for shooting, according to the schedule drawn up by the unit manager.

The organization of filmmaking in the United States still centers for the most part around a producer. This arrangement originated in the need to coordinate the mass production of films; at one time the whole responsibility was so much in the hands of the producer, and so little in the hands of the director, that the latter would be handed a script that was complete, with a cast already chosen. At one time, indeed, the production method was for the producer himself to put the film together after the director had completed the shooting. This system has now virtually died out, and the independent producer is as often as not his own director, or perhaps his own star, since the actor-producer has become a commonplace, along with the producer-director and the writer-producer-director.

4. ECONOMIC CONSIDERATIONS.—While the changes in methods and circumstances of production have resulted, in part, from a desire among writers and directors for greater artistic freedom, they have received their two greatest impulses from the economic situation: (1) increases in income tax, which cripples the salaried filmmaker; and (2) the economic decline of motion pictures, beginning a few years after World War II and caused by rivalry from television, combined with a general falling off in the entertainment quality of the films. Indeed, in 1957 Hollywood was described in a report prepared for the American Federation of Labor Film council as being at the crossroads. In the ten years between 1946 and 1956, the attendance at theaters in the U.S. fell off 50% at a time when the national economy was strong and growing stronger. The number of U.S. features released in the American market declined by 28%, while the number of imported features increased by 233%.

Then, in 1948, by a decree of the Supreme Court of the U.S., the major studios, whose security had been based on their producer-to-consumer organization, were ordered to dispose of their theaters as a result of complaints by independent theater owners.

The situation deteriorated more or less steadily up to 1958. Then in 1959, the tide seemed to turn as a result of a general reorganization and a new policy mapped by executives from New York. Fewer pictures were made, but those made were produced on larger budgets and were given longer runs. There were sales of old motion pictures to television, and the renting of studio space to both television companies and to independent film producers. The returns of the major companies all showed a profit, and the theaters showed a healthy rise in attendance.

5. THEATER MANAGEMENT AND PROMOTION.—The changing conditions of the cinema have called for changes in the running of the theaters and the promotion of films. Prior to the coming of sound, there had to be a certain amount of personal and individual effort in the presenting of films in the theaters.

Then, suddenly, everything arrived in cans—picture, music, and sound. All that was needed now was to set up the projection system. With that, something living went out of theater management and presentation. The effect of this was not apparent during the 1930s and 1940s. Only gradually, in the late 1950s, was it realized that with fewer films being made the exhibitor must give special attention to each film. With the so-called rehousing of the big, expensive productions, on a twice-a-day showing booked in advance, the tide began to turn. Films began again to be presented importantly, with big advertising campaigns and a new element—the personal appearance of stars and directors—to give a flesh-and-blood contact back to audiences.

With the continued development of these methods, a phrase that epitomizes the old approach to cinema-going will fittingly disappear from the language, namely, "This is where we came in."

Television helped in changing the approach to filmmaking and film presentation by taking away the audience for what is called the "grind policy": i.e., the continuous performance with a double feature program, changed twice weekly.

There is evidence of other changes, too. There is a tendency to decentralize production, and Hollywood is said to be located round the world. There are several reasons for this, in spite of the fact that, technically speaking, production is still easier and better in Hollywood. The need for special location, for example, is clear enough. Again, if the script calls for a number of supporting actors for a foreign story, then it is an advantage to go to the country in which the story is set.

A further, and comparatively recent, development has been the drive-in theater. This exists as a matter of social convenience. Young couples can see a film and yet enjoy a sense of being alone. Families unable to get a baby-sitter, or to afford a sitter as well as a film, can take their children with them and put them to sleep in the car. The drive-in also gives a feeling of being a place; less than the theater, but more than television at home. It thus satisfies the urge to go out—a deep-seated urge, which will prevent television from being a final threat to the picture theater.

In the Hall of Mogul Kings

When I arrived in America somewhat over 30 years ago to make *Rebecca,* my first English picture in America, I found myself a minor figure in a vast film industry made up of entrepreneurs who headed the studios, and I became involved in the making of a picture under the producer system.

In those days the individual producer was the man who made the pictures. He was king. The director, the writers, actors, designers, and the like were all subject to his taste and approval. His method usually was to buy, or be handed by the studio head, material for a project. His first job was to "cast" the writer and proceed to put the story into a working script. He would then look around and eventually choose a director. Sometimes, in a major studio, the director would be under contract and therefore assigned at the request of the producer. The same applied to stars and the lesser players. He would then choose what he thought would be the right cameraman for the picture. If the star was an important woman he would choose a "woman's photographer" (in those days many cameramen owed their high salaries to the fact that they were able to photograph a slightly blemished star's face and produce something worthy of an illustration on a chocolate-box cover).

My producer at this time was David Selznick, one of the biggest names in the industry, and one of the few important independent producers. It was a matter of luck for me, I suppose, that my

"In the Hall of Mogul Kings" was originally published in the *London Times,* June 23, 1969, 33.

English reputation had preceded me, because in my case I found the rules were broken a little. I was permitted to participate in the preparation of the script. This was considerate and flattering, except for one thing—the hours. I have a dim recollection of trying to keep awake at 3 A.M. in the producer's summerhouse, while attempting to construct a script with the help of the famous playwright, Robert Sherwood. Naturally Selznick dominated the scene—pacing up and down, apparently oblivious to those around him who were nodding off—he did not even notice that the long, lanky Mr. Sherwood, having imbibed somewhat, was trying unsuccessfully to sail a small boat in the swimming pool. By dawn, of course, nothing much had been accomplished, but that was the producer's way.

I remember, in later years, sitting in Romanoff's restaurant having dinner with Ben Hecht when he said to me: "Don't you think we ought to be going? We have to meet Selznick at your house at midnight." It was now 11:30. I replied, "Don't worry, Ben, he won't be there until half-past three." But Ben insisted we go, and ultimately Selznick turned up. I was 15 minutes wrong. He arrived at 3:15. Kicking off his shoes, he immediately started to pace the room in his stockinged feet. The entire conference lasted 20 minutes.

Now started the actual filming of *Rebecca*. After I had rehearsed the first scene and was ready to shoot, the script clerk hurried up to me and whispered in my ear. I turned with astonishment. "Yes," she repeated, "I have to notify Mr. Selznick because he always insists on seeing every scene rehearsed before it is shot." So we all sat around until he arrived on the set. I thought I was very gracious at the time because, with an airy wave of my hand, I gestured towards the set and the artists and said, "It's all yours, David" and proceeded to walk away. He came after me. "No, no," he said apologetically. "I just wanted to see a run-through." Again I waved my arm. "Go ahead." We rehearsed the scene and I felt all the while that I had an *éminence grise* whispering in my ear. "Don't you think, &c., &c.?" The details were minor. Because of my polite hints, I had very few visits after that. In addition, it was my good fortune that he was extremely busy completing *Gone With the Wind*.

Another important producer's instruction was that during the shooting of the picture no retakes of any kind should be attempted, whether these were necessary because of photography or perhaps some inadequately played scene or even something as essential as scratches on the film. Nothing, absolutely nothing, was to be retaken.

"Why not?" I asked.

"It may not be in the picture." It was explained to me that when the producer had the completely shot material he would then start on what to him was the most important function of all—the reconstruction, the editing, the rewriting, if necessary, the recasting of some minor roles. This was a function in which the director did not play any part whatsoever. As it turned out, in the case of *Rebecca* there was a certain amount of rewriting and two weeks of retakes—the bulk of which were required because of the telescoping of certain passages in the story line.

I should add, however, that this whole process took place after only the first sneak preview. I was astonished that within a mere two weeks of the finish of shooting, temporary titles and temporary music were put on and this rough assembly was sneaked to the public. It was successful enough for Selznick to remark, "I think we have a hit." Nevertheless, this made no difference to the process of reshooting that had to be performed.

I think the most flattering remark I ever heard said about me by Selznick was, "he's the only director that I'd ever trust a picture with."

Today, with the coming of the international film, this whole way of making pictures is impossible. The components of a picture leave as soon as production is finished. For example, in my last picture, *Topaz,* I used artists from Sweden, Denmark, Germany, France, Italy, and the United States. What happened when the picture was finished? All the artists disappeared back to their own countries and were very soon engaged in other pictures. No retakes afterwards, no recasting. In other words, the film has to be completely designed on paper first.

The famous producer of the thirties, Irving Thalberg, has been quoted as saying in a recent biography that films are not made, they are remade. (Even Selznick once said to me of Thalberg: "He's great with a finished picture.") I wonder how Thalberg would fare today? Are we missing some other stimulus that went with those earlier days—the great movie mogul, for example? Only

a few days ago, I read in the *Wall Street Journal* a complaint
by a stockbroker deploring a multi-million dollar loss by Metro-
Goldwyn-Mayer. What, he asked, could one expect of the company's
future when its head was a distiller and its second-in-command a
food merchant? Yet this great industry was started by glove salesmen, furriers, scrap-iron merchants, all of whom came into this
growing business with surging enthusiasms for the medium.

What has taken their place? Because today the industry shows us
a very different picture. What has emerged in the past 10 years is
known as the package deal. It would seem that anyone can be a
producer, provided he is able to purchase a property, interest a star,
and "put it together."

He could take this package to a studio and, if they were sufficiently interested, secure the financial backing. These producers
could be either the agent of the star, the lawyer, the brother-
in-law, or even the wife. After all, we drink instant coffee today,
eat instant mashed potatoes, why should not we have instant producers? And so we have entered the hit-and-miss era of picture-
making.

Naturally the main survivors are the purely creative people:
producers-directors, writer-directors, producer-writers, and so on.

We are told that the audience today is fickle, and does not know
what it wants to see. Perhaps it is our present-day system that is
fickle, and does not know what it wants to make. Naturally, new
talent must be encourged, but who is to encourage them in the
future of the craft of the cinema for world entertainment?

Technique, Style,
and Hitchcock at Work

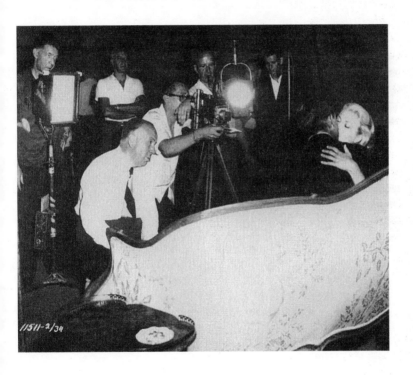

Introduction

These essays overlap with those in the previous section on a variety of points, but here Hitchcock focuses more precisely on the details of his own artistic and technical methods, less concerned with the broad contexts of filmmaking than with the more immediate tasks and materials at hand. He took great delight in talking and writing about how he worked: this not only served publicity purposes, calling attention to his mastery of film art and catering to the public's desire for behind-the-scenes views of how films are made, but also had important critical and theoretical functions. Hitchcock was indeed a theoretician but for the most part, concretely rather than abstractly, and the challenges and problems that most engaged him were practical ones. There are subtexts in the pieces in this section: Hitchcock kept up a continuing dialogue with critics and the filmgoing public and commented regularly, although sometimes slyly and indirectly, on a growing agenda of often-controversial film topics. But if he was always defending and situating himself, he was also, more simply, describing himself and his experiences as they came up, sharing with his readers fascinating stories of his methods, discoveries, and creative uses and adaptations of the materials of filmmaking.

The first four essays in this section are especially good examples of Hitchcock's subtle balancing of text and subtext. "On Music in Films" is his most extensive commentary on a crucial aspect of his art that is sometimes underappreciated because of his characteristic emphasis on visual techniques. The immediate context of the essay is the release of *Waltzes* from *Vienna,* a rarely screened and deservedly neglected film whose main virtue may turn out to be that it helped prompt Hitchcock to examine cinematic uses of music that were elaborated in later, far more successful and innovative films. Perhaps Leonard Leff is right to say that in general, "Hitchcock had few original ideas about music" (*Hitchcock and Selznick,* 165), but originality is not the only basis of artistic achievement. Hitchcock's comments on the atmospheric and psychological functions of music are unexceptional, but his overall awareness of how nonvisual techniques such as music, sound effects, and even silence can support visual techniques of cutting and counterpoint is an extremely important part of his effort to construct thoroughly integrated films, in which all cinematic resources work toward heightening the emotional experience. For this, of course, he needed creative collaborators, such as Bernard Herrmann, whose name is rightly linked to many of Hitchcock's greatest films. In a curious way, "On Music in Films" looks ahead to creative tension as well as collaboration. Part of the underlying argument in this essay is Hitchcock's assertion of the controlling power of the director. Even in the so-called silent era, there was almost always musical accompaniment, normally provided by the theater management, but sound technology placed music "at last entirely under the control of the people who made the picture." That was, as he goes on to say, "surely an advance," but one that was not without its problems, as illustrated by the tumultuous relationship between Hitchcock and Herrmann many years later.

"Close Your Eyes and Visualize!" nicely summarizes some of Hitchcock's most commonly expressed ideas about film in the 1920s and 1930s: his distrust of dialogue, his emphasis on realism that precludes glamour, his use of comedy as a necessary ingredient of the dramatic, and his overall intention of giving the audience "not horror thrills" but "good, healthy, mental shake-ups." As the title suggests, film must always be approached as a visual medium, but it is interesting to note that Hitchcock's rallying cry "It must be pictures first and last" is not so much a fine point of theory as part of an attempt to identify himself as a mainstream film director. His advice echoes that of many popular script-writing manuals of the 1920s, surveyed by Kevin Brownlow in *The Parade's Gone By* ("The Scenario," chap. 22), which crystallized contemporary conventions and formulas. For example, H. H. Van Loan's

How I Did It sets out basic principles strikingly akin to Hitchcock's: establish a premise, he says, then "don't waste any time en route," add action and thrills, and mix comedy with tragedy. And Elinor Glyn's recommendation to amateur photoplay writers in 1922 is almost exactly Hitchcock's nearly fifteen years later: "Close your eyes and concentrate on your play. Don't dream. Visualize!" (quoted in Brownlow, 277).

Even if we do not recognize what may be allusions to these manuals and contemporary commonplaces, Hitchcock draws himself into the mainstream by characterizing his earlier films as filled with "crazy tricks," "arty theories," and "directorial idiosyncrasies" that he no longer approves of. His continuing attraction to cinematic experimentation is not banished completely, and no one who admits "I visualize my story in my mind as a series of smudges moving over a variety of backgrounds" will ever make thoroughly conventional films, but at this point in his life Hitchcock evidently felt the need to confess his cinematic indiscretions and announce "I have stopped all that today." Here as elsewhere, even in the midst of what was a creative and commercially successful period, we catch glimpses of Hitchcock "running for cover" (a term he explains to Truffaut, 186), questioning his methods and looking for at least the temporary comfort of the conventional. One of the most fascinating dramas of his career is this uneasy oscillation between acknowledging and repudiating "the Hitchcock touch."

Hitchcock repeatedly commented that once he had visualized a film and planned out all the shots and sequences, shooting it was of little interest to him. In his short sketch "Search for the Sun," he describes some of the real conditions of making a film, especially outside a studio, and conveys why he might find this aspect of directing tiresome. Should serious artists have to worry about vanishing sunlight, traffic noise, disappearing dogs, and uncooperative babies and sheep? His real underlying complaint, though, is against audiences who, "lying back in upholstered comfort," have little understanding of how films are made. To combat stereotyped notions about the easy and luxurious life of directors and respond to the impatient "clamor" for realistic dramas in recognizably British settings (which, as we have seen in some of the essays in the previous section, he had some sympathy for), Hitchcock humorously but pointedly sets out to educate the "ever critical" public that was "perpetually rising on its hind legs."

He does not envision his audiences in exactly that posture in the following three essays, but still his primary motive is the desire to help make them, as he says in "Search for the Sun," less "apt to take a film for granted"—his films in particular, one might add. In "Direction," he continues his earlier attempt to disassociate himself from "arty" techniques and "obvious camera devices," but his intention is markedly different: instead of apologizing for "directorial idiosyncrasies," he is determined to overcome the likelihood that "anything subtle may be missed." The task, then, is not to stop what he is doing but to do it better. Hitchcock's acknowledgment "I have become more commercially minded" needs to be understood in its full context: it is balanced and explained by his concluding statement, "The art of directing for the commercial market is to know just how far you can go." Unwilling to let the audience or the market completely direct the director, his underlying premise is the manifestolike assertion "The screen ought to speak its own language, freshly coined," and he sets out to describe that language and teach it to his audience by writing about his directorial method and analyzing key scenes in his films. In doing so, Hitchcock becomes a master of the twice-told tale, repeating himself constantly; indeed, "Direction" is a compendium of already familiar and soon-to-be familiar anecdotes and statements. But the important point to note is that these tales are not only twice-told but fascinating as well—the description of "how Mr. Verloc comes to be killed" in *Sabotage,* for example, establishes this sequence as Hitchcock's major *tour de force* of montage until the shower scene in *Psycho*—and serve their dual purpose of instructing the audience and freeing the director to be even more adventurous and subtle.

Much of what is in "Direction" reappears in the two subsequent essays but alongside intriguing new topics and illustrations. For example, in "Some Aspects of Direction," his description of the first sequence of *Secret Agent* calls attention to his slyly cinematic way of beginning his films, a characteristic touch that will become even more prominent in some later films like *Rear Window.* Such sequences instantly acclimate the spectators and, perhaps more important, make them "more receptive to further impressions." He goes on to note that even the title of a film can contribute to this effect. His particular example is *Mutiny on the Bounty,* which, he points out, would have lost a great deal of suspense and audience anticipation if it were instead titled *Boys of the Bounty* or some such thing. As usual, Hitchcock has at least one eye on his own films and on how his titles suggest hidden dimensions to come. Although he does not refer specifically to it, the film current at the time this essay was written provides a perfect illustration. The title *The Lady Vanishes* obviously announces to the audience the main action forthcoming, but it also cleverly introduces what in some respects is the real theme of the film. Miss Froy is not the only lady who vanishes: the lady in Iris—that is to say, the stuffy, privileged, self-centered character that she is at the beginning of the film— disappears, replaced by the down-to-earth heroine that she is at the end of the film. Once we are alerted to this dimension by Hitchcock, the titles of many of his films appear to be that much more witty and significant.

What becomes apparent as we read through the pieces in this section is Hitchcock's dedicated and thoughtful but also disarming way of talking about the art of film. This takes a number of different forms. Sometimes it surfaces in critical disavowals of "artiness," although as we have seen such statements are not as simple as they first appear. At other times what is most disarming is Hitchcock's tone. The talk, for example, at Columbia University is charming and down-to-earth, not so much a formal lecture as a free-flowing conversation on, among many other topics, how the pace of a film depends on editing but more on occupying the audience's mind, the interaction of character and setting, the shape of a film, and the "springboard situation," not the MacGuffin, the false or unspecified background of the action, but the real circumstances from which the plot proceeds. What is so engaging here is his ability to convey the techniques without the technicalities of filmmaking. And in "On Style," Hitchcock patiently instructs an interviewer who, although he represents a national film journal, obviously—at least in Hitchcock's opinion—needs to be gently straightened out about some of the basics of film theory and practice, including intellectual and emotional montage, subjective effects, and Hitchcock's particular use of what he calls "visual counterpoint."

Another way of downplaying or framing cinematic "artiness" is by emphasizing the craft of filmmaking, defining the imaginative in terms of the technical or even the mechanical. *Rope,* a brooding, claustrophobic drama featuring a small cast and shot in a very restricted indoor setting, might not be the first Hitchcock film that comes to mind as his "most exciting picture," but his essay of this title describes not the subject of the film but how the film was designed, produced, and shot. Far from complaining "I wish I didn't have to shoot the picture," he conveys his tremendous delight in executing as well as planning *Rope*. This project began, he explains, with his desire to make an entire film in real time with as few cuts as possible. Hitchcock often insists that cinematic techniques must not call attention to themselves within the context of the film, but there is no reason why outside the film frame he should not take a great deal of pride in detailing the ingenuity that made such a film possible.

Hitchcock revels in the practical, and he and his collaborators, whose contributions he fully acknowledges, are portrayed not as "arty" artists but as inventive technicians, up to every challenge posed by the imagination. Aesthetic sensitivity—to color, for example—counts for little unless it is supported by the technological ability to make clouds out of spun glass, sunsets out of thousands of tiny bulbs, and neon light synchronizers out of war surplus bomb switches. Hitchcock frequently uses musical metaphors to describe the way he makes his films, imagining himself, for example, as a conductor or orchestrator. Here, though, his metaphors are strikingly lowbrow and wonderfully suitable: the choreography of camera movement is like baseball, specifically, a Tinkers to Evers to Chance double play (we can forgive Hitchcock for enthusiastically but mistakenly crediting them with triple plays); and the construction of the film is likened several times to a Rube Goldberg drawing. He is equally lowbrow and technically enraptured in "It's a Bird, It's a Plane, It's . . . *The Birds*," where he describes in great detail the traveling matte process and attributes "one of the most spectacular shots" to the efforts of two women technicians who spent three months laboriously painting birds and silhouettes on tiny film frames.

Because he resolutely avoids high seriousness, critics sometimes underestimate Hitchcock's self-conscious artistry. We tend to want our van Goghs to talk about their intense perception of madness rather than their brush strokes. But for Hitchcock, as for so many others, much of his art is in his craft. Early in the interview "Hitchcock Talks About Lights, Camera, Action," he acknowledges "I'm a *technician* as well as a director," and the practical details he goes on to discuss provide a great deal of insight into not only his current film, *Torn Curtain*, but also his ongoing work with color, image size, and setting to create a "reality effect" that will engage an audience in the fantasies that are his subjects. Mixed in with comments about the history of set lighting is Hitchcock's boldest statement against "deep focus" photography and somewhat incredulous astonishment that the primary image in a shot should ever be merged with rather than separated from the background. André Bazin would not be convinced, but Hitchcock defines his technique as "realistic" and clearly establishes the technical basis for what many consider to be one of his greatest achievements: the simultaneous credibility and incredibility of the Hitchcock world.

It is fitting that the last selection in this section and in the entire volume is "Hitchcock at Work," part of a transcript of one of the many production conferences he participated in during the making of *Marnie*. (There are tapes of other such production conferences in the Hitchcock Collection, which may yet, one hopes, be transcribed and published.) In some respects it is anticlimactic: there are no memorable pronouncements on film technique, and the subject matter is no more momentous than that which Virginia Woolf said used to occupy her for many an hour, getting fictional characters from one room to another. Still, we end where we should, with Hitchcock on the job, in collaboration, meticulously planning, and otherwise deeply engaged in his lifelong activity of turning the ordinary into the extraordinary.

On Music in Films

An Interview with Stephen Watts

When the British student of intelligent cinema turns to survey the creative side of filmmaking in his own country the names available for reference are pathetically few. Even ranging over the whole of the talkie's short history he can probably produce a bare half-dozen, say (alphabetically for safety!) Asquith, Dupont, Grierson, Hitchcock, Korda, and Saville, and only the two last-named of these can be regarded, at the moment, as contributors to the ordinary cinema.

But the arrival of *Waltzes from Vienna* and the news that he has joined the Gaumont-British organization bring back to prominence the name of Alfred Hitchcock.

His return to active direction is almost accidental. After his term as production supervisor at British International—a regrettable, fallow period for the keen intelligence which gave us *Blackmail* and *Murder!*—and his signing a contract for Korda, he was approached by Tom Arnold, the theatrical manager, to supervise the filming of *Waltzes from Vienna*. The step from that to actually directing it was taken because the subject interested Hitchcock so much.

It sounds strange that the most unremittingly cinematic of our directors, the realist and humanist, Hitchcock, should undertake what seemed like simply the rendering into celluloid of a stage musical success.

The clue is in that word "musical." He saw here a chance to do

"On Music in Films" an interview with Stephen Watts was originally published in *Cinema Quarterly* (Edinburgh) 2, no. 2 (Winter 1933–1934): 80–83.

two things: to try out some of his ideas about the relation of music to the film, and try to prove that a film that *is* a film can be created out of a ready-made theater subject.

It was of these beliefs and theories about music and the film that Hitchcock talked to me, illustrating his points with instances from the film he was then busily engaged on cutting.

"The arrival of talkies, as you know, temporarily killed action in pictures," he began, "but it did just as much damage to music. Producers and directors were obsessed by words. They forgot that one of the greatest emotional factors in the silent cinema was the musical accompaniment. They have gradually realized that action should still come first—that, talkies or not, they are still making motion pictures. But music as an artistic asset of the film is still sadly neglected.

"I was greatly interested in music and films in the silent days and I have always believed that the coming of sound opened up a great new opportunity. The accompanying music came at last entirely under the control of the people who made the picture. That was surely an advance on having a separate score played by cinema orchestras. The tremendous advantage of a film being musically accompanied had been demonstrated by 'silents' like *Ben Hur* and *Way Down East*. Yet when it became possible to blend film and music together in an artistic entity the opportunity was overlooked, or at least left undeveloped.

"The result is that the only dramatic use of music in talkies— leaving out of account the 'musicals' which interpolate 'numbers' rather than employ music—is the crude instance of slow music for love scenes. Anything else has been an odd stunt and not a properly worked out scheme.

"But that conventional soft music is the basis of the right idea— expressing the mood of the scene. It is an elementary application of it."

"Do you believe, then, that every film should have a complete musical score before it goes into the production?" I asked.

"I do," Hitchcock replied emphatically. "Though by 'complete' I do not mean continuous. That would be monotonous. Silence is often very effective and its effect is heightened by the proper handling of the music before and after.

"There is, somewhere, the correct musical accompaniment for

almost any scene—music which will improve the scene. But none at all is better than the wrong music."

"But how would you relate music and·action? What would you say was the underlying purpose of all film-music? Can you give me an example?" I asked.

"Well, the first and obvious use is atmospheric. To create excitement. To heighten intensity. In a scene of action, for instance, when the aim is to build up to a physical climax, music adds excitement just as effectively as cutting—but I shall have more to say about that comparison later. Music can also be a background to a scene in any mood and a commentary on dialogue, but, frankly, I have not yet made up my mind about the function of music in relation to dialogue in general. I can only give specific instances where I think it might be profitably used."

"Surely the trouble there," I suggested, "is that an audience cannot listen to and appreciate both words and the musical background at the same time?"

"Partly that. But not entirely. I might argue that I do not want the audience to listen consciously to the music at all. It might be achieving its desired effect without the audience being aware of how that effect was being achieved.

"No. The problem goes deeper than that. Music with certain types of dialogue might be made to achieve a great deal, and here I can give you an apt illustration from *Waltzes from Vienna*.

"There is a dialogue scene between a young man and a woman. It is a quiet, tender scene. But the woman's husband is on his way. The obvious way to get suspense is to cut every now and then to glimpses of the husband traveling towards the house. In the silent days, when the villain was coming, you always had the orchestra playing quickening music. You *felt* the menace. Well, you can still have that and keep the sense of the talk-scene going as well. And the result is that you don't need to insist pictorially on the husband's approach.

"I think I used about six feet of film out of the three hundred feet used in the sequence to flash to the husband. The feeling of approaching climax can be suggested by the music.

"It is in the psychological use of music, which, you will observe, they knew something about before talkies, that the great possibilities lie.

"It makes it possible to express the unspoken. For instance, two people may be saying one thing and thinking something very different. Their looks match their words, not their thoughts. They may be talking politely and quietly, but there may be a storm coming. You cannot express the mood of that situation by word and photograph. But I think you could get at the underlying idea with the right background music. It may sound far-fetched to compare a dramatic talkie with opera, but there is something in common. In opera quite frequently the music echoes the words that have just been spoken. That is one way music with dialogue can be used.

"*Waltzes from Vienna* gave me many opportunities for working out ideas in the relation of film and music. Naturally every cut in the film was worked out on the script before shooting began. But more than that, the musical cuts were worked out too.

"Let me give you an example. As you probably know, *Waltzes from Vienna* tells the story of the conception, composition, and first performance of 'The Blue Danube.' Obviously there has to be a long musical sequence when the piece is first played in public—one of the big scenes of the picture. In what I have been saying about music in films I have supposed the action to be the inspiration of the music. But in this case the music had to inspire the action. All the camera has to work with is the orchestra, the conductor, and the audience. The human angle is the conductor—the younger Strauss—and the people of the story who are listening. So I arranged the cutting to match the rhythm of the music. It is difficult to describe in words. You must visualize the film moving in time with the music. In the slow passages the cutting is slow, when the music quickens the mood of the melody is followed by the quick cutting.

"Then, again, there is a good instance of the sort of thing I have aimed at in the scene when Strauss, a young baker, conceives the tune while at work. There the action—composed of simple things like bakers kneading dough and rolls falling into baskets—moves in time with the music which is forming in the young man's brain.

"Film music and cutting have a great deal in common. The purpose of both is to create the *tempo* and mood of the scene. And, just as the ideal cutting is the kind you don't notice *as* cutting, so with music."

"You think then that cutting, montage, or whatever you like

to call it, cannot do all that is required to establish the mood of a film, Mr. Hitchcock?"

"Exactly, I think cutting has definite limitations. Its best use is in violent subjects. That is why the Russians made such effective use of it, because they were dealing with violence, and they could pile shock on shock by means of cutting. But have you noticed that since they started to make quieter subjects, concerned with agriculture, etc., their montage has not been so noticeable or effective? If I am sitting here with you discussing the Five-Year Plan, no amount of cutting can make a film of us dramatic because the scene is not dramatic. You cannot achieve quiet, restrained effects that way. But you might express the mood and tone of our conversation with music that would illuminate or even subtly comment on it.

"Please make it clear that I am not laying down laws on this subject. I am simply experimenting in theory as I have done in practice in *Waltzes from Vienna*. There are lots of things that I have not made up my mind about. But I do think that any intelligent attempt to harness music to films is a step forward. Words and incidental noises and 'song numbers' are surely not all the sound track was invented for.

"The basis of the cinema's appeal is emotional. Music's appeal is to a great extent emotional, too. To neglect music, I think, is to surrender, willfully or not, a chance of progress in filmmaking."

Close Your Eyes
and Visualize!

In North London, on the banks of the Grand Junction Canal, stands a tall building topped by a giant chimney. In 1924 the film critic of the *Daily Express* said, concerning a film made in this building, that it was "the best American picture made in England."

That film, *Woman to Woman,* starring Clive Brook and Betty Compson, was made at what are now the Gainsborough studios and was produced by the embryonic Gainsborough Company for Famous Players-Lasky. Therein lies my debt to America, for in the beginning I was American trained and under the old F.P.-L. banner dug myself in and studied the branches of the movie game.

On *Woman to Woman* I was the general factotum. I wrote the script. I designed the sets, and I managed the production. It was the first film that I had really got my hands on to. Up till then I had been trained as an engineer, studied art, earned fifteen shillings a week in an advertising agency and, finding this depressing, finally managed to sell myself to the American unit at Islington as a writer of subtitles on the silent films.

Michael Balcon took over the studios from F.P.-L. and under him I made my first film, *The Pleasure Garden.* Others which fol-

"Close Your Eyes and Visualize!" was originally published in *Stage,* July 1936, 52–53. It was also printed, with slight changes, including omitting the last paragraph, as "I Make Suspense My Business," a copy of which is on BFI microfiche no. 10, but with no indication of the place of publication or date. Also on BFI microfiche no. 10, there is a copy of a typescript called "Production Notes—6 July 1936" written by Hitchcock, titled "I Try to Make 'Motion' Pictures." It begins with paragraph four of the above essay and includes a paragraph at the end that is not in the printed version, which I include in brackets here.

lowed were *The Lodger, The Ring, Juno and the Paycock, Blackmail, Murder!,* and *The Skin Game.* I played about with "technique" in those early days. I tried crazy tricks with violent cuts, dissolves, and wipes with everything in the room spinning round and standing on its head. People used to call it "the Hitchcock touch," but it never occurred to me that I was merely wasting footage with camera tricks and not getting on with the film.

I have stopped all that today. I have not the film time to throw away on fancy stuff. I like my screen well used, with every corner filled, but no arty theories clamping the action down. Nowadays I want the cutting and continuity to be as inconspicuous as possible, and all I am concerned with is to get the characters developed and the story clearly told without any directorial idiosyncrasies.

The creed that I chalk up in front of me today is that we are making *Motion Pictures.* Too many men forget that. A film has got to be ocularly interesting and above all it is the picture which is the thing. I try to tell my story so much so in pictures that if by any chance the sound apparatus broke down in the cinema, the audience would not fret and get restless because the pictorial action would still hold them! Sound is all right in its place, but it is a silent picture training which counts today. Naval men have a theory that the finest navigators nowadays are the men who learnt their craft in the out-of-date sailing ships. Similarly I maintain that the young men of America and Britain who strike out into the film game should first go through a course of silent film technique.

There is not enough visualizing done in studios, and instead far too much writing. People take a sheet of paper and scrawl down a lot of dialogue and instructions and call that a day's work. It leads them nowhere. There is also a growing habit of reading a film script by the dialogue alone. I deplore this method, this lazy neglect of the action, this lack of reading action in a film story, or, if you like it, this inability to visualize.

I try to do without paper when I begin a new film. I visualize my story in my mind as a series of smudges moving over a variety of backgrounds. Often I pick my backgrounds first and then think about the action of the story. This was the case in *The Man Who Knew Too Much.* I visualized the snow-clad heights of the Alps and the ill-lit alleys of London and threw my story and characters in amongst it all.

I do not despise sound in my preference for pictures first, but when I am told that the talking picture has a bigger range of subjects, I argue that it also lessens the field of appeal. What appeals to the eye is universal; what appeals to the ear is local.

My methods of filmmaking and the introduction of those legendary Hitchcock touches are quite straightforward. I like to keep the public guessing and never let them know what is going to happen next. I build up my interest gradually and surely and, in thrillers, bring it to a crescendo. There must be no half measures, and I have to know where I am going every second of the time. If there is a secret in doing this, it is perhaps in knowing your script by heart. Then you know automatically the tempo of each succeeding scene and it matters not whether they are shot out of proper order. But also I have to guard against going too fast in a film. This is fatal. I have to remember that, whereas *I* know the story backwards, the audience has got to absorb it gradually. Otherwise the whole thing would be too sketchy to be intelligible.

My artistes, too, must behave as human beings, and in my determination to achieve this ideal perhaps arises the story about my loathing of women in my films. I don't loathe them, but if they are going to appear in one of my pictures, they are not going to look too beautiful or be too glamorous. Glamour has nothing to do with reality and I maintain that reality is the most important factor in the making of a successful film. The very beautiful woman who just walks around, avoiding the furniture, wearing fluffy negligees, and looking very seductive may be an attractive ornament, but she does not help the film any. I hate it when actresses try to be ladies and in doing so become cold and lifeless, and nothing gives me more pleasure than to knock the ladylikeness out of chorus girls. I don't ask much of an actress and I have no wish for her to be able to play a whole list of character roles, but she *must* be a real human person. That is why I deliberately deprived Madeleine Carroll of her dignity and glamour in *The 39 Steps*, and I have done exactly the same thing in *Secret Agent*. In this last film, the first shot you see of her is with her face covered with cold cream!

Next to reality, I put the accent on comedy. Comedy, strangely enough, makes a film more dramatic. A stage play gives you intermissions for reflections on each act. These intermissions have to be supplied in a film by contrasts and, if a film is dramatic or tragic, the obvious contrast is comedy. In all my films I try to supply a definite contrast. I take a dramatic situation up and up to its peak of excitement and then, before it has time to start the downward curve, I introduce comedy to relieve the tension. After that, I feel safe with the climax. If the film petered to an end without any contrast, the climax would probably turn into an anticlimax. Which heaven forbid!

I am out to give the public good, healthy, mental shake-ups. Civilization has become so screening and sheltering that we cannot experience sufficient thrills at first hand. Therefore, to prevent our becoming sluggish and jellified, we have to experience them artificially, and the screen is the best medium for this. In *The Man Who Knew Too Much,* in *The 39 Steps,* and now in *Secret Agent* I have been all out for wholehearted thrills, the more exciting the better. But my thrills are not horror thrills, but full-blooded, healthy stuff for which there is always an eternal demand.

But it must be pictures first and last. A little sound certainly, but used only when the story offers a perfectly natural opportunity for it. I aim today to jolt cinemagoers in their seats with stories that move—with unexpected thrills, with comedy, with reality, and with backgrounds that tell, and finally with human beings, and that means if any actress comes onto my set and dares . . . !

[Finally I have been very lucky. My ideas, my methods, my tricks in film production have all been given free play. I have been allowed to experiment. This I owe to one man, Michael Balcon. Balcon, Director of Productions at the Gaumont-British studios, has been associated with me since I began. It is he who has allowed me to follow my celluloid whims and I am grateful to him.]

Search for the Sun

Filmgoers, lying back in upholstered comfort in the cinemas today, are apt to take a film for granted. In a sense they are right, for they are there to be entertained and not to worry about how the film got there. I sometimes think, however, that if they but know of some of our "headaches" and difficulties behind the scenes, theirs would be a greater appreciation when the film is finally unspooled before their critical eyes.

Largely on account of the machinations of cartoonists and fiction writers, the public in general has a delightfully distorted idea of what goes on in a film studio. Their scanty knowledge is astoundingly applied, as in the case of a lady visitor to a studio who looked at the small microphone suspended above the heads of the artists and said: "What a strange place to put a camera!" I find that the general impression of studio life is that we exist in unparalleled luxury, using gold telephones, employing ravishing secretaries, and doing a little work when the spirit, which is conveyed in our platinum-bound limousines, moves us.

To dispel that illusion, I should like to draw a little word picture. Out in a field near Harrow, "London" stands. It is a complete replica of a London street scene, built for my new Gaumont-British thriller, *Sabotage*. Fully equipped shops, trams, buses, traffic lights, beacons, overhead railway, and hundreds of pedestrians are there, but nothing is happening. The cameras are covered up, the

"Search for the Sun" was originally published in the *New York Times*, February 7, 1937, X, 5.

microphone is shrouded, the crowds stand huddled against the shops. I crouch muffled up and chilled to the marrow in a temporary shelter; my stars, Sylvia Sidney and John Loder, wait desolate and frozen in a doorway. And why? Because it is raining as it has never rained before, rain which drips off my hat and down my collar and which has held us up till tempers are frayed for three nights running.

In short, the greatest difficulty we have in making films in England is to combat the climate. The public, ever critical, is perpetually rising on its hind legs to demand why we don't shake off the shackles of the studio and get out to film the countryside. Might I say in retaliation that the money we have already spent in trying to film the country would make a considerable hole in the national debt, money that has been spent in fruitless excursions with large production units up and down the land in search of the sun, waiting week in and week out for the little gleam of light that will permit us to put a real street or real landscape on the screen.

Scots clamor for Scotland to be put on the screen, but how can we help them when the highlands are invariably swept with mist and rain? Perhaps the only time that the Scottish countryside has really been visible in a film was in *The 39 Steps,* when we decided that it was now or never and made a rapid journey to the highlands in March. By some stroke of fortune the mist held up and the most successful shots of Richard Hannay escaping over the hills were, strangely enough, filmed in a rainstorm.

Weather has terrors aplenty for us, but oddly enough the coming of sound in films has added another difficulty. I have a penchant for including scenes of London in my films and in the old silent days we made endless excursions into the capital, shooting where and when we liked. Today the extra equipment of sound hampers such maneuvers. It is impossible to record dialogue scenes in a crowded thoroughfare with the roar of traffic and clatter of passersby drowning the words of the stars. That is why in the recent case of *Sabotage* I had to build "London" in a field. True, I still had my traffic and pedestrians, but I could control them by building the roadway slightly on the slant. Then I could have buses and vehicles coasting silently by while my artists conducted their conversation on the pavement. Proper traffic sounds were carefully blended in later.

Nevertheless if you ask me which are my three major difficulties in filmmaking, I should say dogs, babies, and boats! Dogs have a will of their own and are impervious to film direction. Also they get lost. On one of my first films, *The Pleasure Garden,* we were using a black-and-tan terrier who quietly vanished halfway through the film. It was imperative that we replace him for further scenes, but the new dog had to be an exact replica. We did the best we could. The new dog was made up to resemble the missing hound and even had a false tail stuck on. The difficulty arose when, the dog's dignity being offended, he proceeded to lick off all the makeup between shots!

Babies unnerve me when they won't cry to order. Somehow I fight back the inherent desire to stick a pin in them and nowadays I have tumbled on the most successful ruse. I get the attendant mother to walk away from her child on the set, which results in the most satisfactory howls!

Boats of any sorts are completely unmanageable. They have an exasperating way of disappearing around bends, leaving you with no way to summon them back for retakes.

Finally there is the sort of difficulty which is the least expected. Such a one occurred during the making of *The 39 Steps.* We had built a realistic Scottish landscape in the G.B. Studios and they thought that the addition of some sheep would increase the effect. Unfortunately realism in this case went too far. A sheep has a very definite appetite. Sixty-two appetites went surging over this bit of "Scotland" and proceeded to eat it before the horror-stricken eyes of the production unit!

Direction

Many people think a film director does all his work in the studio, drilling the actors, making them do what he wants. That is not at all true of my own methods, and I can write only of my own methods. I like to have a film complete in my mind before I go on the floor. Sometimes the first idea one has of a film is of a vague pattern, a sort of haze with a certain shape. There is possibly a colorful opening developing into something more intimate; then, perhaps in the middle, a progression to a chase or some other adventure; and sometimes at the end of the big shape of a climax, or maybe some twist or surprise. You see this hazy pattern, and then you have to find a narrative idea to suit it. Or a story may give you an idea first and you have to develop it into a pattern.

Imagine an example of a standard plot—let us say a conflict between love and duty. This idea was the origin of my first talkie, *Blackmail*. The hazy pattern one saw beforehand was duty—love—love versus duty—and finally either duty or love, one or the other. The whole middle section was built up on the theme of love versus duty, after duty and love had been introduced separately in turn. So I had first to put on the screen an episode expressing duty.

I showed the arrest of a criminal by Scotland Yard detectives, and tried to make it as concrete and detailed as I could. You

"Direction" was originally published in Charles Davy, ed., *Footnotes to the Film*, (New York: Oxford University Press, 1937), 3–15. It was also published in *Sight & Sound* (Summer 1937), reprinted in LaValley, *Focus on Hitchcock*, 32–39, and in slightly abridged form as "My Own Methods" in David Wilson, ed., *Sight & Sound: A Fiftieth Anniversary Selection* (London: Faber and Faber, 1982), 36–42.

even saw the detectives take the man to the lavatory to wash his hands—nothing exciting, just the routine of duty. Then the young detective says he's going out that evening with his girl, and the sequence ends, pointing on from duty to love. Then you start showing the relationship between the detective and his girl: they are middle-class people. The love theme doesn't run smoothly; there is a quarrel and the girl goes off by herself, just because the young man has kept her waiting a few minutes. So your story starts; the girl falls in with the villain—he tries to seduce her and she kills him. Now you've got your problem prepared. Next morning, as soon as the detective is put on to the murder case, you have your conflict—love versus duty. The audience know that he will be trying to track down his own girl, who has done the murder, so you sustain their interest: they wonder what will happen next.

The blackmailer was really a subsidiary theme. I wanted him to go through and expose the girl. That was my idea of how the story ought to end. I wanted the pursuit to be after the girl, not after the blackmailer. That would have brought the conflict on to a climax, with the young detective, ahead of the others, trying to push the girl out through a window to get her away, and the girl turning round and saying: "You can't do that—I must give myself up." Then the rest of the police arrive, misinterpret what he is doing, and say, "Good man, you've got her," not knowing this relationship between them. Now the reason for the opening comes to light. You repeat every shot used first to illustrate the duty theme, only now it is the girl who is the criminal. The young man is there ostensibly as a detective, but of course the audience know he is in love with the girl. The girl is locked up in her cell and the two detectives walk away, and the older one says, "Going out with your girl tonight?" The younger one shakes his head. "No. Not tonight."

That was the ending I wanted for *Blackmail,* but I had to change it for commercial reasons. The girl couldn't be left to face her fate. And that shows you how the films suffer from their own power of appealing to millions. They could often be subtler than they are, but their own popularity won't let them.

But to get back to the early work on a film. With the help of my wife, who does the technical continuity, I plan out a script very carefully, hoping to follow it exactly, all the way through, when shooting starts. In fact, this working on the script is the real making of the film, for me. When I've done it, the film is finished already in my mind. Usually, too, I don't find it necessary to do more than supervise the editing myself. I know it is said sometimes that a director ought to edit his own pictures if he wants to control their final form, for it is in the editing, according to this view, that a film is really brought into being. But if the scenario is planned out in detail, and followed closely during production, editing should be easy. All that has to be done is to cut away irrelevancies and see that the finished film is an accurate rendering of the scenario.

Settings, of course, come into the preliminary plan, and usually I have fairly clear ideas about them; I was an art student before I took up with films. Sometimes I even think of backgrounds first. *The Man Who Knew Too Much* started like that; I looked in my mind's eye at snowy Alps and dingy London alleys, and threw my characters into the middle of the contrast. Studio settings, however, are often a problem; one difficulty is that extreme effects—extremes of luxury or extremes of squalor—are much the easiest to register on the screen. If you try to reproduce the average sitting room in Golders Green or Streatham it is apt to come out looking like nothing in particular, just nondescript. It is true that I have tried lately to get interiors with a real lower-middle-class atmosphere—for instance, the Verloc's living-room in *Sabotage*—but there's always a certain risk in giving your audience humdrum truth.

However, in time the script and the sets are finished somehow and we are ready to start shooting. One great problem that occurs at once, and keeps on occurring, is to get the players to adapt themselves to film technique. Many of them, of course, come from the stage; they are not cinema-minded at all. So, quite naturally, they like to play long scenes straight ahead. I am willing to work with the long uninterrupted shot: you can't avoid it altogether, and you can get some variety by having two cameras running, one close up and one farther off, and cutting from one to the other when the film is edited. But if I have to shoot a long scene continuously I always feel I am losing grip on it, from a cinematic point of view. The camera, I feel, is simply standing there, *hoping* to catch something with a visual point to it. What I like to do always is to photograph just the little bits of a scene that I really need for building up a visual sequence. I want to put my film together on the screen, not simply to photograph something that has been put together already in the form of a long piece of stage acting. This is what gives an effect of life to a picture—the feeling that when you

see it on the screen you are watching something that has been conceived and brought to birth directly in visual terms. The screen
ought to speak its own language, freshly coined, and it can't do
that unless it treats an acted scene as a piece of raw material which
must be broken up, taken to bits, before it can be woven into an
expressive visual pattern.

You can see an example of what I mean in *Sabotage*. Just before
Verloc is killed there is a scene made up entirely of short pieces of
film, separately photographed. This scene has to show how Verloc
comes to be killed—how the thought of killing him arises in Sylvia
Sidney's mind and connects itself with the carving knife she uses
when they sit down to dinner. But the sympathy of the audience
has to be kept with Sylvia Sidney; it must be clear that Verloc's
death, finally, is an accident. So, as she serves at the table, you see
her unconsciously serving vegetables with the carving knife, as
though her hand were keeping hold of the knife of its own accord.
The camera cuts from her hand to her eyes and back to her hand;
then back to her eyes as she suddenly becomes aware of the knife
making its error. Then to a normal shot—the man unconcernedly
eating; then back to the hand holding the knife. In an older style
of acting Sylvia would have had to show the audience what was
passing in her mind by exaggerating facial expression. But people
today in real life often don't show their feelings in their faces: so
the film treatment showed the audience her mind through her
hand, through its unconscious grasp on the knife. Now the camera
moves again to Verloc—back to the knife—back again to his face.
You see him seeing the knife, realizing its implication. The tension
between the two is built up with the knife as its focus.

Now when the camera has immersed the audience so closely in
a scene such as this, it can't instantly become objective again. It
must broaden the movement of the scene without loosening the
tension. Verloc gets up and walks round the table, coming so close
to the camera that you feel, if you are sitting in the audience, almost as though you must move back to make room for him. Then
the camera moves to Sylvia Sidney again, then returns to the subject—the knife.

So you gradually build up the psychological situation, piece by
piece, using the camera to emphasize first one detail, then another.
The point is to draw the audience right inside the situation instead
of leaving them to watch it from outside, from a distance. And you

can do this only by breaking the action up into details and cutting from one to the other, so that each detail is forced in turn on the attention of the audience and reveals its psychological meaning. If you played the whole scene straight through, and simply made a photographic record of it with the camera always in one position, you would lose your power over the audience. They would watch the scene without becoming really involved in it, and you would have no means of concentrating their attention on those particular visual details which make them feel what the characters are feeling.

This way of building up a picture means that film work hasn't much need for the virtuoso actor who gets his effects and climaxes himself, who plays directly on to the audience with the force of his talent and personality. The screen actor has got to be much more plastic; he has to submit himself to be used by the director and the camera. Mostly he is wanted to behave quietly and naturally (which, of course, isn't at all easy), leaving the camera to add most of the accents and emphases. I would almost say that the best screen actor is the man who can do nothing extremely well.

One way of using the camera to give emphasis is the reaction shot. By the reaction shot I mean any close-up which illustrates an event by showing instantly the reaction to it of a person or group. The door opens for some one to come in, and before showing who it is you cut to the expressions of the persons already in the room. Or, while one person is talking, you keep your camera on some one else who is listening. This over-running of one person's image with another person's voice is a method peculiar to the talkies; it is one of the devices which help the talkies to tell a story faster than a silent film could tell it, and faster than it could be told on the stage.

Or, again, you can use the camera to give emphasis whenever the attention of the audience has to be focused for a moment on a certain player. There is no need for him to raise his voice or move to the center of the stage or to do anything dramatic. A close-up will do it all for him—will give him, so to speak, the stage all to himself.

I must say that in recent years I have come to make much less use of obvious camera devices. I have become more commercially minded; afraid that anything at all subtle may be missed. I have learnt from experience how easily small touches are overlooked.

The other day a journalist came to interview me and we spoke about film technique. "I always remember," he said, "a little bit in one of your silent films, *The Ring*. The young boxer comes home after winning his fight. He is flushed with success—wants to celebrate. He pours out champagne all round. Then he finds that his wife is out, and he knows at once that she is out with another man. At this moment the camera cuts to a glass of champagne; you see a fizz of bubbles rise off it and there it stands untasted, going flat. That one shot gives you the whole feeling of the scene." Yes, I said, that sort of imagery may be quite good: I don't despise it and still use it now and then. But is it always noticed? There was another bit in *The Ring* which I believe hardly anyone noticed.

The scene was outside a boxing-booth at a fair with a barker talking to the crowd. Inside the booth a professional is taking on all comers. He has always won in the first round. A man comes running out of the booth and speaks to the barker: something unexpected has happened. Then a cut straight to the ringside: you see an old figure 1 being taken down and replaced by a brand new figure 2. I meant this single detail to show that the boxer, now, is up against some one he can't put out in the first round. But it went by too quickly. Perhaps I might have shown the new figure 2 being taken out of a paper wrapping—something else was needed to make the audience see in a moment that the figure for the second round had never been used before.

The film always has to deal in exaggerations. Its methods reflect the simple contrasts of black and white photography. One advantage of color is that it would give you more intermediate shades. I should never want to fill the screen with color: it ought to be used economically—to put new words into the screen's visual language when there's a need for them. You could start to color film with a boardroom scene: somber panelling and furniture, the directors all in dark clothes and white collars. Then the chairman's wife comes in, wearing a red hat. She takes the attention of the audience at once, just because of that one note of color. Or suppose a gangster story: the leader of the gang is sitting in a café with a man he suspects. He has told his gunman to watch the table. "If I order a glass of port, bump him off. If I order green chartreuse, let him go."

This journalist asked me also about distorted sound—a device I tried in *Blackmail* when the word "knife" hammers on the consciousness of the girl at breakfast on the morning after the murder.

Again, I think this kind of effect may be justified. There have always been occasions when we have needed to show a phantasmagoria of the mind in terms of visual imagery. So we may want to show some one's mental state by letting him listen to some sound—let us say church bells—and making them clang with distorted insistence in his head. But on the whole nowadays I try to tell a story in the simplest possible way, so that I can feel sure it will hold the attention of any audience and won't puzzle them. I know there are critics who ask why lately I have made only thrillers. Am I satisfied, they say, with putting on the screen the equivalent merely of popular novelettes? Part of the answer is that I am out to get the best stories I can which will suit the film medium, and I have usually found it necessary to take a hand in writing them myself.

There is a shortage of good writing for the screen, and is that surprising? A playwright may take a year or more writing a play, but in a year the film industry has to make hundreds of films. More and more pictures, one after the other incessantly, with a certain standard to keep up—it throws a great strain on the creative faculties of every one who has to supply the industry with ideas. Of course there must be cooperation, division of labor, all the time. The old saying, "No one man ever made a picture," is entirely true. And the only answer found so far to the writing problem has been to employ a number of writers to work together on the same picture. Metro-Goldwyn, we are told, employ altogether a staff of eighty or ninety writers, so they can draw at any time on a whole group of writers to see a story through. I don't say there aren't drawbacks in this collective method, but it often makes things easier when time is at stake, as it always is in film production. In this country we can't usually afford to employ large writing staffs, so I have had to join in and become a writer myself. I choose crime stories because that is the kind of story I can write, or help to write, myself—the kind of story I can turn most easily into a successful film. It is the same with Charles Bennett, who has so often worked with me; he is essentially a writer of melodrama. I am ready to use other stories, but I can't find writers who will give them to me in a suitable form.

Sometimes I have been asked what films I should make if I were free to do exactly as I liked without having to think about the box office. There are several examples I can give very easily. For one thing, I should like to make travel films with a personal element in them: that would be quite a new field. Or I should like to do a verbatim of a celebrated trial—of course there would have to be some editing, some cutting down. The Thompson-Bywaters case, for instance. You can see the figures at Madame Tussaud's and the newspapers gave long reports of the trial. The cinema could reconstruct the whole story. Or there is the fire at sea possibility—that has never been tackled seriously on the screen. It might be too terrifying for some audiences but it would make a great subject, worth doing.

British producers are often urged to make more films about characteristic phases of English life. Why, they are asked, do we see so little of the English farmer or the English seaman? Or is there not plenty of good material in the great British industries—in mining or shipbuilding or steel? One difficulty here is that English audiences seem to take more interest in American life—I suppose because it has a novelty value. They are rather easily bored by everyday scenes in their own country. But I certainly should like to make a film of the Derby, only it might not be quite in the popular class. It would be hard to invent a Derby story that wasn't hackneyed, conventional. I would rather do it more as a documentary— a sort of pageant, an animated modern version of Frith's "Derby Day." I would show everything that goes on all round the course, but without a story.

Perhaps the average audience isn't ready for that, yet. Popular taste, all the same, does move; today you can put over scenes that would have been ruled out a few years ago. Particularly towards comedy, nowadays, there is a different attitude. You can get comedy out of your stars, and you used not to be allowed to do anything which might knock the glamour off them.

In 1926 I made a film called *Downhill,* from a play by Ivor Novello, who acted in the film himself, with Ian Hunter and Isabel Jeans. There was a sequence showing a quarrel between Hunter and Novello. It started as an ordinary fight; then they began throwing things at one another. They tried to pick up heavy pedestals to throw and the pedestals bowled them over. In other words I made it comic. I even put Hunter into a morning coat and striped trousers because I felt that a man never looks so ridiculous as when he is well dressed and fighting. This whole scene was cut out; they said I was guying Ivor Novello. It was ten years before its time.

I say ten years, because you may remember that in 1936 M.G.M. showed a comedy called *Libeled Lady*. There is a fishing sequence in it: William Powell stumbles about in the river, falls flat, and gets soaked and catches a big fish by accident. Here you have a star, not a slapstick comedian, made to do something pretty near slapstick. In *The 39 Steps*, too, a little earlier, I was allowed to drag Madeleine Carroll over the moors handcuffed to the hero; I made her get wet and untidy and look ridiculous for the purpose of the story. I couldn't have done that ten years ago.

I foresee the decline of the individual comedian. Of course there may always be specially gifted comedians who will have films written round them, but I think public taste is turning to like comedy and drama more mixed up; and this is another move away from the conventions of the stage. In a play your divisions are much more rigid; you have a scene—then curtain, and after an interval another scene starts. In a film you keep your whole action flowing; you can have comedy and drama running together and weave them in and out. Audiences are much readier now than they used to be for sudden changes of mood; and this means more freedom for a director. The art of directing for the commercial market is to know just how far you can go. In many ways I am freer now to do what I want to do than I was a few years ago. I hope in time to have more freedom still—if audiences will give it to me.

Some Aspects of Direction

The Script

Many people imagine that the director's work begins in the studio and is confined to handling the actors. In my case this is not true: before I go into the studio I like to have the whole film complete in my mind. I like to have the whole story down, shot by shot, on paper, and this means working a lot on the script before I even enter the studio. The preliminary steps are something like this.

First, when I've got my story I like to strip it right down to the bone—just take the essentials and write them down so they only cover about a single sheet of paper. When I have made the picture I like to feel that if a man in the audience is asked what it's about he will describe it just as I did on this one sheet. That is the beginning. Next comes the forming of the pattern the picture's going to take. I have a hand in this, treating the essential ideas in a way which I feel is suited to the film medium and planning out the course the script should take. Now, the writers get to work, filling out the completed plan. This is usually a two months' job and is a highly important stage to which a full understanding of the general plan is essential to all the writers. For example, as soon as the plan of the first sequence is written out it must be shown and explained carefully to the dialogue writer so that he can feel exactly the mood of

"Some Aspects of Direction" was originally published in *National Board of Review Magazine* 13, no. 7 (October 1938): 6–8. It was based on a radio talk, "The Making of a Melodrama," aired on WNYC on July 12, 1938, on a show hosted by Otis Ferguson (Spoto, 201).

speech required. And so, gradually, with all the writing units coop-
erating with each other, the full story is completed.

But there is still another step to come before shooting begins:
when the treatment is on paper and the dialogue added, the whole
script must be cut up into individual shots. When this has been
done I feel the worst is over. I have an exact plan of operation and
can go straight ahead putting it into celluloid. But cooperation between the writers must come first; they must be willing to discuss
and reject their own material when necessary and help to be part
of a single unit. Personally, I prefer writers without reputations; I
find them more agreeable to changes in their work and willing to
learn. An established writer often thinks his way must be best, or
imagines there is no difference between writing a novel or play and
writing for the movies. He forgets that the problems and situations
of the stage are very different from those of the screen. These differences are best illustrated, I think, by analyzing an actual sequence in a movie, so I would like to take the first sequence of my
picture *Secret Agent* as an example.

I had to begin this picture by telling the audience that it was
wartime, and that the British Foreign Office wanted to use a young
lieutenant as a spy in the Eastern war zone. So they pretended the
lieutenant had been killed in France, and secretly brought him to
London to give him his orders. Now if I had told these facts in a
screen caption, in a form of a dialogue, or shown the young lieutenant arriving alive from France, the result would have been pretty
dull. So instead I began the film with a close-up of a coffin. The
coffin stands in a darkened room, covered by a British flag, and immediately creates a mood of total solemnity. This mood is deep-
ened as the camera starts to move backwards, very slowly, almost
as though it were on tiptoe itself, and the audience sees four tall
candles burning at the corners of the coffin, and then the assembled mourners. When this scene has had time to sink in, the mourners slowly file out of the room until only one person is left behind—the one-armed servant, who reverently closes the big doors
when the room is empty. Then, left alone, he fumbles for a cigarette, slips it in his mouth, and lights it from one of the candles.
This lack of reverence is enough to change the mood of the audience from tragedy to suspicion. Then the servant goes up to the
coffin, snatches off the flag, and tries to pull the coffin off its stand.
It is too heavy and clumsy for his one arm; it falls, and the lid flies

off. The coffin is empty! The servant turns away and looks disgust-
edly at the portrait of a young man on the wall. After the group
picture of the mourners, the camera has been brought up close to
the one-armed man. Now it shifts to the portrait on which he is
gazing. Slowly the head in the portrait fades, and I cut to the same
head on the shoulders of a very much alive young man who is sitting in a London office being given his orders for work as a spy. A
little dialogue, a shot of newspaper headlines announcing trouble
in the East, and the audience knows exactly what has happened,
who the young man is, and where he is going. A mood of mystery
has been created at once; the audience gets the idea of what is
going on, and is receptive to further impressions.

In addition to the technical facts and treatment of the situation
described above, you may notice another thing—that the audience
has been let in on the secret of the agent's identity from the start.
When I can I like to do this. I think it adds greatly to the excitement if the audience is let into a secret. They know all about it,
but they know many of the people on the screen don't know, and
that is what gets them excited. Even a small thing like the title of a
film can matter tremendously in this respect. Take *Mutiny on the
Bounty*. The audience knows there is going to be a mutiny. They
see the story develop, they watch Charles Laughton flogging his
men, and much of their excitement is in waiting for the mutiny
that they know must come and of which Laughton knows nothing.
Think what they would have missed if the film had been called *Boys
of the Bounty,* or *Rovers of the South Seas*. Yes, share your secrets
with the audiences and they will pay interest on them.

Director and Actor

One should always give one's audience every chance to know and
understand the characters they are looking at, so they can feel
what's coming and grasp what's happening. Not, of course, by obvious tricks, but by getting good actors who know how to express
a mood or intention with the slightest gesture or change of expression, like Peter Lorre. This is the way to make your characters
stand out effectively. I like an actor to play a part for which his
personal experience in life has raised him. In this way he does not
have to resort to cheap mannerisms and unnatural movements.
The best actors are those who can be effective even when they are

not doing anything. Understatement is priceless, and that is why I make melodramas, because they lend themselves so admirably to understatement.

To get back to the actors, however. A director can help a lot by taking care of his actors' physical positions. For example, suppose a man's enemy enters through a door. If the director has put the actor in an easy chair facing the door it will be more difficult for him to register antagonism than if he had been caught while straining towards an ashtray to stub out a cigarette, or groping for a collar stud under the bed. Or if he is chatting carelessly to a friend with a smile on his face, it is easier for his feelings to be expressed by the sudden vanishing of that smile than it is if he starts registering theatrical terror. It is more true to life and it is more believable. These physical details, no matter how small, are so much a part of life that they can be used with vivid force. It is exciting to show a cop running at topnotch speed to catch a crook, but it is still more exciting if the audience discovers the cop's got asthma! It brings another doubtful element into the chase. It is more natural than his tripping over a fireplug. And the sound picture has greatly increased our ability to register such details.

The Use of Sound in the Film

I believe that there should always be sound effects of some kind throughout the whole film. I don't mean constant talk, but sound. I have found that if you drop your sound effects suddenly, the picture tends to drop with it; it seems to break the continuity. But your sounds should always be as natural as possible; for example, I think we all agree that music and dialogue do not go together. It is not a natural combination. Nor do I like the toning down of sound to suit the convenience of the story—say a factory scene, when the roar of the machines is faded out so that the young man can be heard making wisecracks more distinctly. That is not natural either. Another thing to avoid is using dramatic sound in a scene which is already charged with as much drama as it can hold. It does not increase the drama—it lessens it. No, on the whole I think the chief value of such sound effects lies in giving point to a situation. Some years ago I made a picture called *Blackmail*. A girl committed a murder with a knife, ran home as fast as she could, crept upstairs to change her clothes, and came down to breakfast with the family as though nothing had happened. While she eats, a talkative old woman comes to the door and gossips outside about the murder. "Such a horrible thing" she says, "and done with a knife too," "it's just not British to kill people with a knife . . . something only a foreigner would do . . . no it's not like using a brick or something British like that, a knife isn't." As she chatters away the camera turns on the girl in the room, hearing the mutter of words come through the door with just the word "*knife*" ringing out at the end of every mumbled sentence. And then suddenly the voice of her father, clear and loud across the table: "Pass me the bread knife, Alice, dear" as the final shock, and the camera remorselessly showing it in his hands cutting through the new loaf. I think this example gives a pretty clear idea of what I mean—of how careful use of sound can help strengthen the intensity of a situation.

Lecture at
Columbia University

I have some notes here that are mixed up with a letter from my mother, and I am trying to sort them out. First of all, before we go into melodrama and suspense, about which Mr. Abbott asked me to speak to you, I wish to talk about the method one invariably uses in designing a motion picture script.

When I am given a subject, probably a book, play, or an original, I like to see it on one sheet of foolscap. That is to say, have the story, in its barest bones, just laid out on a sheet of foolscap paper. You might call it the steelwork, or just the barest bones, as I said before. Now you do not have to write down very much, maybe just that a man meets a woman at a certain place, and something else happens. In the briefest possible way, this thing should be laid out on a piece of paper.

From that, of course, we start to build the treatment of that story—the characterizations, the narrative, and even the detail, until we have probably a hundred pages of complete narrative without dialogue. But I do not mean narrative in the abstract, the practical

This talk was delivered at Columbia University for a course taught by John E. Abbott, The History of the Motion Picture (class 9, March 30, 1939, 7:00–8:30 P.M.). Typescripts of this talk are in the Hitchcock Collection at the Herrick Library and at the MOMA Film Study Center. The talk is introduced by Professor Abbott. After the portion of the lecture that I include above, Hitchcock goes on to answer questions from Mr. Abbott and members of the audience. He discusses a wide range of topics: the use of sound, the MacGuffin, Laughton in *Jamaica Inn,* difficulties with the censor in *The Man Who Knew Too Much,* the ending of his films, color in films, the use of close-ups in *Secret Agent* and *The 39 Steps,* the scenario, preplanning, realistic settings, his handling of actors, and rhythmic cutting.

side of what is going to appear on the screen. I always try to avoid having in the treatment anything that is not really visual. In dialogue we indicate it by saying, for instance, that the man goes to the sideboard, pours himself out a drink, and tells the woman that something or other is going to happen to him. We indicate it in the treatment, and this is very full and practically the complete film on paper, in terms of action and movement.

The particular reason why I prefer to do that is because I don't like to kid myself. I do not like to let myself think that there is more in it than there really is, because I believe that one should build up. That is why I prefer to start with the broad narrative, and then from that, develop into this full treatment—but purely cinematic treatment. You must not go into anything like a short story, or anything descriptive, like "with half-strangled cries" and that sort of thing. You just want the actual movement or action, and then indicate the dialogue.

Dialogue is the next phase, and that depends on how much time one has. Once the story line is decided upon and one has a dialogue writer in, one usually deals with it sequence by sequence. After the first sequence, we call the dialogue writer in and hand it to him. While he has the first sequence, we start the first sequence in treatment, and build up as we go along. Finally we have a whole pile of material which is treatment, and a whole pile of material which is dialogue.

From that stage we go into the shooting script, by assembling the dialogue and the treatment. We keep building it even further, and adding to it. We do not do this in a mechanical way, but put up as many ideas as we possibly can. Finally we have a shooting script of the whole thing. Then we cast it, shoot it, and finally it is shown.

A member of the audience sees that film, and probably after seeing it goes home and tells his wife about it. She wants to know what it was like, so he tells her that it was about a man who met a girl—and whatever he tells his wife is what you should have had on that piece of paper in the very beginning. That is the complete cycle that I like to aim for, as far as possible, and that is the process one works on in designing a motion picture script.

Now to talk about melodrama, you know, of course, that melodrama was the original mainstay of motion pictures material, on account of its obvious physical action and physical situation. After

all, the words "motion picture" mean action and movement. Melodrama lends itself very much—perhaps more than before the talkies
came in; more than anything else, I mean.

You know we had the early chase films, and we had those
French pictures where a man used to run around Paris. He was on
a bicycle and knocked people over as he went along. Are there any
of these films in the museum?

Mr. Abbott: Yes.

Of course, in those days, and even up to the coming of the talking picture, the characters were pretty well cardboard figures. One
advantage that the talking picture has given us is that it allowed us
to delineate character a little more, through the medium of dialogue. The talking picture has given us more character, and obviously, in the long run, that is what we are going to rely upon.

There has been a tendency, I feel, in the past, in this development of character, to rely upon the dialogue, only, to do it. We have
lost what has been—to me, at least—the biggest enjoyment in motion pictures, and that is action and movement. What I am trying
to aim for is a combination of these two elements, character and
action.

The difficulty is, I feel, that the two rhythms are entirely different things. I mean the rhythm and pace of action and the rhythm
and pace of dialogue. The problem is to try and blend these two
things together. I am still trying it, and I have not entirely solved
the problem, but eventually, I imagine, it will be solved. The field
of the future motion picture story has obviously got to come from
character, and where the difficulty comes is that character controls
the situation.

That is the one thing that disturbs me a little. You see modern
novels, psychological novels, with frank characterizations and very
good psychology, but there has been a tendency, with the novel
and with a lot of stage plays, to abandon story. They don't tell
enough story or plot. For a motion picture, we do need quite an
amount of story.

Now the reason we need a lot of story is this: a film takes an
hour and twenty minutes to play, and an audience can stand about
an hour. After an hour, it starts to get tired, so it needs the injec-
tion of some dope. One might also say there should be a slogan,
"Keep them awake at the movies!" (Laughter)

That dope, as one might call it, is action, movement, and

excitement; but more than that, keeping the audience occupied mentally. People think, for example, that pace is fast action, quick cutting, people running around, or whatever you will, and it is not really that at all. I think that pace in a film is made entirely by keeping the mind of the spectator occupied. You don't need to have quick cutting, you don't need to have quick playing, but you do need a very full story and the changing of one situation to another. You need the changing of one incident to another, so that all the time the audience's mind is occupied.

Now so long as you can sustain that and not let up, then you have pace. That is why suspense is such a valuable thing, because it keeps the mind of the audience going. Later on I will tell you how I think the audience should participate in those things.

In trying to design a melodrama with these elements of character, action, and movement, of course it does present a pretty big problem, and one has to adopt various methods. One method I have used in the past—I did it with *The Man Who Knew Too Much*—was to select some backgrounds or events that would lend themselves to a colorful, melodramatic motion picture. Of course, this is quite the wrong thing to do, but here is an idea: select the background first, then the action. It might be a race or it might be anything at all. Sometimes I select a dozen different events, and shape them into a plot. Finally—and this is just the opposite to what is usually done—select your character to motivate the whole of the above.

Under the present circumstance, people figure out a character or group of characters, and they allow them to motivate the story, the background, and everything else. Now you see, you are liable, unless you get a very colorful character, like an engine driver, a ship's captain or a diver, to be led into very dull backgrounds.

For example, if you take a society woman, she will obviously lead you into a drawing room, into a lot of talk, you see, and there you are! (Laughter) You might choose many characters of that nature, and it is inevitable, if you follow the regular method. I am not advocating that this should be everybody's method, it is only a feeling I have, myself, because I want to get certain things, you see.

Sometimes you cannot get the characters you want to take you into these places, so you say, "All right, I will have the society woman." The next thing is, of course, what to do with her. You might say, "I would like to have her in a ship's stokehole." Your job becomes very hard, indeed! You have to be really inventive to get a society woman into a ship's stokehole, to get a situation that will lead that way, and a character who, by reason of the situation, would find herself in a ship's stokehole.

Of course, I'd bet a lot of you would say, "It is too much trouble. Let's put her in a yacht's stokehole. A society woman is bound to go there." That, of course, is radical and you must not do it, because the moment you do, you are weakening and not being inventive.

If you can summon up enough courage to select your background and your incidents, you will find you really have something to work out. In *The Man Who Knew Too Much*, I said, "I would like to do a film that starts in the winter sporting season. I would like to come to the East End of London. I would like to go to a chapel and to a symphony concert at the Albert Hall in London."

That is a very interesting thing, you know. You create this terrific problem, and then say, "How the devil am I going to get all those things into it?" So you start off, and eventually you may have to abandon one or two events, as it might be impossible to get some of the characters into a symphony concert, or whatever it is. You say, "Well, can't Stokowski have his hair cut?" or something like that, and you try and blend the characters in the best way you can. By the time you finish the job, it must always—as far as you possibly can—appear to be quite natural that all the events have taken place in those settings because it was necessary for them to do so.

Now in the shape of this thing, it is inevitable that you must design your incidents and your story shape to mount up. I always think the film shape is very much like the short story. Once it starts, you haven't time to let up. You must go right through, and your film must end on its highest note. It must never go over the curve. Once you have reached your high spot, then the film is stopped.

Now one of the things that is going to help you hold all these things together and provide you with that shape is the suspense. Suspense, I feel, is a very important factor in nearly all motion pictures. It can be arrived at in so many different ways. To me, there is no argument that a surprise lasting about ten seconds, however painful, is not half as good as suspense for about six or seven reels.

I think that nearly all stories can do with suspense. Even a love story can have it. We used to feel that suspense was saving someone from the scaffold, or something like that, but there is also the suspense of whether the man will get the girl. I really feel that suspense has to do largely with the audience's own desires or wishes.

There, though, we have another subject—audience identification, and it is so great that I don't think I have time to deal with it here. I might say that it is a very, very important point. For example, you probably get more suspense out of an audience worrying about a known figure than some unknown person. It is quite possible that an audience will have convulsions at the thought of Clark Gable being shot or killed, but if it is some unknown actor, they will say, "Who the hell is he, anyway?" That is one important aspect of suspense.

Then there is the other thing, and that is where suspense is in a title. Take a film like *Mutiny on the Bounty*. Suppose it had not had the word "mutiny" in the title, but that it was called *The Good Ship Bounty*. You would have told the audience nothing. With its real title, however, the audience in the cinema is waiting from the moment the picture starts, wondering when the mutiny is going to start.

That applies again and again with titles. A lot of people are very unconscious of that fact. They do not realize how much suspense the audience is enjoying through a thing like that.

But to revert to the actual writing of suspense, of course in the old days, as I said, it was the race to the scaffold. Griffith did it, you know, in *Orphans of the Storm, The Knife,* and that sort of thing, but I feel that today we can have two types of suspense. We can have suspense like the old chase, which I would call objective suspense, and then there is a subjective suspense, which is letting the audience experience it through the mind or eyes of one of the characters. Now that is a very different thing.

You see, I am a great believer in making the audience suffer, by which I mean that instead of doing it, say as Griffith used to do it, by cutting to the galloping feet of the horse and then going to the scaffold—instead of showing both sides, I like to show only one side. In the French Revolution, probably someone said to Danton, "Will you please hurry on your horse," but never show him getting on the horse. Let the audience worry whether the horse has even started, you see. That is making the audience play its part.

The old way used to be that the audience was presented with just an objective view of this galloping horse, and they just said

they hoped the horse got there in time. I think it should go further than that. Not only "I hope he gets there in time," but "I
hope he has started off," you see. That is a more intensive development. Of course, that is simply dealing with the treatment of
what is the convention of suspense, but to get to suspense for a
film as a whole, as I have said, a title can give it.

And then there is a thing which one might term the springboard situation. In the first reel of a film you establish a given situation. You might take a sympathetic character who gets himself
into some sort of trouble, whatever it might be. The rest of the
film, then, is, "Will he get himself out of that situation?" I always
call that the springboard situation.

For example, this film that Mr. Abbott mentioned, *The Lodger,*
was based on Jack the Ripper. I took the trouble to spread a description of this man all over London. I did it by every known
means of disseminating news. The fact that he only went for fair-
haired girls was broadcast, or that he wore a black cloak or carried
a bag. I spent a whole reel on stuff like that. By the end of the reel
you were shown a house where the gas went out, and just as the
man was putting a shilling into the meter, there was a knock at the
door. The housewife opened the door, and just then the gas came
up with a full flood of light on this figure. Now that is what I call
the springboard situation. You then knew that Jack the Ripper was
in a London boarding house. In the rest of the film, you see, you
were bound to hold on to that.

I have always been, as far as possible, a great believer in that sort
of thing, such as you had in the Chain Gang picture (*I am a Fugitive from a Chain Gang*), where a man escapes and you wonder
what happens to him. Galsworthy's *Escape* is another example. They
are what I call springboard situations, where suspense starts practically in the first reel. I have always found that, generally speaking,
they are the most helpful. That really comes under the heading of
what I would call letting the audience into the secret as early as
possible. Lay all the facts out, as much as you can, unless you are
dealing with a mystery element. That is another matter entirely.

I will give you an example. I have just finished with a film,
Jamaica Inn, with Charles Laughton, and apropos of this, I came
upon a very queer problem. I don't know how many of you have
read the book, but there was a character in it who was a village parson. He was in a village where wrecking took place—the luring of

ships on to the rocks by a gang of wreckers. Their headquarters were at this Jamaica Inn, and the innkeeper was the head of the gang, but he was under the thumb or control of a shadow described in the book.

Actually, of course, it was this parson character who emerged for the last third of the story, and there he took an active part in the film. He had big acting scenes with the girl in the story, and he really took command of the whole picture, he was that strong. But for two-thirds of the picture, he had to appear just as an innocuous figure.

The problem there was, as I saw it, when I came in on this thing, that one would have to have a very important actor to play this character, because of what he had to do in the last third of the picture. The question was, how could one possibly have an important actor playing in an apparently unimportant part in the first two-thirds, when the characters are talking about a mysterious and influential figure?

Well, as you know, in the "who-done-it" story, the murderer turns out to be none other than the butler or the maid! (Laughter) Now this was a sort of "who-done-it" story, but with that difference, that the part was so strong a prominent actor had to be cast for it, because he took possession of the whole film at the end. The question was that you had neither suspense nor surprise. You certainly had one moment of surprise, though, when Laughton turned out to be whatever it was. A good phrase, that, don't you think? (Laughter)

Naturally, then, the story had to be changed. It is one occasion when journalists say, "Those film people have ruined another good story by changing it around." But one can really hold one's head up here, and say that it has been done with every possible reasoning. We had to let the audience into the secret about that figure and change the whole middle of the story, so that you saw this figure behind the scenes and how he manipulated the wreckers. We had to invent new situations. We couldn't just show what he did and how he did it, but had to have new situations, showing him up against it, investigations going on by the detectives of the period— if they had them in 1820. The entire middle had to be changed, so that it became a suspense story instead of a surprise story.

How am I doing? (Applause) Don't you want to ask questions? I sound bored, with nobody interrupting me.

My Most Exciting Picture

Shooting *Rope* was a little like unpuzzling a Rube Goldberg drawing.

A long time ago I said that I would like to film in two hours a fictional story that actually happens in two hours. I wanted to do a picture with no time lapses—a picture in which the camera never stops.

In *Rope* I got my wish. It was a picture unlike any other I've ever directed. True, I had experimented with a roving camera in isolated sequences in such films as *Spellbound, Notorious,* and *The Paradine Case.* But until *Rope* came along, I had been unable to give full rein to my notion that a camera could photograph one complete reel at a time, gobbling up 11 pages of dialogue on each shot, devouring action like a giant steam shovel.

As I see it, there's nothing like continuous action to sustain the mood of actors, particularly in a suspense story. In *Rope* the entire action takes place between the setting of the sun and the hour of darkness. There are a murder, a party, mounting tension, detailed psychological characterizations, the gradual discovery of the crime and the solution. Yet all this consumes less than two hours of real life as well as "reel" life. (Actually, it took us 35 days to wrap up the picture.)

The sight of a "take" under these conditions is something new under the Hollywood sun. It's like being backstage at one of those

"My Most Exciting Picture," as told to Favius Friedman, was originally published in *Popular Photography,* November 1948, 48–51, 96, 98, 100, 103–104.

madhouses that comedian Joe Cook used to devise when he was explaining why he couldn't imitate the four Hawaiians.

Here, for instance, is a brief glimpse of the action in Reel 2 of *Rope*.

For a full nine minutes the roving Technicolor camera poked its nose into every corner of the "collapsible" Sutton Place apartment. Prop men crouched on their knees beneath the camera boom moving furniture and putting it back. Lights dimmed down in one corner of the apartment, went up in another. "Wild" walls slid silently on vaseline-greased rollers. Script supervisors, prop men, electricians, and camera crew waggled their fingers and made faces at each other in a series of soundless, prearranged signals. And the camera, which had started facing south, was now facing north.

One complete reel, 950 feet of film, was in the can. There was a sudden silence. Then came a loud whisper from one of the harried, exhausted prop men.

"This," he announced, "is the damnedest picture I ever worked!"

All of us, including myself, agreed with him.

Yet *Rope* was probably the most exciting picture I've ever directed. Observers called it "the most revolutionary technique Hollywood had ever seen." Some of our problems seemed, at first, totally insurmountable. James Stewart, our star, couldn't sleep nights because of his role in the picture. It wasn't so much the suspenseful drama as it was the bewildering technique that made him worry. Head grip Morris Rosen still was operating the camera boom in his dreams at four o'clock in the morning and wound up at the finish of the picture 12 pounds thinner. Once, Joe Valentine, our cinematographer, had the 6,000-pound camera dolly roll on his foot when he didn't move fast enough. Still another time, the roving camera rolled too far and smashed one wall of the apartment.

To shoot *Rope* with stage technique under sound stage conditions but with continuous action called for months of preparation and days of exacting rehearsals. Every movement of the camera and the actors was worked out first in sessions with a blackboard-like football skull practice. Even the door was marked and plotted with numbered circles for the 25 to 30 camera moves in each reel. Whole walls of the apartment had to slide away to allow the camera to follow the actors through narrow doors, then swing back noiselessly to show a solid room. Even the furniture was "wild." Tables and chairs had to be pulled away by prop men, then set in place again by the time the camera returned to its original position, since the camera was on a special crane, not on tracks, and designed to roll through everything like a juggernaut.

All this technique, of course, was merely a means to an end. The audience must never be conscious of it. If an audience becomes aware that the camera is performing miracles, the end itself will be defeated.

Yet in *Rope* the camera did perform miracles, all because of the superb teamwork of the technical crew and their collaborative genius.

Broadway playwright Arthur Laurents (*Home of the Brave* and *Heart Song*) wrote the screenplay, the first time a scenario was written without time lapses. Laurents' scenes were unnumbered and there was almost no camera direction, merely indications of the changing camera position at major points throughout the story. Joe Valentine and I decided that one lens—a 35 mm—would give us all the coverage we needed, since it would be impossible to change lenses because of the continuous camera movement. Paul Hill, our Technicolor consultant, solved the problem of parallax, successfully modifying the camera for close-ups so that we could move in close enough to shoot the inside of a man's hat and the label on a hatband. And instead of following the camera with a mike boom, which would have created an insurmountable problem, we decided that the simplest solution was not to follow it. Instead, we set up four separate booms and two additional microphones up high. Operated by six sound men, these mikes picked up dialogue anywhere the camera wandered within the three-room apartment.

But the most magical of all the devices was the cyclorama—an exact miniature reproduction of nearly 35 miles of New York skyline lighted by 8,000 incandescent bulbs and 200 neon signs requiring 150 transformers.

On film the miniature looks exactly like Manhattan at night as it would appear from the window of an apartment at 54th Street and First Avenue, the locale of the play. And since all the major action of *Rope* takes place in the living room of this apartment, with the spectators constantly viewing the background, it was impossible to use process shots or a backdrop. Both would have been too flat. We had to remember the core of the arc of view. So we had to employ the scale cyclorama and devise a "light organ" that not only would light the miniature and its panorama of buildings, but also could give us changing sky and cloud effects varying from sunset to dark—all seen from the apartment—to denote the passing of time.

In the 12,000 square feet of the cyclorama, the largest backing ever used on a sound stage, the spectator sees the Empire State, the Chrysler, and the Woolworth buildings; St. Patrick's, Radio City, and hundreds of other landmarks of the fabulous New York skyline. Each miniature building was wired separately for globes ranging from 25 to 150 watts in the tiny windows. (The electrician's eye level was at the 22nd story.) Twenty-six thousand feet of wire carried 126,000 watts of power for the building and window illumination—all controlled by a twist of the electrician's wrist, via a bank of 47 switches, as he sat at the light organ high up and far behind the camera.

Because the roofs of the buildings closest to the apartment were three-dimensional and built to scale, there was still another problem to solve. For verisimilitude, smoke and steam trailed toward the sky from the tiny chimneys. Pipes under the rooftops supplied this steam, but we discovered that the vapor left the chimneys too fast and rose too high for accurate perspective. The normal speed of the jetting steam was completely out of synchronization with the miniature.

One of the prop men rose to the occasion, placing dry ice over the pipes to retard the steam's speed and volume. After that the smoke trailed lazily into the sky at a rate of speed that was wholly in proportion to the size of the buildings in the miniature.

That electrician who sat high on a parallel behind the camera manipulating the light organ controlled the lighting of the miniature like an artist at a console. He could illuminate an entire building or just one window at a time. He could, at the exact and rehearsed line of dialogue which gave him his cue, flood the Manhattan skyline with light from 200 miniature neon signs. By the time the picture went from the setting of the sun in the first reel to the hour of total darkness in the final *denouement,* the man at the light organ had played a nocturnal Manhattan symphony in light.

And then there were the cloud effects. Searching for what I demanded in a natural-seeming sky, I rejected the two routine methods of getting clouds. We could have painted them on the cyclorama, or we could have projected the clouds on the backdrop by means of painted lantern slides. But we did neither. I wanted the clouds to look like clouds even from ten feet away.

It was Fred Ahern, our production manager, who found the solution to the puzzle. Ahern came up with the perfect light-reflecting substance—spun glass. (Cotton wouldn't do because it soaks up and deadens light.) Five hundred pounds of spun glass were woven by scenic artists into chicken wire molds. Then actual clouds were photographed in all kinds of weather. We discovered that clouds are never the same even when the weather is constant, and it makes no difference what shape they are. Finally we decided on the cumulus or storm cloud, because it is white and fleecy before it turns gray and formidable. Every possible shaped cloud was created out of spun glass: wispy and full; fragile and menacing, circular and long.

Rope shows eight complete cloud changes during its nine reels. (The spun glass clouds were hung on standards and on overhead wires behind the buildings in the cyclorama, then slightly varied after each reel.) As a final check on our meteorology, we asked Dr. Dinsmore Alter of the famed Griffith Observatory for his opinion.

The cumulus clouds were fine, Alter told us, because there are more cumulus in the New York sky than anywhere else in the country, except high in the mountains. "And of course," said Alter, "you won't want any cirrus or high ice clouds."

"Cirrusly, I think not," I said, waiting for a laugh which was a lot weaker than a director has a right to expect on his own set.

To get authentic reproductions of changing sun and cloud effects and the falling of dusk, we had still photographers shoot the sun in three different locales. Once from the top of a New York skyscraper, once from the roof of an unfinished building on Wilshire Boulevard in Los Angeles, and once by a camera crew from the edge of the Santa Monica pier on the Pacific Ocean.

Famed John Miehle, our head still photographer, took over the cloud reproduction assignment, using an 8 x 10 and shooting straight into the sun. Miehle recorded the setting sun at five-minute intervals for an hour and 45 minutes to get a continuous effect. All these progressive variations in sun and clouds were charted on a detailed time schedule, then later cued to dialogue and action reel by reel. Miehle's developed films were studied by Technicolor experts who were able to match nature without a flaw.

Oddly enough, we discovered that there were virtually no major differences in cloud and sunset effects between the photographs shot in New York and those obtained on the West Coast.

Miehle knew that in photographing the sun head-on he might get double images, and he did. But he also obtained magnificent effects. These were the effects that were used in *Rope* to denote the passing of time—the yellow glare of the late afternoon sun fading to a soft gray, the light reflections on the fleecy white clouds dying softly—and finally dusk and darkness coming on as the lights of the city appeared.

Rope was a miracle of cueing. Everybody; actors, cameramen, the prop crew, the electricians, the script supervisors, spent two solid weeks of rehearsals before a camera turned. Even before the set was built I worked out each movement on a blackboard in my home. Then in the studio, the stage (actually a stage within a stage, made noiseless by constructing a special floor one and one-half inch above the regular one, soundproofed with layers of Celotex and carpet) was marked with numbered circles. These indicated where each specific camera stop had to be made, and when. Each camera movement—and there were as many as 30 separate ones—had its predetermined focus. Because of this the crew men operating the camera had to hit the floor markings exactly on cue and without deviations. The entire floor plan was laid out in foot squares so that in the event of retakes we could go back to the exact spot.

For the actual take the door markings were removed and plotted on a board. Holding the cue board the script supervisor signalled the camera crew on every movement during the 10-minute take. It was like one of those fabulous "Tinkers-to-Evers-to-Chance" triple plays. To cue each separate camera movement (and everything had to be done in utter silence) the script supervisor would check his cue board, then nod to a crew man on his left who held a long bamboo pointer. This crew man placed the end of the pointer on a predetermined spot on the floor. His action triggered Morris Rosen, the head grip, who dollied the camera to the new position, while the focus puller on the camera crane, watching his own cue sheet, simultaneously changed the focus on the camera lens.

But that wasn't all. Remember I told you that shooting *Rope* was very much like a Rube Goldberg drawing.

That wooden chest in which John Dall and Farley Granger, as the two young intellectual murderers, placed the body, practically played second lead in the picture. This chest with the body inside of it was always in the center of the living room—so far as the audience is aware.

Yet, actually every time the camera crossed the room the chest had to be rolled off stage just in advance of the camera crane. (We couldn't stop to make new camera setups.) Moving the chest was the assignment of the four prop men crouched on their hands and knees beneath the camera. Not only did they have to move the chest aside on cue but they also had to get it back into the scene again as the camera returned.

And all the time the young actor who played the strangled youth had to remain inside the chest! Since there were no time lapses or camera cuts in the usual scene, he was inside the chest for a full ten minutes, the shooting of 950 feet of film. After the third take, this actor began to get, well, a little tired. "I hope to God they get it on this take," he said fervently. "Those ten minutes seem like ten hours."

Every piece of furniture on the stage—every table, chair, plate, dish, and drinking glass—had to be moved on cue just like the wooden chest. Once, while the characters in the play were eating a buffet supper, Joan Chandler, who played the feminine lead, had to put her wine glass down on a table. But the table was gone. Joan merely put the glass down where the table should have been, one of the crouching prop men (unseen by the camera, of course) raised his hand and Joan's glass found a resting place in it. Another time an actor had to reach for a plate off the unseen table. Again a prop man moved in, handed the actor a plate, and the action went on.

It really was uncanny.

Naturally, in rolling a camera back and forth in a three-room apartment for 10 minutes without a halt (from living room to kitchen and back) we had to have a collapsible apartment. Actually, the basic element was the series of wild walls. ("Wild" is a term used to designate moveable or detachable flats.) In *Rope* the walls were quite literally wild. They rolled on overhead tracks heavily greased with vaseline to soundproof the skids. A separate crew stood by to roll each wall at a given cue, admitting the camera when the actors had gone through the door. When the players returned in the same shot, the wall closed and the Technicolor camera dollied back to pick up a new angle during the split second needed to make the room solid again.

That camera was gliding back and forth following actors all over the place. You'd see James Stewart coming suspiciously close to the chest in the living room that hid the body of the strangled youth. And in the next minute Stewart would be drinking champagne in the kitchen—all in the same 950 feet of film and without a halt in the movement of the camera.

There was one rather knotty problem that Jimmy Stewart, recalling his experiences in the Air Force, helped us solve. In the final moments of the story when the body is discovered and the killers are trapped, the apartment living room is flooded at intervals by great pulsations of light from a huge neon "Storage" sign just outside the window. I wanted the effect to add dramatic tension, much like the increasing crescendos of an orchestra at the climax of a symphony.

But for a while our electrical experts were stumped. They knew that in order to get enough light into the room during the sign's pulsations, huge arc lights would have to be hooked up on a special parallel with the actual sign, then synchronized. Then Stewart thought of the bomb release switch used in heavy bombers during the war. This switch controlled electrically the split second intervals during which bombs were dropped over the target. So we bought a bomb release at a war surplus store, adjusted it to synchronize the alternate flashing of the neon "Storage" sign with the opening and closing of these shutters on the three huge floodlights, and got exactly the effect we wanted.

Those 200 miniature neon signs in the New York skyline cyclorama helped me solve a little problem of my own. It's traditional, with me at least, that I appear fleetingly in every one of my pictures. But *Rope*, with a cast of only nine people who never leave the apartment, looked like the end of the Hitchcock tradition. There was just no way that I could get into the act.

Then someone came up with a solution. The result? The Hitchcock countenance will appear in a neon "Reduco" sign on the side of a miniature building!

Because of the way the picture was shot, the actors' performance varied very little from day to day. Actually, they found it a very stimulating experience. Their cooperation during the intensive pre-shooting rehearsals was truly magnificent.

Instead of reading the script through once or twice, the cast spent two weeks walking through the action from the beginning to the end, much like a stage play. Remember we weren't shooting just a line at a time, nor shifting our camera setup after a one-minute take. There were ten to eleven pages of dialogue on each shot. Actually, for the camera rehearsals we used no stand-ins as such. The stars themselves acted as puppets for the camera. After the camera movement rehearsals there were intensive dress rehearsals, when everyone's job, from script supervisor to prop man, was coordinated. Following that we put Reel 1 and Reel 2 on film. The maximum number of takes on any single reel was six and the minimum was three.

Stewart, of course, claimed that *Rope* was the toughest job an actor ever had. And I agreed with him. He told me that he wasn't sleeping nights. "What this means," Jimmy said, "is that if the rest of the cast is perfect and I fluff a line at, say 895 feet, it becomes the colossal fluff in screen history. The only way it can be reshot is to do the whole scene over again."

"Well," I said, "that's exactly why I picked you for the lead."

As it was, Stewart had to hang around the set 18 days before making a *bona fide* entrance for the rolling camera. It was the final dress rehearsal for Reel 3 in which Jimmy makes an entrance while Farley Granger is playing the piano. The piano stopped and silence ensued, as all eyes went to Stewart. He just made it into the room and was ready to open his mouth. "Just a minute," I said. "I'd like you to make your entrance differently."

Jimmy punched the air in a defeated gesture. "Hey, look," he complained, "I've waited three weeks for this!"

What amused everyone was that I never once looked at the action after the camera got rolling. There was no point, because I couldn't do anything about it. Once the camera started it had to keep rolling until the completion of the take. My job was done the moment I called "Action!"

One of the vital cogs in our machinery of advance planning was Film Editor Bill Ziegler. For the first time in his or anyone else's career as a cutter, a full-length feature had to be edited before it got on film. There were no close-ups, medium, or long shots in the conventional sense, that Ziegler could insert for a change of pace. Every move, every jump from reel to reel had to be planned so that the action would not drag on the screen. All of Ziegler's work, which usually takes place after a film is shot, had to take place while the action was going on.

All told we had 10,000 feet of film, shot without cuts, and from beginning to end like a stage play. And I think that in editing *Rope* this way we achieved suspense and an air of mystery without transoms opening, creaky doors, clutching fingers, or a house filled with eerie shadows.

Technicolor helped but it wasn't the star of the picture. *Rope,* incidentally, is the first time I've ever directed a Technicolor picture. I never wanted to make a Technicolor picture merely for the sake of using color. I waited until I could find a story in which color could play a dramatic role, and still be muted to a low key. In *Rope,* sets and costumes are neutralized so that there are no glaring contrasts. The key role played by color in this film is in the background. I insisted that color be used purely as the eye received it. After all, technique is merely a means to an end and the audience must never be aware that the camera, the director, or the photographer is performing miracles. Everything must flow smoothly and naturally.

Rope is a picture in which material has been created definitely for camera movements. Scenes were planned for visual strength, which in turn was blended with movement. The continuous flow of action meant that the eye was occupied constantly. And the elimination of the conventional shifting camera excites the audience by making the picture flow smoother and faster.

All of us had a lot of fun with *Rope,* particularly the publicity people. One press agent suggested that we have a world premiere in the Philippines because hemp comes from there. Another wanted us to hang it on New York's Strand Theatre.

I thought it best to let the boys have their fun. Their work was just beginning; mine was done. You see, I had come to the end of *my Rope.*

On Style

An Interview with Cinema

HITCHCOCK: What is *Cinema?*

INTERVIEWER: *Cinema* is distributed nationally in the United States, a magazine for what we think of as the "intelligent motion picturegoer." Our premise . . .

H: Are there intelligent picturegoers?

I: We presume so . . . Our premise is that there are intelligent motion picturegoers who look to directors as the creators of motion pictures. Now what I'd like to talk to you about is film style. You stated recently that the two things common to all your films are style and suspense, whereas otherwise they are all quite different. I presume your films are all pre-designed by an art director. Do you do the drawings yourself?

H: Well, art director is not a correct term. You see an art director, as we know it in the studios, is a man who designs a set. The art director seems to leave the set before it's dressed and a new man comes on the set called the set dresser. Now there is another function which goes a little further beyond the art director and it is almost in a different realm. That is the production designer. Now a production designer is a man *usually* who designs angles and sometimes production ideas. Treatment of action. There used to be a man . . . is he still alive? William Cameron Menzies. No, he's not. Well, I had William Cameron Menzies on a picture called *Foreign Correspondent* and he would take a sequence, you see, and by a

"On Style" was originally published in *Cinema* 1, no. 5 (August–September 1963): 4–8, 34–35.

285

series of sketches indicate camera set-ups. Now this is, in a way, nothing to do with art direction. The art direction is set designing. Production design is definitely taking a sequence and laying it out in sketches. Now to give you an example, where I do a lot of my own production design (in fact, I do most of it today) . . . would be a sequence like the airplane chasing Cary Grant in *North by Northwest.* You remember that sequence? Well this has very careful design because I designed it purely to avoid the cliché. Now in movies, or in films if we want to call them by a more dignified name, or motion pictures to go a little further: the cliché of the man being put on the spot is usually a place of assignation and it takes the form of a figure under a street lamp at the corner of the street with the rain-washed cobbles shining in the night . . . maybe a cut to a blind being pulled aside, and a face looking out.

I: A cut to?

H: A shot of it . . . a shot of it. Every time I use the word cut . . . I mean a shot, a separate piece of film. And another piece of film that would be a cut would be a black cat slinking along the wall . . . Anyway this is the cliché atmosphere in which you put a man who has been deliberately placed in danger. Somebody is going to come along and bump him off. In the gangster films they went by a black limousine that went da da da da da da with a gun and the guy fell down. Well of course, this is such a cliché thing, you see, that one has to fight shy of it and run as far away from it as one possibly can because it's all predictable. The audience has seen it so many times, students of the cinema are so familiar with it. Now I decide to do something quite different and I say to myself, What shall I do? Well, let's have it with nothing so that the audience will have no conception as to how this man is going to be bumped off or shot. So therefore, I take the loneliest, emptiest spot I can so that there is no place to run for cover, no place to hide, and no place for the enemy to hide, if we can call him that, you see. Now we get him off the bus and we stand him, a little tiny figure, show-ing, establishing very clearly the complete wasteland everywhere.

I: Would this be an establishing shot?

H: It could be. It does two functions: It sets up the man being placed in position, and it sets up the nature of the surroundings so that the mind of the audience says, "Well. This is a strange place to put a man." Now we go down and we go close on him, and this is where design comes in. And he looks around him and cars go by.

So now we start a train of thought in the audience. "Ah, he's go-ing to be shot at from a car." And even deliberately, with tongue in cheek, I let a black limousine go by. And I let it go right by, you see. Now, the car. We've dispensed with the menace of possible cars or automobiles, we'll say. Now a jalopy comes from another direction, stops across the roadway, deposits a man, the jalopy turns and goes back. Now he's left alone with the man. This is the sec-ond phase of the design. Is this going to be the man? Well, they stand looking at each other across the roadway. Grant, our hero, decides to investigate . . . and casually walks across and talks to the man . . . and obviously nothing is going to emerge from this man, or you feel that, until his bus begins to appear. Now the local bus comes and *just* as it pulls up—and this is a matter of timing—just before it gets to the stop, the man says to Grant, "That's funny." And Grant says, "What's funny?" He says "There's a plane, a crop-dusting plane over there dusting a place where there are no crops." Before this can be gone into in any way at all he's on the bus and gone. So now you've got the third phase. The audience says . . . "Ah, the airplane." Now, what's gonna be strange about the air-plane, and you soon know. And from that point on you have a man trying to find cover. There is no cover until he gets into the cornfield. Now, you do in the design a very important thing. You smoke him out with the very instrument that you're using, a crop duster. Theory being, don't have a crop duster without your using it, otherwise you could have any airplane. So the dusting of the crop, the dust rather from the crop duster, smokes him out of the cornfield and he dashes in front of the truck desperately and the plane makes a last dive, mistimes it. Or the truck does come to a stop by his frantic waving and out goes the whole lot. So you see, this is the design. This sequence is very carefully designed step by step both visually and to some extent in its menace . . . the menace of its content. So that's production design, exemplified in terms of its function. What does it do?

I: Selection primarily of the framing of the shot.

H: Of the images and what they do.

I: What about the direction of the subject movement within the frame?

H: That's axiomatic, you see. The action itself is self-evident. For example, as many variations as one can get of a plane attacking a man. Even to the point where the man is running toward the camera, and you go with him and the plane comes down over the top of him into the camera practically. This is giving the audience the sensation of having the plane dive at them. So here we come again, now this brings you into the manner of style. You see. They'll say "Well, only Hitchcock could have thought a thing like that out." So style . . .

I: The entire situation determined it more than an individual cut or . . .

H: Oh, well a cut is nothing. One cut of film is like a piece of mosaic. To me, pure film, pure cinema is pieces of film assembled. Any individual piece is nothing. But a combination of them creates an idea.

I: Is this what is referred to historically as montage?

H: Montage, you can call it that. But there are many kinds of montage. For example, there was a lot of it, more of it in *Psycho* than many pictures I've ever made. *Psycho* is probably one of the most cinematic pictures I've ever made. Because there you had montage in the bathtub killing where the whole thing is purely an illusion. No knife ever touched any woman's body in that scene. Ever. But the rapidity of the shots, it took a week to shoot. The little pieces of film were probably not more than four or five inches long. They were on the screen for a fraction of a second.

I: How long was the entire scene?

H: I would say about a minute and a half, that's all.

I: Would this be speeding up action or slowing it down . . .

H: No . . . no . . . No, this is the action told in terms of pieces of film. Expressing violence by the juxtapositions of the angles, and the pieces of film assembled. In actual practice—this has nothing to do with the final result—but in the course of handling a nude girl, I actually used a nude girl. But I shot her in slow motion, and turned the camera slow as well, so that when it's projected at normal speed this slow motion is speeded up. I made her work very slowly because I wanted the breast, the bare breast to be conveniently covered with the struggling arm at the right moment. Doing it with rapidity, you could never time it right. But having her do it in slow motion, and turning the camera in slow motion, when it went through at the normal speed the arm came up quickly. And the timing was worked out that way. But that's nothing to do with the technique, that was only a means of achieving that covering up, you see.

I: More technical than style.

H: Yes, that was a technical thing. Now let's go back to talk further in terms of style, in the use of film and the juxtaposition of pieces of film. We have two kinds. We can have the pieces of film that are put together to create an idea, or the pieces of film that are put together to create an emotion. Now the bathtub scene was an emotional putting together of film . . . an expression of extreme violence. Now also in *Psycho* you had a scene where the detective was coming up the stairs. Now the audience knew that there was a menace around. A monster. So he came up the stairs and when he got to the top of the stairs, I took the camera very high, extremely high. So that he was a small figure. And the figure of the woman came out, very small, dashed at him with a knife. And the knife went out, and we're still very high, and as the knife started to come down, I cut to a big head of the man. And the knife went right across the face, and he fell back from that point on. Now the reason for going high—and here we're talking about the juxtaposition of size of image. So the big head came as a shock to the audience, and to the man himself. His surprise was expressed by the *size* of the image. But you couldn't get the emphasis of that size unless you had prepared for it by going high. In music going high would be like the tremolo of the violins and suddenly the brass goes GRRR! as it comes out with the big head expressing his shock. Now that's juxtaposition of pieces of the film to create emotion. Now we have the other type of pieces of film *which create ideas*: *Rear Window,* a very cinematic picture. But a static figure—in one position, in one room, for the whole picture. And yet this is pure cinema. I'll tell you why. Mr. Stewart is sitting looking out of the window. He observes. We register his observations on his face. We are using the visual image now. We are using the mobility of the face, the expression, as our content of the piece of film. Let's give an example of how this can vary, this technique, with whatever he is looking at: Mr. Stewart looks out. Close-up. Cut to what he sees. Let's assume it's a woman holding a baby in her arms. Cut back to him. He smiles. Mr. Stewart likes babies. He's a nice gentleman. Take out only the middle piece of film, the viewpoint. Leave the close-ups in—the look and the smile. Put a nude girl in the middle instead of the baby. Now he's a dirty old man. By the changing of one piece of film only, you change the whole idea. It's a different idea. One was a benevolent gentleman, his character *changed* even with that. So this is what I mean by pure cinema. It doesn't relate to what a lot of movies are, which I call photographs of people talking. That's a different thing entirely. I'll tell you another interesting thing in the manner of style or the use of cuts . . . creative imagery . . . and what you convey to an audience by the cuts. One of the people working on the picture asked me could they lay out the sequence of the detective going up the stairs. I said, sure if you want to have a go, lay it out in a series of sketches. I happened to be home sick that day, so I said to the assistant, I said you've got the sketches, it's a hand going up the rail, it's the feet on the tread going up, it's a close-up of the man going up, and now you get feet again and these different things, and I let them shoot them. Then when the cutter put the shots together for me, I realized they couldn't be used. The whole thing was wrong. The reason it was wrong is because these cuts belonged to a furtive individual of a menacing nature. But the detective was an innocent party, therefore you wanted an innocent shot. And I threw the whole thing out. It was a wrong use of the montage. Of this type of montage. So I'm illustrating all of these to show what style is, and how you use it and for what purpose. Every piece of film that you put in the picture should have a purpose. You cannot put it together indiscriminately. It's like notes of music. They must make their point.

I: Can we get an example, say from *The Birds,* of this type of thing?

H: Yes, well, you get a different thing in *The Birds.* In *The Birds* you get a sequence, the main sequence . . . of course, you get the girl in the attic, there is a clear montage. That's the same as the scene in *Psycho* with the girl in the bathtub, the attack . . . by a series of pieces of film assembled together of all facets of the scene. Now the reaction of the people where the birds are attacking the house, and you don't see them, *there* is a matter of shots assembled together to create a panic of people who are running from what? I don't know. I can't see anything. Now I gave two kinds of shots. I gave the mother and child a dotty movement. Can't find cover. They end up in a corner. The girl retreats from nothing. So her image was an emptiness in the foreground, symbolizing nothing. And she backs up against the sofa, and starts to climb the wall, rolls around the lamp. I build her up as she goes along. Well these images are angles chosen to express the fear of the unknown. They're not shot just without any thinking about what the intention is, you see.

I: In seeing the film I was trying to be conscious of this and it got very hard because I got involved in the story, but there was one sequence—I guess you would term it cross cutting—after Tippi Hedren has crossed the bay, and deposited the present of the birds and starts back. Then there is the sequence of her rowing across, and the car, and back and forth . . .

H: That's right, well that's her viewpoint.

I: That's her viewpoint. Now would this be termed cross cutting?

H: Ah, no, no, that's subjective treatment. Subjective treatment is the close-up of the person and what they see. You see I use it a lot. A tremendous lot of subjective treatment in film. I put the camera, as it were, I make the person in close-up and what they see. *Rear Window* is purely subjective treatment—what Jimmy Stewart sees all the time. And how he reacts to it.

I: Could we say that a strong point in your style would be this subjective treatment?

H: Subjective treatment. As against the objective. You see, the objective is the stage. Is the theater. We are audience looking at the people on the stage. We aren't with them, we aren't getting any viewpoint you see.

I: So, with this you're getting the camera within the mind of the viewer.

H: You know the young film director always says, oh, let's do a scene where the audience is the camera. That's the prime cliché of *all* clichés. Bob Montgomery did one called *Lady in the Lake*. It's quite unnecessary. You might just as well do a close-up of who it is. You know, it's a trick and there's nothing to it. You'd much better have a close-up and then what they see. Move with them—do anything you like—make them go through any experience—anything.

I: But Chabrol and Truffaut have in a sense imitated this style of yours, or learned from it.

H: Yes, they have. But after all, the greatest example of that which has been traditional, I think, in movies is the experience of a person on a roller coaster. You know when they brought that out with Cinerama, people said "Oh, my God, isn't Cinerama wonderful? Nothing, of course, nothing like it at all!" That old roller coaster angle has been shot ever since silent films—way, way, back. I remember when they made a film years ago called *A Ride on a Runaway Train* and they put the camera up front and looked the world in the face. I can go back as far as 1912, maybe earlier, maybe 1910, when they used to have a thing in London called "Hale's Tours." And the audience paid their money and they went into a long car, like a pullman car, with rows of seats and a screen at the end. So you sat there, and all they did, they back-projected a film taken on the front of a train in Switzerland. Going through the Alps and so forth, and you sat there, and you were taken for a ride on a train. This is the same thing. This is purely subjective treatment.

I: Well, that would then be one major aspect of your style. We are also defining pretty well what is pure cinema here. What would be another aspect?

H: Let me say this to you. I put first and foremost cinematic style before content. Most people, reviewers, you know, they review pictures purely in terms of content. I don't care what the film is about. I don't even know who was in that airplane attacking Cary Grant. I don't care. So long as that audience goes through that emotion! Content is quite secondary to me.

I: Now is this a philosophical viewpoint? . . . Or is this something that just happened, like the man who makes cartoons likes to make people laugh?

H: Well, I believe this. I believe we still have in our hands the most powerful instrument, cinema, that's been known. I know of no other medium where on a given night in Japan, in Germany, in Paris, and in London and in New York, the different audiences of different nationalities can be shocked at the same moment at the same thing on that screen. I don't know of any other medium. The theater? How far does that get? It never gets to Japan. Well, by God, you go outside of a movie on The Ginza, and you will see a great big head of Hitchcock up there. Because they think so much of the director with oriental eyes! Really! Yes! But this is my point when you say what do I enjoy? I enjoy the fact that we can cause, internationally, audiences to emote. And I think this is our job.

I: As an entertainer? As a creator?

H: As an entertainer. As a creator. What is art? Art is an experience, isn't it? You know? Now the art of the talking picture, I think, belongs to the theater. You see, the only thing wrong with silent pictures was that sound never came out of the mouths. But unfortunately, the moment sound arrived, all these horrible commercial people rushed to the theater, and borrowed from the theater. And they are still doing it today. I've done it myself! They say "Will you make a film of *Dial M For Murder*"? I say O.K., all right. But I refuse to open it up like they do in the movies. I said it's nonsense. What do you do? When you take a stage play, I said? What do you call opening it up? The taxi arrives, we have a long shot of the street. The taxi stops at the front door of the apartment house. The characters get out, cross the sidewalk, go into the lobby, get into an elevator, go upstairs, walk along the corridor, open the door, and they go into a room. And there they are, on the stage again. So, you might just as well dispense with all that, and be honest and say it's a photographed stage play and all we can do is to take the audience out of the orchestra and put them on the stage with players.

I: You didn't do this completely though. In *Dial M*?

H: Yes, and I'll tell you why. Because I've seen so many stage plays go wrong through opening up, loosening it, when the very essence is the fact that the writer conceived it within a small compass.

I: But you would still treat it cinematically?

H: Within its area. If I can. As much as I can.

I: Do you design each production? Design each film in advance completely? With drawings, and . . .

H: Yes, *Psycho*, yes, to some extent with drawings, but you see *Psycho* was designed, first of all to lead an audience completely up the garden path. They thought the story was about a girl who stole $40,000. That was deliberate. And suddenly out of the blue, she is stabbed to death. Now, a lot of people complained about the excessive violence. This was purposely done, because as the film then proceeded, I reduced the violence while I was transferring it to the mind of the audience. By that first impact, so the design of the film was very clearly laid out. So that that audience, by the time we got toward the end when the girl was going over the house, wandering, they didn't particularly care who she was . . . They will yell LOOK OUT! when a burglar is going around the house. They will still have the same fear of being caught or being attacked or what have you. So, I was transferring by establishing the violence strong in the beginning and then got less and less violent as the film went on, thus letting their minds carry. That's what the pattern of the film was. The pattern of *The Birds* was deliberately to go slow. And with an unimportant kind of relationship.

I: This has been highly criticized by some critics.

H: I deliberately made it slow.

I: You deliberately made it slow?

H: Oh, no question about it.

I: But it was still—to me, interesting.

H: But the point is, that's where the critics were wrong, you see, because the effect on an audience isn't there unless I've made them wait deliberately and gone slow.

I: This is timing?

H: This is truer timing. Well, it's just like designing composition in a painting. Or balance of colors. There is nothing accidental, there should never be anything accidental about these things. You've got to be very clear in what you are doing and why you're doing it. You know, for example, I think it was the *New Yorker* once—they don't review pictures. They don't review them, they make jokes about pictures anyway. They always have a man who's supposed not to like the movies—But they had the ridiculous effrontery to say a picture like *North by Northwest* was unconsciously funny. You know. They really did. Or, Hitchcock is doing a parody of himself. Of course, I'm doing it with the tongue in cheek. *Psycho* was the biggest joke to me. I couldn't make *Psycho* without my tongue in my cheek. If I'd been doing *Psycho* seriously, then it would have been a case history told in a documentary manner. It certainly wouldn't have been told in terms of mystery and oooooh, look out audience, here comes the bogey man! This is like telling a story to a little boy. I'ts like telling a fairy story. You tell it in hushed tones: "Ssh! and then the woman went up the stairs!" That's all I'm doing. And you've got to have a sense of humor to do this.

I: In *The Birds* then, there is really no—what you would call theme or message?

H: All you can say about *The Birds* is nature can be awful rough on you. If you play around with it. Look what uranium has done. Man dug that out of the ground. *The Birds* expresses nature and what it can do, and the dangers of nature, because there is no doubt if the birds did decide, you know, with the millions that there are, to go for everybody's eyes, then we'd have H. G. Wells' Kingdom of the Blind on our hands.

I: I think you took advantage of a natural human trait though, that when, say uranium, or the Bund movement in the '30s, or the plague in the medieval times starts to descend upon a given group of people, they don't want to believe it. They fight against it.

H: Well, or they're helpless with it. You see, the idea of the people in the house, when the birds are attacking and not knowing what to do . . . I only had the shutter blow open and the young man try to close the shutter, to tell the audience what it was really like outside. Otherwise, I was asking too much of their imagination. So, I gave them a little sample: White shadows go for his hand . . . bloody it up. I'm saying "Audience, that's what it's really like outside." Only by the millions, not just two, as I've just shown. Now the helplessness of the people is no different in that sequence than people in an air raid with nowhere to go. Now, that's where the idea came from. I've been in raids . . . in London and the bombs are falling, and the guns are going like hell all over the place. You don't know where to go. Where can you go? Can't go down to the basement. That's kind of sissy, you know.

I: I see . . . So you're just caught.

H: You're caught! You're trapped!

I: In regard to the use of talent: Do you have any special attitude towards talent? . . . They do not dominate, in any way, your film. You are in complete control?

H: Well, first and foremost, what I look for in talent, especially when we are in the area of the purely cinematic, is the mobility of the face. In other words, expression. The register of expression. Especially in subjective treatment it's a very vital thing you see . . . The reaction . . .

I: Now let me tie this together. You are selecting talent so that they will work with one of your basic stylistic manners, that is the subjective treatment.

H: Yes. Well, you take, for example, the work that I gave to Tippi Hedren in *The Birds,* you see. Her face was used entirely to register impressions. Because the story was being told from her point of view. In other words, when after the 2,000 finches have come into the room, the mother is beginning to crack, she's not the strong woman we thought she was, and it's the girl who watches her. The girl's expressions. You see her watching this woman and finally she says "I think I'd better stay the night, don't you?" She didn't say a word until she spoke. But she was taking all that in. Visually.

I: You got the story visually.

H: Yes, and I believe that one should at all cost try and use that face in the visual, as much as possible.

I: It's part of the subjective.

H: Yes, definitely. It's part of imagery. It's part of what our medium is. The visual image registering thought, mind . . . whatever you like to call it.

I: Do you have any attitude toward the more beautiful woman in a situation like that? Is this a more believable thing for people, or less believable—

H: Well, to me the contrast is important. In other words, Cary Grant standing in that wasteland in a business suit was more important than in a tweed jacket and slacks. See, there is a certain amount of value to be got from what one might term visual incongruity. I think, for example, the girl getting into a boat with two birds in a cage, wearing a mink coat in an outboard, is kind of ridiculous, you see. But that again is counterpointing. A visual counterpoint to what would normally happen.

I: Now I've read several criticisms of Miss Hedren's lack of mobility in the face.

H: Oh, they are wrong. They are wrong. I controlled every movement on that face.

I: Her reactions were subtle though and they were not cliché.

H: They were subtle and that was the thing that pleased me about the girl. You know, she never acted before.

I: Is this a help in this case?

H: Of course it is. She had nothing to unlearn. Better than when you have a girl who is mugging all over the place and you say "Please don't mug." I need that face to register an expression, but I only want the one.

I: Unlearned. As opposed to theatrical learning? Theatrical acting?

H: Well overacting—call it what you like. Hedren was doing purely cinematic acting of very fine shadings all of the time. Oh, I held those down. She wasn't allowed to do anything beyond what I gave her.

I: So, this was your control, not a lack, say, on her part.

H: No, my control entirely.

I: And, this is the case with every actor or actress that you use?

H: As far as possible—Yes. I say "Too much, too much." Because the image is too big. It's enormous on the screen there. And don't forget that you've got to keep it down so that you get a range. It's like the timbre of the voice. If the voice is too high, when you want it to go high, there is nowhere to go. And it's just the same way to keep the expression to a minimum.

I: And you are attempting though to shock more with the camera—with the use of the camera, rather than with the use of the person's face registering . . .

H: Well, that belongs, quite obviously, when the girl has birds flung at her, you know.

I: You get that reaction but it's a sequence more than letting her just carry it . . .

H: Yes. Yes. Oh, yes, sure.

I: . . . as she might have to on a stage.

H: Oh, no. Oh, no. No, no, no, that comes under the heading of the theater. You see there is so much theater that's crept into films, that, you know, films are reviewed on the basis of their content and not on their style.

I: Yes. Now this is a point I'm interested in. Content and style.

H: Well, let me say this as a maker of films. Maybe it's a conceit on my part. I think content belongs to the original story of the writer, whoever wrote the book, that you are adapting. That's his department.

I: That's an interesting statement. You don't feel then that the director, as such, is responsible for content, as you would select any different . . .

H: Well look, I make a film—*Dial M for Murder*—and what have I really had to do with that? Nothing. It was a stage play, written for the stage, written by an author. All I had to do there was to go in and photograph it.

I: But the success or the failure on the screen is going to be dependent upon you—not upon the writer. But . . .

H: No.

I: . . . You don't believe that?

H: No, because if that original material hadn't been there, I might . . . I could have done all kinds of things with it. It wouldn't have helped.

I: But a bad director could have ruined it.

H: Ah! Maybe! Yes, but you see, but my craft is that I handle the camera. It's second nature. It is no effort for me.

I: You see *Cinema* has taken the position, frankly, that the director is the responsible person despite the material . . .

H: Right. Well, let me give you an example.

I: . . . because he can so easily destroy it.

H: That is true. Oh, yes. Oh, yes. That is true.

I: And the excitement is going to come primarily from the visual . . . the "visual writing" rather than the paragraph writer.

H: That is true. But you see you take a film like *North by Northwest*. That's true Hitchcock. Because he wrote it. With Ernie Lehman. Ernie Lehman and I sat in the room. Ernie Lehman got noted for writing fantasy melodrama.

I: That's what you would term . . .

H: Oh sure. Cinematic nonsense if you like.

I: Now isn't it true that Truffaut is writing all of his own material—if I'm not mistaken?

H: Well, it's hard to say. You see Truffaut did *The 400 Blows*, which was biographical . . . autobiographical you know. Now I don't know how Truffaut is getting on. I saw *Jules and Jim*. Now I said "Truffaut, why did I feel that the film could have ended and then it restarted, and so forth." He said "Well, I was following a novel." I said "Truffaut, I don't think you should do that, you know, why should you follow a novel?"

I: Did you see *Jules and Jim*? Did you like that?

H: Yes. A lot of the things I liked in it very much, but I did feel that it lacked the shape. Construction to me, it's like music. You start with your allegro, your andante, and you build up. Don't forget even a symphony breaks itself into movements, but a motion picture doesn't. The nearest form to it is the short story. You've got to take it in at one sitting. A play you break into three acts. A book you pick up and put down again. A short story, you read through from beginning to end. That's why the motion picture is the nearest in its shape to the short story.

I: What was Truffaut's response to you?

H: Well, he agreed. But he said he had a reason for it. He was following a novel. I mean he even went so far as to make the photography look like period photography. And I'm not sure whether that's valid . . . any more than if they make a film called *Ivanhoe* and the castles are 20th-century ruins. And it ought not to be. Peo-

ple forget this. You see a costume picture or a picture laid in a period and it happens to be, we'll say medieval Germany or Tudor
England, they go to the ruins that exist today. The settings ought
to look brand new, you know. And sometimes, I feel sure that the
pictures that were made in Rome, of the period—the "Ben Hur"
period. The only reason they look new is because they aren't exist-
ing any more and had to be built anew. But I wouldn't be surprised if those cities did exist they wouldn't go to the Forum and
fix it up a bit.

I: To go back a bit, content to you then is not necessarily a message, but a story line.

H: A story line—yes.

I: That is the thing that counts. And telling that story. Not necessarily that it conveys a political . . .

H: No.

I: . . . or a religious . . .

H: No.

I: . . . or any kind of message.

H: I don't interest myself in that. I only interest myself in the
manner and style of telling the story. But as for the story itself,
I don't care whether it's good or bad, you know. If it serves my
purpose.

I: Would you say that Truffaut has that same opinion?

H: I don't know—I don't know whether we ever discussed it.
You know he's doing a book on me.

I: I know about that. I understand you spent a couple of weeks
with him.

H: Oh, we were in that room there—twenty-six hours the talk
we had.

I: Twenty-six hours! What did you discuss?

H: Everything. He went through every film I'd ever made.

I: Film by film? That's got to be pretty fascinating.

H: Yes, picked out certain things, you know.

I: I'd like to ask a question here about believability, reality in
your films. You are constantly trying to destroy the audience's confidence in what they think is going to happen.

H: I'm having a fight with them all of the time.

I: Yet you've got to maintain a reality, a believability at all times.

H: Oh, at all times. As authentic as you can possibly be, because
you're dealing with fantasy. When you tell that little boy the story

on your knee, whether it's Red Riding Hood, you've got to make it sound real.

I: Now, this would then be a part of your style, your effort in this area. Is it detail?

H: Oh—the utmost—When I went to Bodega Bay, to shoot *The Birds,* I had *every* school child photographed in the area and *every* living person photographed, so that there would be no mistake in the wardrobe. And had the characters photographed. And went to the place, the location before writing any script.

I: Was the area—the bay and the road around it . . . to that house . . .

H: Exactly the same—that house was a derelict farm.

I: Did that give you the idea for—

H: Oh yes, of course, the whole thing was based on the geography. That house was a derelict farm, we built it up again.

I: Let me get that on tape—The geography gave you the idea of her crossing in the boat while he's racing in the car. And of course that built up to the sequence where the birds gather . . . and you had the audience completely off balance by that time.

H: Yes, that's right—that's right.

I: They were involved in her subjective relationship with him.

H: In light and very inconsequential comedy—making nothing much of it. Then BOOM!

I: Now there have been a great many things said about symbolism within your films. One interview discussed Tippi Hedren as symbolical of . . .

H: Well, she represents complacency—Smug complacency, and too many people are complacent today. You know they're smug and they don't realize what catastrophe . . .

I: That is a symbol as such—the personality of Tippi. Now there was also a comparison of her buying birds in a bird shop. Love birds caged up and then having her caged in the telephone booth again. So it is definitely in your mind . . . intended as symbolism . . .

H: Oh, definitely—the telephone booth was the bird surrounded by humans. The roles were reversed.

I: A complete reversal of the roles. Now, in the sequence, when they finally come upon the man at the farm—that is the man that the birds have killed. Just discussing the technical process there, what did the camera do to give us the . . .

H: It jumped in—it was a staccato movement, you see.

I: Ah, yes, and very quick so you didn't really know whether you saw it all or not.

H: Well, I did it for several reasons. I wanted a change from the zooming in, but I wanted to be prepared for censorship problems. If I ran into censorship anywhere—you, like so, you can tape it out you see. And another item interesting about that moment, I never show the woman's reaction to it. I cut to the shoulder.

I: Her shoulder?

H: Going out behind the door. I never show her face. I knew I couldn't. I knew very well I could never get an expression strong enough.

I: So you let it stay in the audience's mind.

H: Then I come down the corridor in silhouette. Not until she got to the man—she was inarticulate—couldn't express it. And then I made the truck carry on for her. The whizzing truck and the cloud of dust.

I: This is a visual thing again. We've got no dialogue here really.

H: No, and the speed of that truck expresses the anguish of the woman, and the dust that it creates. Because when I drove the truck in, I had made it go much slower and no dust—we watered it down. I watered all the road down when the truck went in.

I: I can see here now where you are designing these things in advance, you can premeditate these things. Do you use any improvisation in your actors at all?

H: No, not much.

I: You let them give you a picture as such . . .

H: No, you know, if we are doing a dialogue scene or a conversation scene, I let the actors see how . . . I may ask them, Does he feel comfortable here? What do you like to do? You know. But I mustn't—I don't let them get out of hand, you know. I do it as a kindness toward them.

I: I've heard a lot of comments about your comments about actors.

H: Actors are cattle. Children. They are. They're all right, I get along all right with them.

I: Well, they seem to have a great respect for you.

H: Well, I don't direct them on the stage. I don't believe in that, you know. I discuss the thing in the dressing room. They're artists . . . they can go in and do their scene . . . I more or less tell them what points they're making, storywise or cinematically.

I: Much as we are discussing here, so that they know what it is that . . .

H: They know what part of the film this little piece is going to be. I don't care . . . to tell them the whole thing . . . why they are doing this and what contribution it makes toward the whole.

I: Have you ever had to fire an actor because he or she wouldn't cooperate?

H: Well—Oh yes, I wouldn't tolerate for a minute anything like that. As a matter of fact, I ran into it once with an actor when I wanted him to look up. He said, well I don't know whether I would. I said, well you've got to look up—I need the look. 'Cause I want to show what you see.

I: Are most actresses and actors aware of how much control a camera has over their total effect?

H: I make them aware of it—Yeah—sure.

I: Because in discussing it with talent, they don't seem to be aware of . . .

H: They don't. In the most they don't. They just perform.

I: The way that you move the camera could completely destroy . . .

H: They're not conscious even of the size of the image . . .

I: They are not.

H: No. They just do their stuff and go home at 6 o'clock.

I: Well, let's see here. How are we on time?

H: What time do you have now?

I: About five after four.

H: Oh, you're right, then I must stop! I've got a four o'clock game of chess!

Hitchcock Talks About Lights, Camera, Action

An Interview with Herb A. Lightman

What factors are involved in your decision to employ a specific style of photography to realize a particular script in visual terms? For example, what led you to adopt the "reflected light" approach to filming Torn Curtain?

Away from here one often hears complaints about what is called "Hollywood Gloss." When we were preparing to film *Torn Curtain,* I began casting about for a photographic style that would help us tell the story in a more realistic, not so "glossy" way. Actually, I've felt for a long time that our color films were being photographed in almost the same manner as black-and-white films. I believe there is a hangover from one to the other, especially when it comes to separating the image from the background.

What do you believe are the reasons for this?

To answer that, one must delve a bit into the history of lighting for the cinema. Back in 1919 and 1920, or even further back than that, long before incandescent lights ever came, we used to light from the floor with Klieg arc lights and our general lighting came from banks of mercury vapor lamps. We used in Europe a particular lamp called a "swan neck" which had a diagonal bank of lamps mounted atop a vertical bank. When incandescent light was introduced, the lamp units were used, at first, on the floor, and then almost all lighting left the floor and went up on the rail everywhere.

"Hitchcock Talks about Lights, Camera, Action" was originally published in *American Cinematographer* 48, no. 5 (May 1967): 332–335, 350–351.

It was always high—and that is when the "top-spot type" of back-light came into general use.

This may sound like a history of lighting, really, but I'm only doing this to point out how one element hung over to another. When sound came in, of course, we went all out for incandescent lighting until they were able to silence the arcs, but I can remember that in the days of the very earliest sound films the stage was like a bake oven. It was a mass of these large incandescent lights everywhere. Then of course, finally, they were able to silence the arcs and the spots.

A lot of this took place before you became actively engaged in direct-ing films. What was your actual production function during the early days of your motion picture career?

Well, of course, I'm a *technician* as well as a director, and back in 1923, I functioned as the writer of the picture and also the art director and production designer—always on the same picture. I always did both jobs. In addition to that, I was even sent out to turn the camera now and again.

How did that come about?

I can remember I was on one picture in 1927 when the camera-man went sick and we didn't have a replacement, so I had to do it myself. I was doing both the directing, and the lighting, and it was rather amusing because I would say to the Assistant Director, "We're ready to go" and he would say, "Well, you haven't *lit* it yet." I'd actually forgotten to light it, and I thought, "Oh dear, now I've got to light it. I forgot that." And on another occasion, I would light the scene and say, "Let's go." And they would say "But you haven't *rehearsed* it yet." So the ability to do the two jobs was rather difficult. I was able to do lighting, but I did take the precaution of grinding off a few feet of every scene and send-ing it across to the lab, which was on the lot, to have them hand test it. I mean, I wasn't all that confident of my ability as a lighting man. But even so, it worked out quite well. That was in the days of lighting from the floor with the Kliegs, and the back spot from the top creating the halo around the head, what they call the "liner" today. What was always at the back of the lighting man's mind was the separation of the image from the background. Then, also he used to go in for a great deal of modeling. In other words, there was this yearning to get a stereoscopic effect. But one wondered, was it worth it, really? Was it worth creating an artificial effect in lighting simply to achieve this separation of the figure from the background? Because, there are other ways of doing it—by focus for example. You can focus on your primary subject and let your background fall out. You have to do it in close-ups anyway.

How do you feel about the practice of having the subject sharp and the background fuzzy in a close-up, rather than having everything sharp from subject to background?

My argument has always been: Who wants to see around the close-up? Why should it be sharp behind the close-up? But there was always this aim, and this seemed to me to create an unreal effect—this yearning for the modeled figure, and this separation of the image from the background.

What about the danger of the subject "falling into" the background—becoming confused with it, so to speak?

There was sometimes that danger in monochrome and, therefore, a fairly good reason for striving to achieve separation. That's why, in the old days, we never put wallpaper on the walls of a set—because the pattern would grow out of a man's head. So there was a valid reason, in the days of predominantly black-and-white cinematography, for separating the subject from the background. People may disagree with me, but I'm not sure that reason holds good for color.

Why not?

Because I've always felt that color should be used as its own separation, and we should not need to back light so much to separate the image from the background as we do in black-and-white. Now, of course, there's another "habit." I call it, of lighting, which has been used since lighting from the rail came into being. There has developed a tendency, for example, if there were flowers, in the set, to take a top light and put it on the flowers. It's often done on a practical lamp, as well. It's common to see a lit lamp throwing a black shadow on the wall. Now, there's no reason for that, at all; it's just habit. The result is that you have black shadows all over the walls. You should say to yourself, "In real life, in *reality* where does this light source come from?" You find a scene, let's say, in a farm cottage or somewhere, with objects individually lit around the room, instead of having the light come from one natural source, a single window—because the sun doesn't always come through *every* window. Although I remember in the old days, when we used to light a set, there would be about six moons shining through— one for each window.

How did this search for more natural lighting finally lead to your decision to use reflected light for filming Torn Curtain?

It came to the point where one asked: "What *is* natural light?" That's when I brought Jack Warren in and I said, "Look at the way we're sitting here. What is the light like in this room? Are there black shadows anywhere? We're living in a reflected light. In this office, as we sit here, there's not one bit of direct light on us, even from the window because the curtains have softened it. The colors are not shouting at us. Everything is soft and there is no artificial element of light in this room. Why can't we put the same effect on the screen in *Torn Curtain?*" So Jack went to work, and decided that the best way to arrive at it was by two methods. By reflecting the light and, where we had to use direct light on faces and things, to soften it sufficiently to match the generally reflected light.

In the American Cinematographer *article on* Torn Curtain, *Director of Photography John Warren, ASC, mentioned that he utilized gray gauze in front of the lens. What prompted the use of that technique?*

In order to further reduce the risk of color taking over too much, we shot through a gray gauze, which cut the color down. People talk about delicate color or vulgar color, depending upon whichever end of the scale you lean toward. However, that camera will record whatever you give it, so it's always a matter of taste. Some people think that because it's a color picture, the girl's got to wear a dress with flowers all over it. That's nonsense. When we did *Torn Curtain,* we set up a rule: the moment we got into East Germany, we'd go to gray and beige tones only. No bright colors—except a spot of red now and again which would reflect the red of the uniforms worn by the Vopos. That was a decision we made, coordinated with the costume designer. All these decisions really relate to the photography. You can't expect a cameraman to give you a beautiful effect when the thing given him to photograph is vulgarized and unbalanced by excessive color. For example, the set dresser will put in a green settee and then the costume designer, without any consultation, will put the girl in a purple dress or a pink dress and sit her in the green settee. I'm all for the cinematographer becoming more involved in production design. I think he should be brought into it much more than he is.

How would that differ from usual present procedure?

According to our system as it is today, the cameraman comes on the set and he is given a thing to photograph. The manner in which a set is dressed, wherever they put the lamps is very important. Supposing for example, a cameraman is going to have to shoot a scene which relies on certain lighting effects. Now, he hasn't had a word to say about where the practical lamps should go in the set. Actually he should get a rough idea from the director where the movement is going to be, and then say, "Don't put that practical lamp there, place it somewhere else." But the poor cameraman doesn't have a chance, because the set dresser's already put it there. He's got to follow that. What's wrong with bringing the cameraman in much earlier so that you could say to him, "Jack, are these light fixtures all right? Do you think you're going to run into any difficulties here and there?" The same with the production designer. He should work in close contact with the cameraman. But in some studios, the cameraman comes on the lot maybe only a week before they begin to shoot. It's ridiculous. He should have at least a month or more to prepare.

At what point in your pre-planning do you begin the actual, functional visual design of the production?

When I'm writing script, I bring in the production designer very early on, and when I'm sitting there with a writer and we're designing a scene, I'll say, "I wonder whether we can do that. What sort of setting should we write this for?" We bring in the production designer while the script is being written. We have another strange anomaly in our business: the art director leaves the set the moment it's painted. Then the set dresser comes on. And yet the art director plays no part in the set dressing. That's standard practice. That's why, on *Torn Curtain*, I brought in Hein Heckroth as an overall coordinator of production design—also because the film had a German setting and we needed someone who was thoroughly familiar with that particular atmosphere.

Can you cite a particular sequence in Torn Curtain *which required especially precise coordination of the functions of the art director and the cinematographer?*

There was one very effective sequence in the film that I purposely played entirely in long shot. It took place in that East Berlin hotel room where we had the evening sun shining in—just a faint yellow shaft of warm sunlight; the rest was that awful heavy brown, a mood effect. That sequence represents very close coordination between the visual conceptions of the production designer and the cameraman. The lighting, and the color of the light, work in relation to the somber tones of the room.

You are noted for your technique of "pre-cutting" a film. Can you explain just how this works?

Yes, I can give you an example. In designing certain scenes, one of the important elements you have to take into account is the period of time that scene will actually remain on the screen. Sometimes a scene is only about a 6-foot flash. The eye doesn't have time to take it in, and needs a very sharp delineation, a sharp structure within the composition, to make it arresting to the eye for the short period of time it's on the screen. In the theater, the eye roves around the set; they've got forty minutes for an act, but we don't have that on the screen; things flash by so quickly.

How do you arrive at the choice of image size?

The size of image is a very important consideration. To spring a surprise, like when Paul Newman in *Torn Curtain* goes out to the farm, I have a little tiny figure crossing the field and when he arrives there, it goes *voom!* to the big head. That's a change in image size which is very vital. *Psycho* is full of that sort of thing. There I had the detective coming up the stairs inside the old house. The audience knows there's a monster lurking around, a female monster. The first shot is quite an ordinary one as he climbs the stairway, but when he gets to the top of the stairs I jump the camera to the ceiling. The murderer comes rushing out in a straight-down rather long shot. Then I drop down and jump to a big head of the detective as the knife slashes across his face. The long high shot serves to accentuate the close-up.

Were you allowed to go into East Germany to film those establishing shots which appear in Torn Curtain?

No. We had to do a lot of trick cutting and mixing—actual scenes with those staged in the studio. We shot most of our exteriors for the film right on the backlot of the Universal City Studios—but these scenes were intercut with real ones filmed in East Germany. Paul Newman comes out of the hotel in the morning just before going to that museum. He looks up the street. I cut to a real East Berlin shot of a yellow bus coming along. Then he runs across the street and gets on the yellow bus. I match that shot with one of a duplicate bus on the backlot. Those shots made in East Berlin were photographed by a cameraman we sent in from the West who just got us a few pre-described scenes on the pretext that he was doing a travelogue.

What do you feel are some of the important elements to be considered if actual location shots are to be smoothly intercut with scenes filmed on the backlot?

There is an important key to creating reality on the backlot. If you're content to do a small portion of the set very accurately, it's much better than trying to do a whole street. This is a principle which I've stuck to every since I was an art director. I was working on the UFA lot in Germany in its heyday and there I picked up a great deal of insight into the techniques of set building and perspective of every kind. Once I had a scene to do against the doorway entrance into Milan Cathedral. It's one of the biggest Gothic piles in Europe. I only had to have a shot of a man going through the door into the black interior, so I had to decide how I was going to do it. I would never have been able to build the entrance of the Milan Cathedral; the doors are probably 100 feet high. What I did do was solve the problem by building, in actual scale, the real thing—just one column on the left, but I made it about 8 or 9 feet high only. Its proportions were enormous, and I included half a dozen steps accurately measured, so that we got this big base of a Gothic column and the beginning of the door with a huge hinge on it and the eye did the rest for you. The lines went up out of the picture following the Gothic column and the lines of the set went out to the right. I went to the zoo there and asked for a few pigeons. So I had these few pigeons and they flew around and sat on the stone work, but the point was to do a little piece of the building accurately and well, rather than try to do a sort of cheaply built whole structure. I believe if you're doing a thing on the backlot, you have to go out and get photographs of the real thing and reproduce a portion of it—but with complete accuracy.

The museum "chase" sequence in Torn Curtain *gave an impression of tremendous production value, but those apparently huge sets would have been enormously expensive had they actually been constructed full-scale. What did you do instead in order to achieve the effect?*

That was a very good technical job—that sequence in the museum, but those were all matte shots—except for the few intercut close shots. The trick there—which is another thing that comes out of my training as an art director—is to shoot your long shots from up high with a painted floor (that's all we painted; the rest was a matte) and then have a little background piece built for a close shot of the actor against it. It's important not to go from one long shot directly to the next long shot. Put something real in the middle between your matte shots. I go: long shot, matte—then real background for the close-up. I alternated them all the time.

What are some of your principles regarding the use of the moving camera?

I believe in using camera movement when it helps tell the story more effectively. I suppose the most outstanding example of that is a picture I made called *Rope,* in which each sequence was actually a full 10-minute reel filmed without interruption but with a multitude of camera moves to achieve the various angles. It wasn't actually very cinematic; it was really an extension of theater. It was like giving the audience opera glasses, all of them, and letting them follow the characters around. I think one of the first essentials of the moving camera is that the eye should not be aware of it. In other words, the eye should be on the character moving, but I'm all for the moving camera when it's properly used. For example, let's say you have a scene between two people in a quarrel, a man and a woman. And you've got them on a sofa in a close shot cutting just below head and shoulders, the two of them, and the girl gets up angrily and walks across the room. I'll follow her in close-up across the room to maintain the mood. But very often this isn't done; a cut-back to a longer shot is used instead. And why? I don't understand that. Why shouldn't you stay close? Because the mood of the woman's emotional disturbance is there, you should never cut back—at least not until she gets over it and calms down. Then you can ease the camera out, ease it back unobtrusively.

Are there any definite rules which you follow without deviation, as far as shooting technique is concerned?

There are very, very strict rules that I adhere to. For example, never, never use a shot without its having a clear dramatic purpose. But, on the other hand, I don't shoot "master" scenes. I just shoot the one that's necessary, unless there's a dualogue. If you've got two people talking at a table, you shoot over-the-shoulder shots and you have to repeat the scene, but otherwise not. Also, to me, it seems that the size of the image on the screen must contribute. You cannot shoot long shots indiscriminately unless you're establishing a locale. But I think the long shot can be very dramatic when you need it.

For a long time you seemed to prefer making pictures in black-and-white rather than in color. How do your preferences lie currently in that regard?

I think that I prefer making films in color. The reason I didn't do *Psycho* in color was because of the blood. That was the only reason. With all the blood in that bathtub, I knew very well I'd have had the whole sequence cut out—if it had been filmed in color. It just couldn't have been done.

What do you think of the statement often made that certain films should be made only in black-and-white because even muted color would be too obtrusive, dramatically speaking?

There *is* a theory that certain pictures should be made in black-and-white because of the mood of the picture—which may be true in a few cases, but I think a similar mood can be achieved in color. For example, if you take a country scene in the winter, with a gray mist to it, just fields and bare trees, nothing in bright color, that's just as effective as black-and-white because you can feel the coldness from the bleak color. There is also the fact that in a color film, if you want to reduce a scene to black-and-white you can use nothing but grays. There were several such sequences in *Torn Curtain*. For example, there was the scene in the Security office at the airport. It was all gray, everywhere. The only color was in the faces. Just the faces, that's all. So really, you're back to black-and-white except for the faces. The set and the clothes and the decor are all gray. It all goes back to my previous comment, that whatever you give that color camera, it'll photograph for you.

What do you feel are the most important elements to be considered in the establishment of mood on the screen?

I think, to sum it up in one way, the risk you run in trying to get mood is the *cliché*, the shadows in the room and what have you. I spend half of my time avoiding the *cliché*, in terms of scenes. In *North by Northwest*, the girl sends Cary Grant to a rendezvous where we know an attempt will be made to kill him. Now the *cliché* treatment would be to show him standing on the corner of the street in a pool of light. The cobbles are washed by the recent rains. Cut to a face peering out of a window. Cut to a black cat slithering along the bottom of a wall. Wait for a black limousine to come along. I said *no*. I would do it in bright sunshine with no place to hide, in open prairie country. And what is the mood? A *sinister* mood. There's not a sign of where the menace can come from, but eventually it turns up in the form of a crop duster airplane. Someone inside the plane shoots at Cary Grant and he has nowhere to hide.

Do you feel that lighting is perhaps the most important single element in the creation of cinematic mood?

Motion picture mood is often thought of as almost *exclusively* a matter of lighting, *dark* lighting. It isn't. Mood is *apprehension*. That's what you've got in that crop duster scene. In other words, as I said years and years ago, I prefer "murder by the babbling brook." You've got some of that in *The Trouble With Harry*. Where did I lay the dead body? Among the most beautiful colors I could find. Autumn in Vermont. Went up there and waited for the leaves to turn. We did it in counterpoint. I wanted to take a nasty taste away by making the setting beautiful. I have sometimes been accused of building a film around an effect, but in my sort of film you often have to do that if you want to get something other than the *cliché*.

You have spoken of working with the production designer in the selection of locales during the scripting phase of a production. What is your primary consideration in the choice of setting for a particular sequence?

A rule that I've always followed is: Never use a setting simply as a background. Use it one hundred percent. For example, in *Torn Curtain*, Paul Newman goes to a ballet. Who discovers him? A ballerina, in the middle of her dance. How does he get the idea to shout "Fire!"? From a scenic fire on the stage. You've got to make the setting work dramatically. You can't use it just as a background. In other words, the locale must be functional. In the crop duster sequence in *North by Northwest*, the crop duster is used as a weapon carrier. That is to say, someone in the plane shoots at Cary Grant; but this is not enough. If we are using a crop duster—then it must dust crops. In this particular case, the crops are the hiding place of Cary Grant. So I don't use a crop duster with only a gun. That's not enough. It must be used according to its true function. *All backgrounds must function.*

Certainly one of the most off-beat settings you've ever used was in that same film, the Mount Rushmore Memorial.

Yes, but unfortunately, I couldn't use the Mount Rushmore Memorial to function according to my established pattern. The authorities wouldn't let me work on the faces at all. I had to work *between* them. I wanted Cary Grant to slide down Lincoln's nose and hide in the nostril. Then Grant has a sneezing fit, while he's in the nostril. *That* would have made the setting very functional.

Isn't there sometimes a very fine line between a setting that is most unusual and one that is credible to the audience?

The basic principle to be observed is to be as life-like as one can—especially in my sort of material. I deal in *fantasy*. In other words, I don't deal in slice-of-life stories. My suspense work comes out of creating nightmares for the audience. And I *play* with an audience. I make them gasp and surprise them and shock them. When you have a nightmare, it's awfully vivid if you're dreaming that you're being led to the electric chair. Then you're as happy as can be when you wake up because you're relieved. It *was so* vivid. And that's really the basis of this attempt at realistic photography, to make it look as real as possible, because the effects themselves are actually quite bizarre. The audience responds in proportion to how realistic you make it. One of the dramatic reasons for this type of photography is to get it looking so natural that the audience gets involved and believes, for the time being, what's going on up there on the screen.

It's a Bird, It's a Plane,
It's . . . *The Birds*

I suppose that *The Birds* is probably the most prodigious job ever done. I don't know whether you are aware of what we call double printing, but we have a system called the traveling matte process.

Let us assume that we're going to photograph two men talking on the corner of Fifth Avenue, New York, and we're shooting the picture in June, but the story requires a snow-covered street. Now, normally in a scene like this they'd shoot the background, and we'd put it on a screen and stand the two men in front of it. In this particular case you can't do that because you're making the picture in June. So what you do is photograph the two men against a white background, and then the film is put away.

Now, say the picture isn't going out until the following year. The first snows come to New York in November. The cameraman goes out and sets the camera up roughly where the two men have stood and photographs Fifth Avenue in the snow. That film is brought to the studio—the lab—and they work on what is called the optical printer. The first film that goes into the printer is the raw stuff—the unexposed film—and against that the negative of Fifth Avenue.

Now, a print is made of the two men in front of the white backing and is overdeveloped to such a degree that the two men become silhouettes. So you add that as a third film to go through the

"It's a Bird, It's a Plane, It's . . . *The Birds*" was originally published in *Take One* 1, no. 10 (1968): 6–7.

printer. Thus you have a raw film, Fifth Avenue, and this black silhouette of two men talking.

In the printer, the black portion of the men has prevented the light from going through, so that the only part exposed onto the raw film is Fifth Avenue around the two men. If you were to develop that film at that moment and run it on a screen, you would get Fifth Avenue and two white silhouettes. Of course you don't develop it, you just rewind the film and start again.

Now, what is the negative of the two men? We shot them against a white background, therefore the white background in the negative is black. So you just put this negative and the already partly exposed raw film through a printer the second time and now you have the men being printed in the space provided for them—the unexposed portion of the film. That is what is called a traveling matte.

Now, of course over the years that's all changed. When we come to do *The Birds,* this is what we are going to do: We're going to have children running down the street and we have the problem of overlaying the ravens. We had about thirty or forty ravens who were trained to fly from one perch to another in the studio against a plain background.

But *now* we're in color. So, in order to get a silhouette (we must have a silhouette, otherwise it will ghost—like two snaps on one film), we photograph in color against a yellow background (the same light that they use for fog lamps on cars). This sodium light, as it is called, is a color that is the narrowest band on the spectrum of light and comes out black. It's the only color that won't photograph.

So now you have your colored image and a black background. At the same time there is a prism—a lens which makes two images. One goes through in color and the other is reflected through a red filter onto an ordinary black-and-white film, so that you make your silhouette at the same time as you're making your scene. So that when you put the two together you have the negative of the children running down the street and the silhouette of the birds printed first and the real birds afterwards. So they're overlayed.

Now, you don't hold that scene for very long—you hold it for a flash. Then you go to a close-up of one of the children and you throw a live trained bird onto the shoulder of the child. And it's the intercutting, the quick intercutting, that gives you the illusion of the scene in close-up and in distance and so forth.

One of the most spectacular shots in *The Birds* was a high shot showing seagulls going down to attack a town. Now, we didn't have a full town out there, we had a dockside and so forth. So we put the camera on a hill of the studio where they were building a new car park. In our scene we had a gas station on fire and a trail of flaming gas toward a car park. That we staged way below the studio. But all the rest was nothing—we just marked it out with lines so that people could only run in a certain direction. The matte-artist painted a painting of the view from above the harbor, except he blacked out the live portion—the flame and the people running. These two—live portion and matte—are printed together. So that now, when we look at it on the screen, it's as though you're in a helicopter or high up in a balloon. There's a whole town, there's a blaze, and people running.

Now the next problem: having the birds fly down. We hired an island off the coast and put a camera on a high cliff. We brought the gulls around with fish behind the camera and then threw the fish over the cliff. And with the camera on the beach below. When this film was shown we looked at it and there it was: a cliffside, surf, beach, with gulls going down.

Now, two women took this film frame by frame—each little frame. Only fifteen feet in all, but it took them three months to transfer by painting each individual bird onto a plain background. They also painted the silhouette of each bird. And that's the way the birds were printed over the scene and they were seen going down. That lasted ten seconds on the screen—we took three months to do it.

Hitchcock at Work

MR. HITCHCOCK: The film is going to open with a girl, back view, going into a railroad station at Hartford, Connecticut. At present, I don't know what time of the day we can shoot it because we don't want it full of crowds because it may cover her up. The essential part is that we follow her back view into the station as she goes to the desk or booking office.

EVAN HUNTER: The ticket window. But Hitch, it should be on a Friday evening because she goes directly there from robbing the safe.

MR. HITCHCOCK: Well, we needn't say it's Friday evening as long as we don't people it with too many people; we're going to have to put our extras in it anyway however we shoot it there. And she goes to the ticket window and buys a ticket. We still follow her into the station as she looks up and we go up to New York, you see. We go close enough to her to see the color of her hair, and finally she goes on to the platform down toward the train. Or it can be empty waiting for the train to come in. I don't know, we've got to look into that, you see, or you can probably be going east to find out all this information for us. And we end up with a close shot on a rather bulky handbag under her arm. So that would constitute the first scene which we'll have to investigate whether we

"Hitchcock at Work" was originally published in *Take One* 5, no. 2 (May 1976): 31–35. It was edited from a transcription of a production conference during preparations for *Marnie*.

shoot it all in the station, whether we make a traveling plate of it or what is the best way to handle that, you see. I feel that we ought to cheat like they do in the Italian films and have nobody around if we can. Because otherwise we don't draw enough attention to the girl. The next sequence cuts immediately to an open safe and a crowd around it in an office. This would require an impression of an office, and maybe we can have one of those kind of offices with glass screens around it. So we get an impression of an office beyond, which we can either make as a backing or something because we needn't show too much activity or we can fake a set behind it. And the essence of this scene is that the safe has been robbed and there is a group of people. Mainly that constitutes the scene in which the manager or proprietor or the high official, whoever he may be, he is known in the story as a Mr. Strutt, is the self-conscious figure who apparently gave this girl a job, without proper references and we indicate that he was obviously impressed by her other than her ability as a clerk or whatever she was, so he becomes a central guilty figure. So pictorially it's a group scene, you see.

MR. HUNTER: Also, it's an accounting firm, Bob.

MR. BOYLE: Wouldn't Hartford—would it be insurance? Probably would be insurance, wouldn't it?

MR. HUNTER: Well, we want it to be accounting because he comes in later on—

MR. HITCHCOCK: He comes in later on in the story. This man is a very important figure, because he comes in, that's why we—the scene will be concentrated on this man and we read a complete picture of this man falling for the girl when he shouldn't have done. It's the chief cashier who's a girl—almost accuses him of having an affair with her—which he didn't. As we shall find later—but nevertheless he feels very guilty about the whole thing and he's right on the spot. There're police around and so forth, etc. Now, from that we continue the next scene down a hotel corridor—still back view on the girl and she's now carrying a suitcase which is brand new, wrapped in brown paper and—

MR. HUNTER: Excuse me, may I break in here a minute—do we need to tell Bob what we need in the way of a physical thing in the office since *modus operandi*'s going to figure in this, you know. Her access to the safe.

MR. HITCHCOCK: I don't think so.

MR. HUNTER: We don't?

MR. HITCHCOCK: Not for our opening scene. As long as we show the safe as being robbed but our dialogue will tell us a lot there. Now in this next scene, following the office scene as I said, we're going down a corridor in a hotel and we can establish this as a hotel by possibly a clear—a floor weight or, I don't know, depends what type of hotel we use. I don't think it should be a big hotel. It should be a small hotel, rather cheesy. But we have to establish within this corridor what it is, you see.

MR. HUNTER: Not too cheesy, you know. Not like the 47th Street ones, off Broadway.

MR. BOYLE: Where are we in this hotel?

MR. HUNTER: New York City.

MR. BOYLE: New York City.

MR. HUNTER: But not a luxury hotel, either.

MR. HITCHCOCK: No. And she finally goes into a room and there we see another suitcase, clothes on the bed, and now she tears the paper in which is the brand new suitcase and there are other boxes on the bed showing purchases, and the scene in this little bedroom constitutes her change of clothes and the cutting out of labels and so forth, you see, and then eventually we go and follow her into a bathroom and she goes round behind the door and by this time she's taken off probably part of her clothes and we hear the water go on and so forth and eventually we go into the bathroom and we just go to the head and we've never seen her face yet and right on the head down into the basin and we see the dark, very dark brown dye flowing out of the hair into the basin. And it just swirls around this dye—and for the first time she lifts her face. The hair is now blond and we see her face, for the first time. Now—we go then to Penn Station or a Greyhound station—have we decided . . .

MR. HUNTER: I think the bus terminal would be better. You know, we've had one railroad station—

MR. HITCHCOCK: Whatever it is—it will probably be the bus terminal.

MR. HUNTER: The Port Authority Bus Terminal on, I think, it's 38th and 8th.

MR. BOYLE: Not to leave the hotel room so soon—she has no reason. She's just trying to pick something that's a nonentity, isn't she? It's neither too poor nor too rich. It's some lost hotel.

MR. HITCHCOCK: Quality of the hotel—you're talking about the quality of the hotel?

MR. BOYLE: Well, yeah, I'm going back to the hotel. What kind of a hotel she would pick. Obviously, she has money, so she could live anywhere.

MR. HUNTER: Yes, but she doesn't want to call attention to herself, in any way, you see; she's going in there to change her identity really.

MR. HITCHCOCK: That's all she is—so that she would choose a very quiet hotel. Very quiet, very unobtrusive hotel. So you can debate this again, you know. A girl can get lost in the biggest hotel, just as well. You know, so that you see that there are many people up and down the corridors and the elevator and so forth, but . . .

MR. BOYLE: Yes that's true.

MR. HITCHCOCK: We could debate that, but we don't have to decide that finally now.

MR. BOYLE: Could be a business hotel.

MR. HITCHCOCK: Like the New Yorker or the Commodore.

MR. BOYLE: People come and go all the time.

MR. HITCHCOCK: As a matter of fact . . .

MR. BOYLE: Or the Biltmore across from . . .

MR. HITCHCOCK: The way to establish that is to establish a facade of a hotel with so many windows, you know.

MR. BOYLE: Yeah.

MR. HITCHCOCK: So if you state that fact, you know, a mass of windows . . .

MR. BOYLE: The Commodore would be very good.

MR. HITCHCOCK: The Commodore—Anyway. We can debate that afterwards. Now—the only reason I bring up the question, Evan, as to whether it should be a railroad station or bus station. Can you leave a suitcase there—for good? In the lockups, it's no good.

MR. BOYLE: Well, sure it is. Why not?

MR. HITCHCOCK: Because they empty them every 24 hours.

MR. BOYLE: Well, what does she care what they do with it? It'll vanish from sight. She's going to throw the key away, anyway. So they'll take the bag out of the locker and take it someplace else. She's never going to claim it. What does she care?

MR. HITCHCOCK: Right. Well, anyway this bus depot. She deposits the old bag. She arrives with two bags, you see. An old one and a new one. The old bag is deposited and then she goes to the bus with the new bag, you see. And the bus drives off. I think we're going to label it to Maryland, Laurel—

MR. HUNTER: Well, no, I play a scene where she buys a ticket. There's dialogue. At the window, she buys a ticket to Laurel, Maryland. And he tells her when the bus is leaving and when it's going to arrive and all that.

MR. HITCHCOCK: On arriving at her destination there's a station wagon belonging to a hotel waiting for her at the destination, which we've got at present as . . .

MR. HUNTER: Laurel, Maryland.

MR. HITCHCOCK: Laurel, Maryland, you see. This isn't final, you see. Laurel, Maryland, of course, is a well-known race track center and so forth. From here there's a station wagon waiting with the name of a hotel on the side. And she's driven . . . and we may have a couple of establishing shots of going through the countryside to establish we're in the country, you see. And then it eventually arrives at what we call the Old Colonial Hotel. This hotel has to have a bit of class about it, you know, it's where retired people can live, there are horse people. It's in—it should be a hotel within its own small grounds in this area and it should be related to racing, hunting, you know, that's the atmosphere that we take her into.

Because don't forget we've got a strange mysterioso working for us. Because after all you've seen a girl who's a petty thief or a small thief changing her hair, clothes and so forth, and now she's arriving in completely contrapuntal surroundings—beautiful countryside and a rather smart or traditional hotel—

MR. HUNTER: And she's been here—you know—she's recognized here—she's been here many times before.

MR. HITCHCOCK: Now we come into the lobby. The lobby of this hotel conveys the same quality. And when she goes to the desk a man carries her bag in and the woman clerk recognizes her immediately, addresses her by name and says "Your riding clothes came back a week ago" or something or yesterday or whatever we establish "and they're in your room" or she asks, you know. We establish anyway she's left clothes there, which still sets up a mystery. And now she goes from there and we see her change—is that right?

MR. HUNTER: No, I think we should simply show her coming right into where the horse is kept.

MR. HITCHCOCK: That's what I meant.

MR. HUNTER: Oh, I thought you meant showing her change.

MR. HITCHCOCK: No, no, she goes upstairs and from there that indicates she's going upstairs to change and now we go right to the stables, where she arrives.

MR. HUNTER: This is another place now. It's not a part of the hotel grounds.

MR. HITCHCOCK: That's why we might have to show the station wagon taking her there. So she might get out of the station wagon at some stables. Now, these stables should be—I think they're a type of stable where they train yearlings and other people are allowed to keep horses. This is very important to find out—what kind of stables this would be. She keeps a horse there. But it's vital to our story that she knows about the training of horses, especially race horses. And we have to get that over. You see, what happens now with a regularly trained race horse . . . it goes to stables from one meet to another, that's how it works out now. That, I found out—they don't go back to training stables. In England they do.

But they don't necessarily—once a horse has been trained—so this should be a training stable—

MR. BOYLE: And also a boarding stable.

MR. HUNTER: It's a boarding stable. She's not training a horse there, she's just boarding it.

MR. BOYLE: Exercise boys and people like that who work with the horses.

MR. HITCHCOCK: And also they might—we might choose a place where they have a track—a training track.

MR. HUNTER: They would have.

MR. BOYLE: Or training rings, at least.

MR. HITCHCOCK: Well, I know tracks where they have them out here in Northridge. Lot of these people have training tracks. Starting gate, schooling, what they call schooling, and so forth. Now—we show her riding, which calls for some beautiful landscapes and her riding in the distance on this horse. Not any particular way—around and so forth and then we go to close-ups, which will mean plates and things . . . for her close-ups showing her enjoying it and her hair blowing and it's very important that we establish here one big close-up of the hair blowing and as she's riding—

MR. BOYLE: And come back to that.

MR. HITCHCOCK: And it's a motif, you see—it's a leitmotif that goes through the film. Again, it's going to be presented in such a way that you say, well I don't get this—we want to mystify the audience. The contrast between the thievery and the way she was dressed . . . quite modestly, as a clerk, and so forth, with this proprietary interest in this particular horse-riding thing she has. Now, from there we go to visit her mother. Her mother is going to live in Baltimore. In one of those streets where they have all those steps—you know—the whitewash steps? This again is a tremendous contrast 'cause you see, we've practically shown, we've done all this cinematically—we've told the mystery of this girl in a series of images of pictures and settings and backgrounds. That's why they're all very important because they do make statements all the time. Now we get this cheesy, long Baltimore residential street. It's almost like a—you haven't been to Baltimore, have you? Well, it's like the north of England street—just the same—oh yes, just like the north of England. Rows of houses and chimneys but the one feature of Baltimore is that people take great pride in their steps 'cause all the houses have one step up from the sidewalk. And they're always done with pumice stone or whitewashed or painted white. You get this vista of all these steps, you see, and she drives down the street, maybe in a taxi . . .

MR. HUNTER: If we can, Bob, if we can get it near the water someplace . . .

MR. HITCHCOCK: What would be nice if at the end of the street we could see masts of ships 'cause this is very important later on. And they do have them, there're probably streets around there with this terribly sordid atmosphere—the saloon at the corner and the ships down at the bottom. And the taxi stops and she gets out. Then, you know, opens the door—or the door's opened for her. Now she's in her mother's home, which is pretty . . . it has to be the size of the real house—quite small, narrow passage, the sitting room in the front and the one story up to the bedrooms, staircase up in the hallway. There, of course, we have the scene where she meets her mother and the little woman who looks after her. And we play the whole scene—and the girl's familiar with the place and there'll be a kitchen required.

MR. HUNTER: This should be a pretty dowdy place.

MR. HITCHCOCK: Oh, it will be dowdy. Bob, we'll eventually get the photographs of the real interior there. That'll all be done. We'll get all that. But the external atmosphere is very important, to show again, the contrast of the riding and she's now in a nice suit, not too showy but fairly conservative and she's blond. And she goes in and now we introduce the mother and now something of her—the fact that she brings gifts to them and that she works for a millionaire and her mother believes her. We characterize her mother as a cautious woman. . . .

A Bibliography of the Writings of Alfred Hitchcock

The following is a list of all of Hitchcock's published writings that I have either located or seen cited, excluding the brief prefaces to the many volumes of horror and mystery stories that came out under his name. I interpret the category of "Hitchcock's published writings" fairly broadly to include not only items that came out under his name but also those that quote him extensively. I do not attempt to list all interviews with Hitchcock or all items that quote him briefly, however substantively; Jane Sloan's *Alfred Hitchcock: A Guide to References and Resources,* while not complete, is a useful guide to these. But I do call attention to a few substantive writings not listed by Sloan.

Entries appear chronologically by date of publication. When original publishing information is not available, or if an item not reprinted in this volume is extremely rare and hard to locate, I include the location of the microfilm, microfiche, or clipping file where I examined it. BFI fiche refers to the British Film Institute Hitchcock clippings file on microfiche; Herrick Library refers to the Hitchcock Collection at the Margaret Herrick Library, Academy of Motion Picture Arts and Sciences; MOMA refers to the Hitchcock clippings folders at the Film Study Center of the Museum of Modern Art; and NYPL refers to the New York Public Library clippings file. A • before an item indicates that it is included in this volume.

• "Gas." *The Henley: Social Club Magazine of the Henley Company Ltd.* I, no. 1 (1919).
• "Films We Could Make." *London Evening News,* November 16, 1927. Listed by Sloan, 345, as "Americans: A Letter," following Spoto's citation, 113–114, 599.
"The Talkie King Talks." *London Evening News,* June 25, 1929.
"How a Talking Film Is Made." *Film Weekly,* November 18, 1929, 16–17.
"Two English Film Producers on British Girls We Want for the Talkies." *Daily Mail,* March 10, 1930. [MOMA clipping file.]

- "How I Choose My Heroines." In *Who's Who in Filmland,* by Langford Reed and Hetty Spiers, xxi–xxiii. London: Chapman and Hall, 1931.
- "Are Stars Necessary?" *Picturegoer,* December 16, 1933, 13.
- Watts, Stephen. "AH on Music in Films." *Cinema Quarterly* (Edinburgh) 2 (Winter 1933–1934): 80–83. [Interview.]
- "Half the World in a Talkie: A Chat with Alfred Hitchcock." *London Evening News,* March 5, 1934. [BFI fiche no. 9.]
- "Stodgy British Pictures." *Film Weekly,* December 14, 1934, 14.
- "If I Were Head of a Production Company." *Picturegoer,* January 26, 1935, 15.
- Buchanan, Barbara J. "Women are a Nuisance." *Film Weekly,* September 20, 1935, 10. [Interview.]
- "Why Thrillers Thrive." *Picturegoer,* January 18, 1936, 15.
- "My Screen Memories: I Begin with a Nightmare," written in collaboration with John K. Newnham. *Film Weekly,* May 2, 1936, 16–18. [Five-part series, including the following 4 items.]
- "My Screen Memories: The Story Behind 'Blackmail.'" *Film Weekly,* May 9, 1936, 7.
- "My Screen Memories: My Strangest Year." *Film Weekly,* May 16, 1936, 28–29.
- "My Screen Memories: Making 'The Thirty-nine Steps.'" *Film Weekly,* May 23, 1936, 28–29.
- "My Screen Memories: My Spies." *Film Weekly,* May 30, 1936, 27.
- "Close Your Eyes and Visualize!" *Stage* 13 (July 1936): 52–53. [Also printed with slight changes as "I Make Suspense My Business," on BFI fiche no. 10; no source given.]
- "More Cabbages, Fewer Kings." *Kinematograph Weekly,* January 14, 1937, 30. [Also printed with slight changes in *Kine Weekly,* April 1937.]
- "Search for the Sun." *New York Times,* February 7, 1937, X, 5. [Also printed as "Why British Countryside Is Not Filmed," *Film Pictorial,* December 5, 1936.]
- "Life Among the Stars." *London News Chronicle,* March 1, 1937. [Five-part series, including the following 4 items; on BFI fiche nos. 9 and 10.]
- "Life Among the Stars: Nita Naldi, Vamp." *London News Chronicle,* March 2, 1937.
- "Life Among the Stars: One Scene that Made a Girl a Star." *London News Chronicle,* March 3, 1937.
- "Life Among the Stars: Handcuffed, Key Lost!" *London News Chronicle,* March 4, 1937.
- "Life Among the Stars: How I Make My Films." *London News Chronicle,* March 5, 1937.
- "Much Ado About Nothing." *The Listener,* March 10, 1937, 448–450.
- "Direction." In *Footnotes to the Film,* ed. Charles Davy, 3–15. New York: Oxford University Press, 1937. [Also printed as "My Own Methods," *Sight & Sound,* Summer 1937.]
- "Directors Are Dead." *Film Weekly,* November 20, 1937, 14.
- "Director's Problems." *The Listener,* February 2, 1938, 241. [Also printed in *Living Age* 354 (April 1938): 172–174.]

- "Nova Grows Up." *Film Weekly,* February 5, 1938, 5.
- Perkoff, Leslie. "The Censor and Sydney Street." *World Film News,* March 1938, 4–5. [Interview.]
- "Crime Doesn't Pay." *Film Weekly,* April 30, 1938, 9.

Benedetta, Mary. "Britain's Leading Film Director Gives Some Hints to the Film Stars of the Future." [*Evening Standard?*], July 14, 1938. [Interview; BFI fiche no. 10.]

- Williams, J. Danvers, "The Censor Wouldn't Pass It." *Film Weekly,* November 5, 1938, 6–7. [Interview.]
- "Some Aspects of Direction." *National Board of Review Magazine* XIII, no. 7 (October 1938): 6–8. [MOMA clipping folder.]
- Williams, J. Danvers. "What I'd Do to the Stars." *Film Weekly,* March 4, 1939, 12–13. [Interview.]
- Lecture at Columbia University, lecture, March 30, 1939. [Typescripts at Herrick Library and MOMA Film Study Center.]
- "Old Ruts Are New Ruts." *Hollywood Reporter* 54, no. 28 (October 28, 1939, 9th Anniversary Issue).

Introduction. In *Intrigue: Four Great Spy Novels of Eric Ambler,* by Eric Ambler, vii–viii. New York: Knopf, 1943.

Hitchcock, Alfred, and Harry Sylvester. "Lifeboat." *Collier's,* November 13, 1943, 16–17, 52-54, 56–58. [Story.]

"The Film Thriller." In *Film Review 1946–1947,* ed. F. M. Speed, 22–23. London: McDonald & Co., 1947.

"The Hitch Touch," *Band Wagon,* July 1946, 27–28. [BFI fiche no. 10.]

Clayton, David. "Hitchcock Hates Actors." *Filmindia,* July 1947. [Interview.]

"The First British Talkie." In *The Elstree Story,* 80–82. London: Clerke & Cockeran/Associated British Picture Corp., 1948.

- "Let 'Em Play God." *Hollywood Reporter* 100, no. 47 (October 11, 1948, 18th Anniversary Issue).
- "My Most Exciting Picture." *Popular Photography,* November 1948, 48–51, 96, 98, 100, 103–104.
- "The Enjoyment of Fear." *Good Housekeeping* 128 (February 1949): 39, 241–243.
- "Production Methods Compared." *Cine-Technician* 14, no. 75 (November–December 1948): 170–174. [Printed also in *American Cinematographer* 30, no. 5 (May 1949), and in *Hollywood Directors 1941–76,* ed. Richard Koszarski, 156–161. New York: Oxford University Press, 1977.]
- "Master of Suspense: Being a Self-Analysis by Alfred Hitchcock." *New York Times,* June 4, 1950, II, 4.
- "Core of the Movie—The Chase." *New York Times Magazine,* October 29, 1950, 22–23, 44–46. [Interview.]

"Death in the Crystal Ball." *Coronet* 29 (December 1950): 38.

"The Role I Liked Best. . . ." *Saturday Evening Post,* December 12, 1950. [4 brief paragraphs on his role in *Lifeboat.*]

"The Wise Man of Kumin." *Coronet* 30, no. 2 (June 1951): 38–39.

Preface, *Cahiers du Cinema,* no. 39 (October 1954): 11–13. [Preface written for a collection of detective stories.]

"The Chloroform Clue: My Favorite True Mystery." *American Weekly,* March 22, 1953, 18–20. [NYPL clipping file.]

"My Five Greatest Mysteries." *Coronet* 38 (September 1955): 75–77.

● "The Woman Who Knows Too Much." *McCall's* 83 (March 1956): 12, 14.

"H Speaking." *Cosmopolitan* 141 (October 1956): 66–67.

"How I'd Worry the Kremlin." *This Week Magazine,* November 11, 1956, 8–9.

● "Murder—With English on It." *New York Times Magazine,* March 3, 1957, 17, 42.

"The Great Hitchcock Murder Mystery." *This Week Magazine,* August 4, 1957, 8–9, 11.

"Why You Need Thrills and Chills." *This Week Magazine: The National Sunday Magazine,* September 22, 1957, 2. [NYPL clipping file, "Not Dated" folder. According to the introductory blurb, this is abridged from his introduction to an anthology, *This Week's Stories of Mystery and Suspense.*]

"Hitchcock in the Lion's Den." *This Week Magazine,* October 26, 1958, 22, 24.

"AH and his fan mail," *New York Herald Tribune,* January 6, 1959, 2, 14.

"Alfred Hitchcock." *Films and Filming* 5, no. 10 (July 1959): 7, 33.

● "Would You Like to Know Your Future." *Guideposts Magazine* 14, no. 8 (October 1959): 1–4.

● "Why I Am Afraid of the Dark." *Arts: Lettres, Spectacles,* no. 777, June 1–7, 1960, 1, 7. In French: "Pourquoi j'ai peur la nuit."

● "Elegance Above Sex." *Hollywood Reporter* 172, no. 39 (November 20, 1962, 32nd Anniversary Issue).

● "A Redbook Dialogue: AH and Dr. Fredric Wertham." *Redbook* 120 (April 1963): 71, 108, 110–112.

● "Hitchcock on Style." *Cinema* (Beverly Hills) 1, no. 5 (August/September 1963): 4–8, 34–35.

"Hitchcock Came to College." *Hollywood Reporter* 178, no. 1 (November 19, 1963, 33rd Anniversary Issue). [Reprinted in Hurley, 304–308.]

Wheldon, Huw. "Hitchcock on His Films." *The Listener,* August 6, 1964, 189–190. [Interview.]

● "Award-Winner Hitchcock Performs Brilliantly." *Morning Telegraph,* March 12 and 13, 1965. Herb Stein's column reprints the talk. [See "The Real Me," listed below, August 9, 1966, which uses material from here.]

Foreword. In *The Filmgoer's Companion,* ed. Leslie Halliwell, 7. London: MacGibbon and Kee, 1965.

"Hitchcock and the Dying Art: His Recorded Comments." *Film,* no. 46 (Summer, 1966). [Reprinted in *Film,* no. 79 (November 1979): 25–28.]

"The Real Me (The Thin One)." *Daily Express,* August 9, 1966, n.p. [BFI clipping file/microfiche.]

"Hitch." *Take One* (Montreal) 1, no. 1 (September/October 1966): 14–17. [Reprinted in LaValley as "I Wish I Didn't Have to Shoot the Picture."]

● "Hitchcock Talks About Lights, Cameras, Action." *American Cinematographer,* May 1967, 332–335, 350–351.

"Director Hitchcock Tells Young Film Directors How Easy It Is." *Making Films in New York* 2–4 (August 1968): 38. [Reprinted from interview in *Action* 3, no. 3 (May–June 1968): 8; also reprinted in *Directors in Action,* ed. Bob Thomas, 26–31. Indianapolis: Bobbs Merrill, 1973.]

•"It's a Bird, It's a Plane, It's . . . *The Birds*," *Take One* 1, no. 10 (1968): 6–7.

"*Rear Window.*" *Take One* 2, no. 2 (1968): 18–20. [Reprinted in LaValley, 40–46.]

•"Film Production." In *Encyclopaedia Britannica* (1968), vol. 15, pp. 907–911. [First printed in 1965 edition; partially reprinted in "Symposium," *Arts in Society* 4 (Winter 1967): 66–68; at BFI.]

•"In the Hall of Mogul Kings." *Times* (London), June 23, 1969, 33.

"Hitch." *Films in London* 1, no. 7 (October 19/October 25, 1969): 6–7. [Quotations from a transcript of a John Player celebrity lecture H gave at the National Film Theatre; interviewer: Bryan Forbes.]

Batdorf, Emerson. "Let's Hear It for Hitchcock: The Definitive Interview with Movie-Maker Doing Most of the Talking." *Plain Dealer Sunday Magazine,* February 1, 1970. [BFI, fiche no. 8.]

"On Suspense and Mystery." *Harper's Bazaar* 104, no. 70 (July 1971). [A long quotation from another source on these familiar topics.]

"Your Fears Are My Life." *Reveille,* September 23–September 29, 1972. [Fiche at Herrick Library.]

"AH: The German Years." *Action,* January–February 1973, 23–25. [Interview.]

•"Address to the Film Society of Lincoln Center." *Film Comment* 10, no. 4 (July–August 1974): 34–35.

"Alfred Hitchcock Cooks His Own Goose." *Harper's Bazaar* 109 (December 1975), 132–133.

•"Hitchcock at Work." *Take One* 5, no. 2 (1976): 31–35.

Foreword. In *The Flicks, or Whatever Became of Andy Hardy* by Charles Champlin. Pasadena: Ward Ritchie Press, 1977.

•"Surviving." *Sight & Sound* 46 (Summer 1977): 174–176. Interview with John Russell Taylor.

Foreword. In *The Movies Grew Up 1940–1980,* by Charles Champlin. Chicago: Swallow Press, 1981. See Foreword to Champlin 1977, above.

Works Cited

Berger, John. *The Success and Failure of Picasso*. Baltimore: Penguin, 1965.

Brill, Lesley. *The Hitchcock Romance: Love and Irony in Hitchcock's Films*. Princeton: Princeton University Press, 1988.

Brownlow, Kevin. *The Parade's Gone By*. Berkeley, Los Angeles, and London: University of California Press, 1968.

Freeman, David. *The Last Days of Alfred Hitchcock*. Woodstock: Overlook Press, 1984.

Hurley, Neil P. *Soul in Suspense: Hitchcock's Fright and Delight*. Metuchen: Scarecrow Press, 1993.

Kapsis, Robert E. *Hitchcock: The Making of a Reputation*. Chicago: University of Chicago Press, 1992.

Kuhn, Annette. *Cinema, Censorship and Sexuality 1909–1925*. New York: Routledge, 1989.

LaValley, Albert, ed. *Focus on Hitchcock*. Englewood Cliffs: Prentice-Hall, 1972.

Leff, Leonard J. *Hitchcock and Selznick: The Rich and Strange Collaboration of Alfred Hitchcock and David O. Selznick in Hollywood.*. New York: Weidenfeld & Nicolson, 1987.

Leitch, Thomas M. *Find the Director and Other Hitchcock Games*. Athens: University of Georgia Press, 1991.

Modleski, Tania. *The Women Who Knew Too Much: Hitchcock and Feminist Theory*. New York: Methuen, 1988.

Montagu, Ivor. "Working With Hitchcock." *Sight & Sound* 49 (Summer 1980): 189–193.

Robertson, James C. *The Hidden Cinema: British Film Censorship in Action, 1913–1975*. New York: Routledge, 1989.

Rosenbaum, Jonathan. "The Invisible Orson Welles: A First Inventory." *Sight & Sound* (Summer 1986): 164–171.

Ryall, Tom. *Alfred Hitchcock and the British Cinema*. Champaign: University of Illinois Press, 1986.

Sloan, Jane E. *Alfred Hitchcock: A Guide to References and Resources.* New York: G. K. Hall, 1993.

Sontag, Susan. *On Photography.* New York: Dell, 1977.

Spoto, Donald. *The Dark Side of Genius: The Life of Alfred Hitchcock.* New York: Ballantine Books, 1983.

Truffaut, François, with the collaboration of Helen G. Scott. *Hitchcock.* 1967; rev. ed. New York: Simon & Schuster, 1984.

Wood, Robin. *Hitchcock's Films Revisited.* New York: Columbia University Press, 1989.

Yacowar, Maurice. *Hitchcock's British Films.* Hamden, Conn.: Shoestring Press, 1977.

Index